Mental Health Law in China

This book provides an important critique of mental health law and practice in China, with a focus on involuntary detention and treatment.

The work explores China's mental health law reform regarding treatment decision-making in the new era of the UN Convention on the Rights of Persons with Disabilities (CRPD). It adopts a socio-legal approach, not only by undertaking a comprehensive desk-based analysis of the reforms introduced by China's Mental Health Law (MHL) but also examining its implementation based on evidence from practice. The book seeks to investigate whether China's first national MHL takes a step closer to the requirements of the UN Convention on the Rights of Persons with Disabilities on mental health treatment decision-making, and, if not, why not?

The book will be of interest to those working in the areas of mental health law and policy, medical law and disability, human rights law, and Asian Studies.

Bo Chen is Assistant Professor in the Faculty of Law, Macau University of Science and Technology.

Routledge Research in Health Law

Workplace Mental Health Law
Comparative Perspectives
Takenori Mishiba

Mental Health Law in China
A Socio-legal Analysis
Bo Chen

For more information about this series, please visit: https://www.routledge.com/Routledge-Research-in-Human-Rights-Law/book-series/RRHL

Mental Health Law in China

A Socio-legal Analysis

Bo Chen

Routledge
Taylor & Francis Group
NEW YORK AND LONDON

First published 2023
by Routledge
605 Third Avenue, New York, NY 10158

and by Routledge
2 Park Square, Milton Park, Abingdon, Oxon OX14 4RN

Routledge is an imprint of the Taylor & Francis Group, an informa business

British Library Cataloguing-in-Publication Data
A catalogue record for this book is available from the British Library

Library of Congress Cataloging-in-Publication Data
A catalog record has been requested for this book

ISBN: 978-1-032-07906-6 (hbk)
ISBN: 978-1-032-07908-0 (pbk)
ISBN: 978-1-003-21203-4 (ebk)

DOI: 10.4324/9781003212034

Typeset in Galliard
by Taylor & Francis Books

Contents

Tables

Foreword

China played a leading role in the drafting the UN Convention on the Rights of Persons with Disabilities (CRPD). And China is now a key part of the global conversation about how to make practical provisions to respect the rights-based perspective on disability.

Any revolution in ideas takes time to work itself through in domestic law and policy. The UN CRPD has huge ripple effects throughout a broad swathe of laws and policies inherited from the past. Mental health law is no exception. It is one of those critical frontiers of disability reform not only in China but around the world.

This book provides an original, important, and captivating critique of mental health law and practice in China, with a focus on coercive detention and treatment. The book is essential reading for those seeking to understand the evolution of mental health law in China. This is achieved by providing the reader with an understanding of the medical and socio-legal culture and context within which mental health law has developed and evolved in China. The author brings both a scholarly and practical approach to the subject matter, assisting the reader in understanding the implications of international human rights law for the future of Chinese mental health law. This provides a road map as to how the non-coercive standards articulated in the CRPD can be realised in practice.

This work will no doubt assist scholars, activists and policymakers in undertaking similar analysis of mental health laws in other jurisdictions and regions throughout the world and support them in attending to the core task of transposing the values of the CRPD into the domestic policy mix. History, culture and society are always important and inform the search for meaningful ways to make universal norms relevant in the domestic context.

The author skilfully presents the international debate on mental health law and the implications of the CRPD for mental health laws. The author also provides expert analysis of mental health law in China highlighting the strengths of that law while identifying and addressing its shortcomings and weaknesses. The author employs the use of legal doctrinal and desk-based research to explain and contextualise the development, scope and content of mental health law and its regional forerunners (the municipal mental health regulations). Importantly the author also draws on qualitative data and analysis of the relevant case law in unpacking and critiquing the operation of Chinese mental health law.

A core message is that recent legislation, on its face, brings China more closely into conformity with the CRPD. However, significant implementation challenges remain which are created in part by a lack of specificity in the law. The research is novel in identifying and critiquing factors that have restricted the effectiveness of the new Mental Health Law. These factors include the power imbalance between psychiatrists and service-users, the important role of families of service-users and barriers that restrict service users' access to justice through the Chinese judicial system. All of these barriers can be surmounted.

A treaty is essentially a collection of words, a collection of majestic generalities. Treaties such as the CRPD must be translated into concrete lines of action. The author reminds us that there is a world of difference between the 'law in the books' and the 'law in action'. Human rights law must reach the 'small places' where people live their own lives. This book is to be welcomed in seeking to translate the majestic generalities of the CRPD as it applies to persons who experience psychosocial disability into concrete lines of action for China.

I hope and expect this book will encourage reflection as well as innovation in China in this policy space. We all share in the vision of building a better and more inclusive future. This is a difficult task, and the first step is to identify the challenges, which the author has done expertly in this work. This research should encourage and stimulate conversations on how China can implement its obligations under the CRPD in the field of mental health. The main task of a researcher is to expand our policy imagination. This book certainly achieves that.

As UN Special Rapporteur on the rights of persons with disabilities I congratulate the author for this research, which makes a highly original and important contribution to this underexplored field of research.

Gerard Quinn
UN Special Rapporteur on the rights of persons with disabilities

Acknowledgements

My doctoral supervisor Dr Charles O'Mahony wrote in his PhD that Dr Mary Keys is 'one of the best supervisors in the world' and 'the world is a better place because of her'. I cannot agree more since Mary is my doctoral supervisor too. Now I have two of the best supervisors in the world. Their continuous support has been invaluable to my life in Galway and beyond.

I would like to thank everyone in the Centre for Disability Law and Policy and the School of Law, NUI Galway, from which I have received my PhD. In particular, I would like to thank Emeritus Prof Gerard Quinn, Prof Ray Murphey, Prof Eilionóir Flynn, Prof Gabor Gombos, Prof Donncha O'Connell, Prof Shane Darcy, Dr Catriona Moloney, Dr Maureen O'Sullivan, Dr Lucy-Ann Buckely, Dr Liz Brosnan, Dr John Bogue, Dr Ciara Smyth, and Dr Shivaun Quinlivan for offering me opportunities of research or working with them on different occasions. I would also like to thank Prof Zhang Wanhong, Dr Ma Zhiying, Dr Harry Yi-Jui Wu, Mr Ni Zhen, Prof Anna Lawson, Prof Peter Bartlett, Prof Brandon Kelley, Ms Daisy Cheung, my colleagues at the Faculty of Law, Macau University of Science and Technology, two anonymous reviewers, and many other peer scholars for their feedback, support, and inspiration.

Special thanks to all the participants in the research for your invaluable experience and insights that have informed this book. I would also like to thank everyone who appears on the footnotes in the book. The research would be impossible without your contribution. I would like to thank my friends in China who are still working hard to impact the lives of persons with disabilities in different capacities.

I thank Macau University of Science and Technology and National University of Ireland Galway for providing funds. I am also grateful to the wonderful editors Ms Alison Kirk, Ms Emily Summers, and Ms Joanna Hardern.

Finally, I owe a big thank you to my family. In particular, I would like to thank my parents, who will probably never read this paragraph in English, for their unconditional support and love. Also, Jieying and I are always joking about whether I should write something like 'without my wife this book would be finished much earlier'. The truth is, without your love and company, this book and many other things would not be possible at all.

Abbreviations

CIA	Central Intelligence Agency
CoE	Council of Europe
CRPD	UN Convention on the Rights of Persons with Disabilities
CRPD	Committee UN Committee on the Rights of Persons with Disabilities
CPC	Communist Party of China
CPL	The Civil Procedure Law of the People's Republic of China
ECHR	Convention for the Protection of Human Rights and Fundamental Freedoms
ECtHR	European Court of Human Rights
EU	European Union
GProvisionsCL	The General Provisions of Civil Law of the People's Republic of China
GPrinciplesCL	The General Principles of Civil Law of the People's Republic of China
LAOSC	The Legislative Affairs Office of the State Council of the People's Republic of China
ICCPR	International Covenant on Civil and Political Rights
ICESCR	International Covenant on Economic, Social and Cultural Rights
MHL	Mental Health Law of the People's Republic of China (First National Mental Health Law)
MI	Principles Principles for the Protection of Persons with Mental Illness and for the Improvement of Mental Health Care
NGOs	Non-Government Organisations
NPC	National People's Congress of the People's Republic of China
SCNPC	The Standing Committee of the National People's Congress of the People's Republic of China
UDHR	Universal Declaration of Human Rights
WHO	World Health Organisation

List of Cases

ECHR Cases

Aerts v Belgium (1998) 29 EHRR 50
Amuur v France (1996) 22 EHRR 533
DN v Switzerland (2003) 37 EHRR 21
H.L. v United Kingdoms, App No 45508/99 (ECHR, 5 October 2004)
Herczegfalvy v Austria (1993) 15 EHRR 437
Kawka v Poland App No 2587/94 (ECHR, 9 January 2001)
Plesó v Hungary App No 41242/08 (ECHR, 17 January 2012)
Stanev v Bulgaria (2012) 55 EHRR 22
Storck v Germany, App No 61603/00 (ECHR, 16 June 2005)
Winterwerp v the Netherlands (1979) 2 EHRR 387
Witold Litwa v Poland (2001) 33 EHRR 387
X v United Kingdom (1981) 4 EHRR 188

Chinese Cases[1]

Beijing Anding Hosptial v Yang – Medical Service Contract Dispute First Instance Case, Basic People's Court of Xicheng District, Beijing Municipality, Civil First Instance No 24789, 19 December 2014 [《首都医科大学附属北京安定医院与杨X等医疗服务合同纠纷一审民事判决书》，北京市西城区人民法院，(2014)西民初字第24789号]

Delin Wang v Anding Hosptial of Tianjin Municipality – Medical Damage Liability Dispute First Instance Case, Basic People' Court of Hexi District, Tianjin Municipality, Civil First Instance No 4915, 21 July 2017 [《王德林与天津市安定医院医疗损害责任纠纷一审民事判决书》，天津市河西区人民法院, (2017)津0103民初4915号]

Ding v Mental Hosptial of Xuzhou Municipality and Ding – Medical Damage Liability Dispute First Instance Case, Basic People's Court of Gulou District,

1 The titles of the cases below are translated by the author from Chinese into English. The titles of cases in the Chinese language are removed from the footnotes in the main text of the book, for the benefit of the reader. The same arrangement also applies to the instruments, the journal articles and books (chapters) referenced in the book.

Xuzhou Municipality, Jiangsu Province, Civil First Instance No 3401, 29 June 2017 [《丁某与徐州市某某医院、丁某某医疗损害责任纠纷一审民事判决书》，徐州市鼓楼区人民法院, (2015)鼓民初字第3401号]

Feng Liang v Zhongpei Wu Memorial Hospital of Shunde District, Foshan Municipality – Right to Life, Right to Health and Right to Body Intergrity Dispute Appeal Case, Intermediate People's Court of Foshan Municipality, Civil Appeal No 37, 7 March 2014 [《梁锋, 佛山市顺德区伍仲珮纪念医院与生命权、健康权、身体权纠纷二审民事判决书》，佛山市中级人民法院, (2014)佛中法民一终字第37号]

Guo Zhu v Shu Zhu and Wanchun Mental Hosptial of Wenjiang District, Chengdu Municipality – Medical Damage Liability Dispute First Instance Case, Basic People's Court of Wenjiang District, Chengdu Municipality, Sichuan Province, Civil First Instance No 2035, 29 September 2014 [《原告朱某国与被告朱某树、成都市温江区万春精神病医院医疗损害赔偿纠纷一案民事判决书》， 成都市温江区人民法院, (2014)温江民初字第2035号]

Zhenyang Han v Psychiatric Hospital of Zhumadian Municipality – Medical Damage Liability Dispute Appeal Case, Intermediate People's Court of Zhumadian Municipality, Henan Province, Civil Appeal No 179, 7 April 2017 [《韩镇阳、驻马店市精神病医院医疗损害责任纠纷二审民事判决书》， 驻马店中级人民法院, (2017)豫17民终179号]

Hong Xia v The Third People's Hospital of Panzhihua Municipality – Tort Liability Dispute First Instance Judgment, Basic People's Court of Renhe District, Panzhihua Municipality, Sichuan Province, Civil First Instance Case No 1260, 18 November 2013 [《原告夏宏诉被告攀枝花市第三人民医院侵权责任纠纷一案一审民事判决书》，攀枝花市仁和区人民法院, (2013)仁和民初字第1260号]

Hongmei Gou v Physical and Mental Health Hospital of Nanchong Municipality – Right to Health Dispute, Basic People's Court of Yingshan County, Nanchong Municipality, Sichuan Province, Civil First Instance No 957, 18 August 2014 [《苟红梅与南充市身心医院健康权纠纷一审民事判决书》， 营山县人民法院, (2014)营民初字第957号]

Lianqiong Zhang v Stomatological Hospital of Jinmen Municipality – Right to Health Dispute First Instance Case, Basic People's Court of Dongbao District, Jinmen Municipality, Hubei Province, Civil First Instance No 238, 11 March 2016 [《原告张联琼与被告荆门市口腔医院健康权纠纷一案一审民事判决书》，荆门市东宝区人民法院, (2016)鄂0802民初238号]

Lianshui Du v Chinese Medical Psychiatric Hospital and others – Personal Liberty Dispute, Basic People's Court of Lixia District, Jinan Municipality, Shandong Province, Civil First Instance No 1219, 08 September 2015 [《杜连水与济南中医精神专科医院等人身自由权纠纷一审民事判决书》， 济南市历下区人民法院, (2015)历民初字第1219号]

Lixin Xu v Shanghai Qingchun Mental Rehabilitation Hospital and Canxing Xu – Right to Personal Liberty Dispute Appeal Case, First Intermediate People's Court of Shanghai Municipality, Civil Appeal No 2108, 15 September 2015 [《徐立新与上海青春精神病康复院、徐灿兴人身自由权纠纷二审判决书》，上海市第一人民法院, (2015)沪一中民一(民)终字第2108号]

Mengyan Jing v Mental Hospital of Luohe Municipality – Tort Liability Dispute First Instance Case, Basic People's Court of Yancheng District, Luohe Municipality, Civil First Instance No 219, 24 May 2016 [《蒙艳景与漯河市精神病医院侵权责任纠纷一审民事判决书》, 漯河市郾城区人民法院, (2016)豫1103民初219号]

Wenjie Mai v Third People's Hospital of Foshan Municipality – Medical Damage Liability Dispute Appeal Case, Intermediate People's Court of Foshan Municipality, Guangdong Province, Civil Appeal No 1887, 18 September 2015 [《麦文杰与佛山市第三人民医院医疗损害责任纠纷二审民事判决书》, 广东省佛山市中级人民法院, (2015)佛中法民一终字第1887号]

Qiao Jing v Third People's Hsopital of Mianyang Municipality – Personal Liberty Dispute Retrial Application Case, High People's Court of Sichuan Province, Civil Retrial Application No 3745, 10 March 2017 [《敬乔、绵阳市第三人民医院人身自由权纠纷再审审查与审判监督民事裁定书》, 四川省高级人民法院, (2016)川民申3745号]

Shuhua Sun v Fourth People's Hospital of Linyi Municipality – Medical Damage Liability Dispute First Instance Case, Basic People's Court of Lanshan District, Linyi Municipality, Shandong Province, Civil First Instance Case No 2487, 16 November 2015 [《孙淑华与临沂市第四人民医院医疗损害责任纠纷一审民事判决书》, 临沂市兰山区人民法院, (2015)临兰民初字第2487号]

Shuibing Cao v The Seventh People's Hospital of Hangzhou Municipality – Medical Damage Liability Dispute Appeal Ruling, Intermediate People's Court of Hangzhou Municipality, Zhejiang Province, Civil Appeal No 1176, 17 March 2016 [《曹水兵与杭州市第七人民医院医疗损害责任纠纷二审民事裁定书》, 杭州市中级人民法院, (2016)浙01民终1176号]

Tongbo He v Third People's Hospital of Mianyang Municipality – Personal Liberty Dispute Retrial Application Case, High People's Court of Sichuan Province, Retrial Application No 3761, 20 February 2017 [《何通博人身自由权纠纷再审审查与审判监督民事裁定书》, 四川省高级人民法院, (2016)川民申3761号, 2017年2月20日]

Weihua Yao v Beijing Anding Hospital attached to the Capital Medical University – Medical Damage Liability Dispute First Instance Ruling, Basic People's Court of Xicheng District, Beijing Municipality, Civil First Instance 31441, 24 November 2017 [《姚卫华与首都医科大学附属北京安定医院医疗损害责任纠纷一审民事裁定书》, 北京市西城区人民法院, (2017)京0102民初31441号]

Xu v The Hospital attached to Central South University – Medical Damage Liability Dispute Case, Basic People's Court of Furong District, Changsha Municipality, Civil First Instance No 2938, 22 July 2015 [《许某某与中南大学某某医院医疗损害责任纠纷一审民事判决书》, 长沙市芙蓉区人民法院, (2014)芙民初字第2938号]

Yangdi Zhu v Lishui Shan and others – Traffic Incident Liability Dispute First Instance Judgment, Basic People's Court of Zengcheng Municipality, Guandong Province, Civil First Instance No 2761, 24 April 2014. [朱杨娣与单丽水、单潮海、华安财产保险股份有限公司广州市海珠支公司、中国太平洋财产保险股份

有限公司广州市新塘支公司机动车交通事故责任纠纷一审民事判决书, 增城市人民法院, (2013)穗增法民一初字第2761号]

Yonghao Yu v Yongbo Yu, Feng Zhang and others – Tort Liability Dispute Appeal Case, Intermediate People's Court of Zibo Municipality, Shandong Province, Civil Appeal No. 551, 18 April 2016 [《于永浩与于永波、张锋等侵权责任纠纷二审民事判决书》, 淄博市中级人民法院, (2016)鲁03民终551号]

Yu v Mental Hospital of Zhumadian Municipality – Right to Personal Liberty Dispute First Instance Case, Basic People's Court of Yicheng District, Zhumadian Municipality, Henan Province, Civil First Instance No 4122, 26 June 2017 [《余某诉驻马店市精神病医院人身自由权纠纷一案一审民事判决书》, 河南省驻马店市驿城区人民法院, (2016)豫1702民初4122号]

Zhengxi Wang v Min Wang – Tort Liability Dispute Appeal Case, Intermediate People's Court of Yichang Municipality, Civil Second Instance No 1311, 26 June 2017 [《王正喜、王敏侵权责任纠纷二审民事判决书》, 宜昌市中级人民法院, (2017)鄂05民终1311号]

Zhengxi Wang v Min Wang and Yuanzheng Wu – Tort Liability Dispute, Basic People's Court of Sanxiaba District, Yichang Municipality, Hubei Province, Civil First Instance No 13, 10 February 2017 [《王正喜与王敏、吴远征侵权责任纠纷一审民事判决书》, 宜昌市三峡坝区人民法院, (2016)鄂0591民初13号]

Zhenhua Qi v Peng Fu and Beijing Huilongguan Hospital – Personality Right Dispute Appeal Case, First Intermediate People's Court of Beijing Municipality, Civil Appeal No 09354, 16 December 2015 [《齐振华与付鹏等人格权纠纷二审民事判决书》, 北京市第一中级人民法院, (2015)一中民终字第09354号]

Xiangyu Wang v Kangning Veteran Hospital of Liaoning Province and Qiuyue Wang – Medical Contract Dispute Appeal Case, Intermediate People's Court of Huludao Municipality, Liaoning Province, Civil Appeal No 01257, 11 February 2015 [《上诉人王翔宇与被上诉人辽宁省复员军人康宁医院、王秋月医疗服务合同纠纷一案二审民事判决书》, 葫芦岛市中级人民法院, (2014)葫民终字第01257号]

List of Instruments

International and Regional Instruments

Council of Europe Committee of Ministers, 'Recommendation No. R (83) 2 of the Committee of Ministers to Member States concerning the legal protection of persons suffering from mental disorders placed as involuntary patients' (1983)

Council of Europe Parliamentary Assembly, 'Recommendation 818 on Situation of the mentally ill' (1977)

Convention for the Protection of Human Rights and Fundamental Freedoms (opened for signature 4 November 1950, entered into force 3 September 1953)

International Covenant on Civil and Political Rights (adopted 16 December 1966, entered into force 23 March 1976) 999 UNTS 171

International Covenant on Economic, Social and Cultural Rights (adopted 16 December 1966, entered into force 3 January 1976) 993 UNTS 3

UN Convention on the Rights of Persons with Disabilities (adopted 13 December 2006, entered into force 3 May 2008) 2515 UNTS 3

UN General Assembly 'Principles for the Protection of Persons with Mental Illness and for the Improvement of Mental Health Care' (17 December 1991) UN Doc A/RES/46/119

Universal Declaration of Human Rights (adopted 10 December 1948) UNGA Res 217 A(III)

International Bodies' Comments and Recommendations

CRPD Committee, 'General Comment No 1 Article 12: Equal Recognition Before the Law' (11 April 2014) UN Doc CRPD/C/GC/1

CRPD Committee, 'Concluding observations on the initial report of China'(15 October 2012) CRPD/C/CHN/CO/1

CRPD Committee, 'General comment No. 6 (2018) on equality and non-discrimination' (26 April 2018), CRPD/C/GC/6.

CRPD Committee, 'Guidelines on article 14 of the Convention on the Rights of Persons with Disabilities The right to liberty and security of persons with disabilities' (September 2015)

Human Rights Committee, General comment No. 35 Article 9 (Liberty and security of person) (16 December 2014) CCPR/C/GC/35

Other International or Regional Documents

China, 'Implementation of the Convention on the Rights of Persons with Disabilities Initial Reports Submitted by States Parties under Article 35 of the Convention' (2011) CRPD/C/CHN/1

China, 'Implementation of the Convention on the Rights of Persons with Disabilities 2nd and 3rd Reports Submitted by States Parties under Article 35 of the Convention' (2018) CRPD/C/CHN/2–3

Human Rights Council, 'Report of the Special Rapporteur on the right of everyone to the enjoyment of the highest attainable standard of physical and mental health' (28 March 2017) A/HRC/35/21.

Human Rights Council, 'Report of the Special Rapporteur on the rights of persons with disabilities' (11 January 2019) A/HRC/40/54

Human Rights Council, 'Report of the Special Rapporteur on torture and other cruel, inhuman or degrading treatment or punishment' (1 February 2013) A/HRC/22/53

Working Group on Arbitrary Detention, 'United Nations Basic Principles and Guidelines on the right of anyone deprived of their liberty to bring proceedings before a court' (4 May 2015) WGAD/CRP.1/2015

Constitution and Statutes

Mental Health Act 2001 (Ireland)

Mental Health Care Act 2017 (India)

The Civil Procedure Law of People's Republic of China [《中华人民共和国民事诉讼法》]

The Constitution of the People's Republic of China [《中华人民共和国宪法》]

The Criminal Procedural Law of the People's Republic of China [《中华人民共和国刑事诉讼法》]

The Election Law of the National People's Congress and People's Congresses at Different Levels of the People's Republic of China [《全国人民代表大会和地方各级人民代表大会选举法》]

The General Principles of Civil Law of the People's Republic of China [《中华人民共和国民法通则》]

The General Provisions of Civil Law of the People's Republic of China [《中华人民共和国民法总则》]

The Legislation Law of the People's Republic of China [《中华人民共和国立法法》]

The Medical Practitioners Law of the People's Republic of China [《中华人民共和国执业医师法》]

The Mental Health Law of the People's Republic of China [《中华人民共和国精神卫生法》]

Other Domestic Regulations or Documents

Guidelines for National Mental Health Work (2008–2015) [《全国精神卫生工作体系发展指导纲要（2008－2015）》]

National Mental Health Plan (2002–2010) [《中国精神卫生工作规划(2002–2010年)》]

National Mental Health Work Plan (2015–2020) [《中国精神卫生工作规划（2015－2020年）》]

Opinions on Further Strengthening Mental Health Work (2004) [《关于进一步加强精神卫生工作的指导意见》]

Opinions on Strengthening Mental Health Work (1987) [《进一步加强精神卫生工作的若干意见》]

The Mental Health Regulation of Beijing (2007) [《北京市精神卫生条例》]

The Mental Health Regulation of Hangzhou (2007) [《杭州市精神卫生条例》]

The Mental Health Regulation of Ningbo (2006) [《宁波市精神卫生条例》]

The Mental Health Regulation of Shanghai (2002) [《上海市精神卫生条例》]

The Mental Health Regulation of Wuhan (2010) [《武汉市精神卫生条例》]

The Mental Health Regulation of Wuxi (2007) [《无锡市精神卫生条例》]

The People's Supreme Court's Opinions on Implementing the General Principle of Civil Law of the People's Republic of China (1988) [《最高院关于执行〈民法通则〉的若干意见》]

The Psychological Health Regulation of Shenzhen (2011) [《深圳经济特区心理卫生条例》]

The Supreme People's Court's Interpretations of the Application of the Civil Procedure Law of the People's Republic of China [《最高人民法院关于适用〈中华人民共和国民事诉讼法〉的解释]

1 Introduction

1.1 Chapter Introduction

This book explores China's mental health law reform regarding treatment decision-making in the new era of the UN Convention on the Rights of Persons with Disabilities (CRPD or the Convention).[1] It adopts a socio-legal approach, not only by undertaking a comprehensive desk-based analysis of the reform introduced by the Mental Health Law (MHL)[2] but also examining its implementation based on evidence from practice.

The international context of this research is that, since the CRPD entered into force, the future of mental health laws internationally is at a crossroads. China ratified the CRPD in 2008 and submitted its first state report to the Committee on the Rights of Persons with Disabilities (CRPD Committee) in 2010 on the implementation of the Convention. In its Concluding Observations in 2012, the CRPD Committee expressed its concern about the 'involuntary commitment system' in China for not respecting the 'individual will of persons with disabilities'.[3] The CRPD Committee also stated:

> The Committee advises the State party to adopt measures to ensure that all health care and services provided to persons with disabilities, including all mental health care and services, is based on the free and informed consent of the individual concerned, and that *laws permitting involuntary treatment and confinement, including upon the authorization of third party decision-makers such as family members or guardians, are repealed.*[4]

Subsequently, this recommendation has not appeared to raise much attention or concern in the related law-making processes in China. When the Concluding

1 UN Convention on the Rights of Persons with Disabilities (adopted 13 December 2006, entered into force 3 May 2008) 2515 UNTS 3 (CRPD).

2 Mental Health Law of the People's Republic of China (passed by the Standing Committee of the National People's Congress on 26 October 2012, entered into force on 1 May 2013) (MHL).

3 CRPD Committee, 'Concluding observations on the initial report of China' (15 October 2012) CRPD/C/CHN/CO/1.

4 Ibid., para 38. Emphasis added.

DOI: 10.4324/9781003212034-1

Observation was adopted, China was close to the end of its 28-year-long law-making journey to introduce its first national MHL. The lack of legislative debate or reaction to the CRPD Committee's recommendation in the MHL's legislative history may be explained by the narrow window between the Concluding Observations' adoption on 15 October 2012 and the final review of the MHL under the Standing Committee of the National People's Congress on 26 October 2012.

However, there has been an international trend where States Parties to the CRPD have enacted legislation in which involuntary mental health interventions are still permissible, for example India.[5] Other States Parties, such as Ireland, Australia, and Canada, entered declarations or reservations in relation to provisions in the CRPD requiring abolishing involuntary interventions upon their ratification of the Convention.[6] As will be addressed in this book, a straightforward and popular explanation to the fact that most, if not all, States Parties are not following the CRPD Committee's recommendation on the abolition of involuntary mental health interventions is its radical and unrealistic nature.[7]

Given this context, this book seeks to explore in depth the tension between the CRPD requirements and the MHL. The research is timely. After many years of implementation of the MHL, there are rich materials in both medical and legal practice, enabling a comprehensive understanding of both the law in the book and the law in action. Moreover, as China submitted its state report, combined for the second and third reporting cycles, on 31 August 2018 to the CRPD Committee,[8] the research seeks to help the mutual understanding between the newest international human rights standards and the MHL. As will be addressed in Chapter 3, China is home for over 170 million adults having at least one type of mental disorder and 16 million people having severe mental illness.[9] A comprehensive examination of the MHL and its practice will assist an honest and beneficial dialogue between the international human rights community and the Chinese

5 Mental Health Care Act 2017 (India). For more discussion, see Mukul Inamdar, Michael Stein and Joske Bunders, 'Does "Supported Decision-Making" in India's Mental Health Care Bill, 2013, Measure up to the CRPD's Standards?' (2016) 1 *Indian Journal of Medical Ethics* 229; Richard M Duffy and Brendan D Kelly, 'India's Mental Healthcare Act, 2017: Content, Context, Controversy' (2019) 62 *International Journal of Law and Psychiatry* 169.

6 See 'Declarations and Reservations' to the CRPD < https://treaties.un.org/Pages/ViewDetails.aspx?src=TREATY&mtdsg_no=IV-15&chapter=4&lang=_en&clang=_en > accessed 1 July 2021. It is also interesting to note that the United States of American whose civil mental health law has significant impact on the laws of many other countries, has not yet ratified the CRPD. See Michael Perlin, *Advanced Introduction to Mental Health Law* (Edward Elgar Publishing 2021).

7 See, generally, John Dawson, 'A Realistic Approach to Assessing Mental Health Laws Compliance with the UNCRPD' (2015) *International Journal of Law and Psychiatry* 70.

8 China, 'Implementation of the Convention on the Rights of Persons with Disabilities: 2nd and 3rd Reports Submitted by States Parties under Article 35 of the Convention' (2018) CRPD/C/CHN/2–3.

9 Chapter 3, Section 3.2.

government. In return, a better understanding of the CRPD requirements may help avoid wasting time and investment into the approach that has been proved a failure in other countries. As will be addressed in Chapter 3, China does not have a long history of institutionalisation,[10] but there has emerged a worrying trend of prioritising institutional care over community-based care.[11] This research attempts to contribute to the discussion around the worrying trend by providing a baseline study of the current MHL and its implementation.

The book also aims to present the above analysis of China's law reform process as a case study to engage international debate around mental health laws and the CRPD. The international debate on whether involuntary detention and treatment authorised by mental health laws can comply with international human rights law is seemingly intractable. As a result, several approaches have been suggested to resolve the different perspectives, including the exploration of alternative measures to coercion in psychiatry,[12] the fusion model of mental health and capacity law,[13] and the disability-neutral approach in state intervention to save lives.[14] One of the proposals is to develop good quality, voluntary mental health services before involuntary detention and treatment can be abolished. Arguably the hope is, if the voluntary services are sufficiently resourced, there would be no need to initiate the involuntary track even if it is still in place.[15]

The examination of China's mental health law reform in this book seeks to provide a detailed and insightful case study to evaluate the above approach. The MHL not only introduced the 'voluntary principle' and narrowing the scope of involuntary detention and treatment but also called for increased attention and resources for the voluntary services. However, the analysis in the book suggests the law reforms in China have not achieved its aims due to the barriers identified in the later chapters. This informs the international debate that the 'improving voluntary services before abolishing involuntary detention and treatment' approach is unlikely to work unless the surrounding conditions, such as power imbalance and guardianship (formal or informal) are changed.

10 Chapter 3, Section 3.2.

11 Chapter 7, Section 7.3.1. Also, see Jiajia Liu, 'Dependent and Non-Community Living: Rethinking the Institutionalization Trend of Chinese Policies Regarding Persons with Mental Disabilities', in Wanhong Zhang (eds) *Disability Rights Study in China 2015* (Social Science Academic Press 2015).

12 Piers Gooding, Bernadette McSherry and Cath Roper, 'Preventing and Reducing '"Coercion" in Mental Health Services: An International Scoping Review of English-Language Studies' (2020) 142 *Acta Psychiatrica Scandinavica* 27.

13 John Dawson and George Szmukler, 'Fusion of Mental Health and Incapacity Legislation' (2006) 188 *The British Journal of Psychiatry* 504.

14 Eilionóir Flynn and Anna Arstein-Kerslake, 'State Intervention in the Lives of People with Disabilities: The Case for a Disability-Neutral Framework' (2017) 13 *International Journal of Law in Context* 39.

15 Bernadette McSherry and Penny Weller (eds), *Rethinking Rights-Based Mental Health Laws* (Hart Publishing 2010).

1.2 Structure of the Book

The book is guided by the question: Does China's first national MHL take a step closer to the CRPD requirements on mental health treatment decision-making? If not, why not?

After this introduction, Chapter 2 sets out to explore the CRPD requirements on treatment decision-making in mental health services. It will begin by reviewing how international human rights law has addressed the rights of persons with mental health issues before the adoption of the CRPD. The chapter acknowledges the current reality that a) the CRPD Committee calls for an absolute ban on involuntary detention and treatment in its No. 1 General Comment on Article 12 Equal Recognition before the Law; and b) no State Party has met this standard. Since CRPD-compliant mental health law have yet to be developed, the question becomes: What evaluative framework could be adopted to determine whether China's mental health law reform takes a step closer to the CRPD requirements?

Chapter 2 will emphasise the 'necessary but safeguarded' approach to involuntary mental health interventions adopted by the Principles for the Protection of Persons with Mental Illness and for the Improvement of Mental Health Care, known as the MI Principles,[16] and the case law of the European Court of Human Rights. Then it will examine in depth the provisions of the CRPD and relevant interpretation and scholarly debate on the CRPD requirement of abolishing involuntary mental health interventions. Chapter 2 looks beyond a doctrinal conclusion about whether involuntary mental health intervention, as a last resort, is CRPD-compliant but draws the consensus out of the heated debate. By doing so, Chapter 2 will develop a standard or a tool to assess whether or not the MHL makes a step closer to the CRPD requirement that is maximising the decision-making autonomy of persons with mental health issues in treatment. It is not intended to challenge the interpretation of the CRPD Committee or a part of the debate; rather, it aims to learn from the debate and provide a clearer context for readers.

Before moving to the doctrinal study of the MHL and applicable guardianship law, Chapter 3 provides essential context by explaining that because of the long period of wars and political movements, there were only a few trained mental health professionals in China and the governments of different regions had no desire or available resources to develop their community services. After the reform into a market economy, the government prioritised the problem of untreated patients as a major threat to social stability and economic growth, thereby promoting policies that control people with mental health issues, through their families at home or in institutions. In recent years, with the increased public funds available to the Chinese government and the enactment of the MHL, the investment into mental health services has increased. However, as there is no voice advocating for the development of community-based mental health services, the

16 UN General Assembly, 'Principles for the Protection of Persons with Mental Illness and for the Improvement of Mental Health Care' (17 December 1991) UN Doc A/RES/46/119.

majority of public expenditure has been targeted at the construction of psychiatric hospitals/institutions that segregate persons who experience mental health issues.

Chapter 3 also explains that China's legal system is part of a centralised political system, closer to the continental European legal tradition than to the common law systems, lacking an effective mechanism to solve the conflicting norms, conservative to human rights claims, and deeply embedded in the Party/State's social agenda. The status of treaties, including the CRPD, in China's domestic legal system will also be introduced. Chinese courts do not have a culture of determining that government policies or rules contravene the Constitution or the MHL. This context helps the reader understand the conservative approach adopted by the Chinese courts in balancing 'social stability' and the autonomy and human rights of mental health service users.

Chapter 4 delivers a comprehensive review of the MHL and applicable adult guardianship law in China. It does so by reviewing the municipal mental health regulations and national drafts before the enactment of the MHL. It also highlights the major changes introduced by recent reforms in both the MHL and the Civil Law. It will discuss how the 'voluntary principle' in the MHL is laudable for moving in the direction of maximising respect for service users' autonomy and decision-making rights. Several potential pitfalls in the implementation of this principle will be discussed, such as guardians' decision-making power, the lack of independent oversight, and allied issues. The chapter will also critically engage with recent law reform, identifying that, at least in theory, there is an opportunity for better respect for service users' decision-making rights in the context of mental health treatment. However, to understand the impact of this law reform in practice, it is necessary to move beyond a doctrinal examination of the law. It also requires evidence from the ground.

Chapter 5 turns to explore the implementation of the positive law reform with the empirical data and courts' judgments. Using the data collected from the qualitative interviews, this chapter provides a detailed examination of the different stages of decision-making in the context of mental health treatment. This is also supported by the analysis of the MHL-related cases in which the judicial system responds to medical practice across the spectrum of legal issues relating to assessment, involuntary treatment, discharge, the complaints mechanism, and guardianship. This chapter concludes that the positive provisions in the MHL have not been fully translated into practice. A common theme emerging from the findings is that psychiatrists and family members share the decision-making power in China. Where a person with a diagnosis of a severe mental disorder is considered to pose harm or danger to others, psychiatrists are the ultimate decision-makers with respect to detention for treatment. However, even in this scenario, family members are still the most important stakeholders. Psychiatrists understand their role as proposing treatment plans and rely on family members for final decisions. By contrast, in other jurisdictions the decision to detain for treatment is a clinical decision made by a psychiatrist. On the other hand, the courts in general are not actively responding to legal issues arising and are reluctant to question clinical decision-making. It will be concluded that the courts adopt a more substantive approach in respect of some issues and are more deferential to psychiatrists' professional discretion and the family members' decision-making role in others. In general, the courts are not prone to intervene, unless a serious breach of the MHL is found.

Chapter 6 provides further analysis, suggesting that the slow translation of the progressive elements of the MHL can be explained in part by the power imbalance within and beyond the decision-making structure and that the process remains unchanged, conceptualised as 'shared power and silenced service-users'. This chapter concludes that considerable discretion is afforded to psychiatrists who share the decision-making power with the service user's family members. This dynamic explains the barriers facing service users in accessing justice and why the MHL has been inadequately implemented. Psychiatrists still retain enormous power and authority, displayed at various levels. Family members earn their decision-making power by paying the fees for mental health services and bearing all responsibilities, including compensating third parties for any loss caused by service users. The lack of effective mechanisms to challenge the decisions made for them against their will effectively silences the service user's voice. It will be suggested that the logic underlying the MHL's decision-making framework for mental health detention and treatment is no different from the system that existed before the MHL entered into force. Therefore, no meaningful change is possible unless these surrounding conditions are changed.

Chapter 7 pulls together the findings and conclusions of the previous chapters. The book concludes that mental health law reform in China requires structural changes on a larger scale, with close participation of all stakeholders, to be effective. To achieve this, the book provides three CRPD-informed recommendations for further research and law or policy initiatives: developing community-based services and non-coercive support measures, awareness-raising of the CRPD and its human rights model of disability, and enhancing the participation of service users to all stages of decision-making.

1.3 A Note on Terminology

'No term in the history of madness is neutral – not mental illness, madness, or any other term'.[17] The terminology used throughout this book merits explanation. The usual terms adopted in mental health laws internationally are 'mental illness' or 'mental disorder'. These terms have long been criticised as 'adopting an uncritically medical model of disability'.[18] This medical model of disability, including mental health issues, is argued to be inappropriate for not capturing the experience, in particular, the social stigma and prejudice of the persons affected by psychiatric diagnosis.[19]

17 Geoffrey Reaume, 'Mad People's History' (2006) *Radical History Review* 170, 182.
18 Peter Bartlett, Oliver Lewis and Oliver Thorold, *Mental Disability and the European Convention on Human Rights* (Martinus Nijhoff Publishers 2007).
19 Ibid.

The CRPD adopts a social model or human rights model of disability,[20] focusing on the interaction between one's impairment and various barriers to full and effective participation in society on an equal basis with others.[21] Without addressing the subjects of this book directly, the relevant term adopted in the CRPD is 'mental' impairment or disability, differentiated from 'intellectual' impairment or disability.[22] The book does not follow this terminology mainly because the term 'mental disability' may lead to confusion. On the one hand, it has been used to refer to both persons with intellectual disabilities and persons with mental health difficulties in human rights.[23] On the other hand, in disability literature, mental disability is more likely to be perceived as a transitional term after 'mental retardation' but before 'intellectual disability' in history.[24]

Another term that has been more used in the CRPD-related literature is 'psychosocial disabilities or impairments'.[25] Though there is some controversy of the applicability of the social model of disability to mad people,[26] the term has been deliberately used in the international disability movement by the groups of users and survivors of psychiatry in human rights advocacy.[27] This book, however, does not use the term 'psychosocial disability' either, because most participating service users in the research found the term too strange and alien.

Therefore, the book will use 'persons with mental health issues' and 'service users' interchangeably. 'Mental health issues' intends to cover both persons having mental health difficulties and persons who are deemed or labelled with mental health difficulties. 'Service users' is a compromising choice for clarity in expression, including those whose engagement with mental health services is without their consent. In addition, the term will also vary if it is in a quote – for example, 'patients of mental disorders' is used in the MHL – or context specific – for example 'persons under guardianship' will be used in the discussion of the

20 Theresia Degener, 'A Human Rights Model of Disability' in Peter Blanck and Eilionóir Flynn (eds), *Routledge Handbook of Disability Law and Human Rights* (Routledge 2016).

21 CRPD, art 1.

22 Ibid.

23 See, generally, Bartlett, Lewis, and Thorold (n 18).

24 Robert L Schalock, Ruth A Luckasson and Karrie A Shogren, 'The Renaming of Mental Retardation: Understanding the Change to the Term Intellectual Disability' (2007) 45 *Intellectual and Developmental Disabilities* 116.

25 Anna Lawson, 'People with Psychosocial Impairments or Conditions, Reasonable Accommodation and the Convention on the Rights of Persons with Disabilities' (2008) 26 *Law in Context: A Socio-Legal Journal* 62.

26 Helen Spandler and Jill Anderson, *Madness, Distress and the Politics of Disablement* (Policy Press 2015).

27 Tina Minkowitz, 'The United Nations Convention on the Rights of Persons with Disabilities and the Right to Be Free from Nonconsensual Psychiatric Interventions' (2007) 34 *Syracuse Journal of International Law and Commerce* 405; and Tina Minkowitz, 'Advancing the Rights of Users and Survivors of Psychiatry Using the UN Convention on the Rights of Persons with Disabilities' in Helen Spandler, Jill Anderson and Bob Sapey (eds), *Madness, Distress and the Politics of Disablement* (Policy Press 2015).

guardianship system. Regardless of what term is used, this book adopts a human rights model of disability that 'places the individual centre stage in all decisions affecting him/her and, most importantly, locates the main "problem" outside the person and in society'.[28]

Another set of capacity-related terms also require clarification. Legal capacity is a key concept in the CRPD[29] and interpreted explicitly to contain both the capacity to have rights and the capacity to exercise rights.[30] Involuntary mental health interventions constitute an arguably unjustified limitation to one's legal capacity to refuse treatment. Due to the limitation of scope and length, the book will not cover the literature around legal capacity and the CRPD unless they are directly relevant to mental health laws.

For the purpose of this book, however, a very often discussed issue is mental capacity and its role in mental health services. The CRPD Committee makes a clear distinction between mental capacity, which is essentially decision-making skills of a person, and legal capacity. More importantly, the CRPD Committee noted in the General Comment No. 1 that 'perceived or actual deficits in mental capacity must not be used as justification for denying legal capacity'.[31] As will be addressed in Chapters 4–6, the related terms adopted in Chinese law include 'capacity for civil conduct' in civil law and 'capacity to litigate' in Civil Procedure Law. Leaving their definitions and implication to be addressed later, it is useful to briefly note that these two capacity-related terms have a similar meaning to the mental capacity for different tasks but lead to a result of denying legal capacity to exercise their civil rights or civil procedural rights.

1.4 Chapter Conclusion

As an introduction to the book, this chapter sets out the background of this book and outlines the structure of the following chapters. It also explains the terminology used throughout the book. The next chapter will examine involuntary mental health interventions under the framework of international human rights law.

28 Gerard Quinn, Theresia Degener and Anna Bruce, *Human Rights and Disability: The Current Use and Future Potential of United Nations Human Rights Instruments in the Context of Disability* (United Nations Publications 2002), 14.

29 Gerard Quinn, 'Civil Death: Rethinking the Foundations of Legal Personhood for Persons with a Disability' (2016) 56 *The Irish Jurist* 286.

30 CRPD Committee, 'General Comment No 1: Article 12: Equal Recognition Before the Law' (11 April 2014) UN Doc CRPD/C/GC/1, para 13.

31 Ibid.

2 Evaluative Framework and International Human Rights Law

2.1 Chapter Introduction

This book aims to provide a comprehensive examination of the decision-making of mental health detention and treatment under the Mental Health Law (MHL)[1] in light of the United Nations Convention on the Rights of Persons with Disabilities (CRPD or the Convention).[2] It is, therefore, necessary to explore in depth its requirements in respect of mental health laws, particularly as interpreted by the United Nations Committee on the Rights of Persons with Disabilities (CRPD Committee). As will be discussed below, the CRPD's approach and the interpretation of the CRPD Committee have created enormous controversy, being criticised for being too radical and unrealistic.[3] This chapter aims to help understand these controversies, by examining the relevant CRPD provisions and authoritative interpretations, the criticism towards the CRPD approach, and the efforts in finding a middle ground.

By doing so, this chapter does not aim to simply conclude whether or not involuntary mental health interventions are permissible under the CRPD, since the answer from the CRPD Committee is, consistently, a clear 'No'. Instead, the goal is to find the consensus out of the complex controversies: maximising service users' autonomy in mental health decision-making by providing non-coercive supports. The discussion and conclusion in this chapter aim to serve as an evaluative framework for Chapter 4 that examines whether the law reform in China has taken a step closer to the CRPD approach.

This chapter begins with Section 2.2 which reviews the approaches to involuntary mental health interventions adopted by the international and regional human rights mechanisms before the CRPD's entry into force. Following a brief

1 Mental Health Law of the People's Republic of China (passed by the Standing Committee of the National People's Congress on 26 October 2012, entered into force on 1 May 2013) (MHL).

2 UN Convention on the Rights of Persons with Disabilities (adopted 13 December 2006, entered into force 3 May 2008) 2515 UNTS 3 (CRPD or the Convention).

3 See, for example, John Dawson, 'A Realistic Approach to Assessing Mental Health Laws Compliance with the UNCRPD' (2015) *International Journal of Law and Psychiatry* 70.

DOI: 10.4324/9781003212034-2

introduction of the CRPD in Section 2.3, the chapter will have a close examination of the arguments for and against the claimed 'too radical and unrealistic' requirement of abolishing involuntary interventions overall in Section 2.4.

2.2 Involuntary Mental Health Interventions and the International Human Rights Law prior to the Convention

The section will focus on two major mechanisms in relation to their position of addressing involuntary mental health interventions, namely the Principles for the Protection of Persons with Mental Illness and for the Improvement of Mental Health Care (MI Principles)[4] and the European Convention on Human Rights (ECHR).[5] Before proceeding to them in more detail, it will first give a brief overview of the lack of formal recognition of rights of persons with mental health issues under the international human rights law before the CRPD's entry into force. Then it considers the specific requirements raised by the MI Principles and the ECHR, respectively. As will be suggested below, the human rights instruments prior to the CRPD require the recognition of the rights to dignity, autonomy, and due process as safeguards of persons with mental health issues, but still allow involuntary interventions.

2.2.1 Insufficient protection in the 'International Bill of Human Rights'

Since the Second World War, international human rights law has grown rapidly as a response to the massive human rights violations which occurred during the war.[6] The Universal Declaration of Human Rights,[7] the International Covenant on Civil and Political Rights[8] and the International Covenant on Economic, Social and Cultural Rights[9] were adopted between the 1940s and the 1960s as the 'International Bill of Human Rights', recognising a wide range of human rights.[10]

4 UN General Assembly, 'Principles for the Protection of Persons with Mental Illness and for the Improvement of Mental Health Care' (17 December 1991) UN Doc A/RES/46/119.

5 Convention for the Protection of Human Rights and Fundamental Freedoms (opened for signature 4 November 1950, entered into force 3 September 1953) (ECHR). Technically, since it is considered to be a living instrument, the ECHR and its case law is parallel with, rather prior to, the CRPD. The point here is that the CRPD represents a new approach compared to the position adopted in the MI Principles and the ECHR.

6 See, generally, Daniel Moeckli et al. (eds), *International Human Rights Law* (Second Edition, Oxford University Press 2014).

7 Universal Declaration of Human Rights (adopted 10 December 1948) UNGA Res 217 A(III) (UDHR).

8 International Covenant on Civil and Political Rights (adopted 16 December 1966, entered into force 23 March 1976) 999 UNTS 171 (ICCPR).

9 International Covenant on Economic, Social and Cultural Rights (adopted 16 December 1966, entered into force 3 January 1976) 993 UNTS 3 (ICESCR).

10 John P Humphrey, 'The International Bill of Rights: Scope and Implementation Bicentennial Symposium: Constitutional Government – Strengths, Weaknesses, Future' (1975) 17 *William and Mary Law Review* 527.

However, none of the three earliest and most fundamental human rights documents explicitly mention persons with mental health issues. Although the principle of non-discrimination is included and the condition of mental health issues is arguably a protected ground against discrimination, the effectiveness of such protection was believed to be unsatisfactory. In the landmark study of whether existing human rights instruments had been adequately utilised in the context of disability, including the condition of mental health issues, Quinn and Degener observed:

> More often than not, invisibility has meant that a universal right is simply not applied equally (if applied at all) to persons with disabilities. For example, in the case of education, violations can have as much to do with the right to an equal and effective education as with the right to education as such. Likewise, in the case of civil commitment, the issue can be that relevant due process principles are not applied equally (*mutatis mutandis*) to persons with mental illness. Reform of the law on mental disability can be campaigned for as requiring restoration of equal rights and equal protection of the rule of law.[11]

Leaving the issue of civil commitment to be considered later, the problem of human experimentation serves as another vivid example of how this omission resulted in human rights abuse to people with mental health issues in real life. Article 7 of the ICCPR requires that 'no one shall be subjected without his free consent to medical or scientific experimentation'.[12] However, the fact was that human experimentation, including those without any intended benefit, were conducted on people with intellectual disabilities and mental health issues routinely, without consent from participants.[13] The generic recognition of human rights under the ICCPR failed to protect persons with mental health issues from non-consensual human experimentation, because of the long history in which persons with mental health issues have been considered as a 'separate class' with 'lesser rights'.[14] More importantly, these abuses 'have generally not been recognized as violations of human rights even by organizations that are engaged in human rights work',[15] reflecting the deep-rooted marginalisation of persons with mental health issues even within the mainstream human rights community.

11 Gerard Quinn, Theresia Degener and Anna Bruce, *Human Rights and Disability: The Current Use and Future Potential of United Nations Human Rights Instruments in the Context of Disability* (United Nations Publications 2002) < www.ohchr.org/Documents/Publications/HRDisabilityen.pdf > accessed 5 July 2021, 27.

12 ICCPR, art 7.

13 Clarence J Sundram, 'In Harm's Way: Research Subjects Who Are Decisionally Impaired' (1998) 1 *Journal of Health Care Law and Policy* 36, 40.

14 Piers Gooding, *A New Era for Mental Health Law and Policy: Supported Decision-Making and the UN Convention on the Rights of Persons with Disabilities* (Cambridge University Press 2017), 42.

15 Ibid.

Additionally, other human rights violations, many of which are still lawful under domestic laws, include arbitrary detention (sometimes for life) without due process of law, forced sterilisation, being chained and caged both at home and in institutions, unmodified electro-convulsive treatment without anaesthesia, and other cruel, inhuman, and degrading treatment.[16]

As a result of the worldwide outrage towards these human rights violations and the social movements against institutionalisation and abusive psychiatric practice, dedicated responses from international human rights standards were put forward.[17] For example, the United Nations General Assembly adopted the *Declaration on the Rights of Mentally Retarded Persons* in 1971.[18] The resolution 'starts by pointing out that persons with disabilities enjoy a parity of human rights protection with all other persons'; and the fact that 'it needed saying in the first place' reflected the ineffectiveness of the generic protection.[19]

That said, it is equally worth noting that the human rights contained in the ICCPR and ICESCR have been invoked by persons with mental health issues and advocates, which in turn facilitated the development of dedicated mechanisms of human rights protection for the group of people. For example, the freedom from arbitrary arrest or detention 'has bolstered efforts to require adequate procedural protections' for those persons who are subject to mental health detention.[20] Similarly, many social and economic rights, particularly the right of everyone to the enjoyment of the highest attainable standard of physical and mental health,[21] have provided a powerful legal, and also moral, basis in advocating for increasing the access to community services and suitable training that benefits persons with mental health issues.[22]

2.2.2 MI Principles: a pre-CRPD guide to mental health laws and human rights

As a response to the marginalisation in the mainstream human rights treaties and in particular the international concerns on the political abuse of psychiatry in the Soviet Union and beyond,[23] the rights of persons with mental health issues have

16 Piers Gooding, 'Change and Continuity: A Historical Overview of the Significance of the United Nations Convention on the Rights of Persons with Disabilities to Mental Health Law' (2014) 20 *European Journal of Current Legal Issues* < webjcli.org/article/view/367 > accessed 5 July 2021.

17 Jennifer Brown, 'The Changing Purpose of Mental Health Law: From Medicalism to Legalism to New Legalism' (2016) 47 *International Journal of Law and Psychiatry* 1.

18 UN General Assembly Resolution 2865 (XXVI), 20 December 1971.

19 Gerard Quinn, 'A Short Guide to the United Nations Convention on the Rights of Persons with Disabilities' in Gerard Quinn and Lisa Waddington (eds), *European Yearbook of Disability Law*, vol 1 (Intersentia 2009), 93.

20 Lawrence Gostin and Lance Gable, 'The Human Rights of Persons with Mental Disabilities: A Global Perspective on the Application of Human Rights Principles to Mental Health' (2004) 63 *Maryland Law Review* 20, 34.

21 ICESCR, art 12.

22 Gostin and Gable (n 20), 34–35.

23 Samantha Maingay et al., 'Mental Health and Human Rights: The MI Principles–Turning Rhetoric into Action' (2002) 14 *International Review of Psychiatry* 19.

gradually received dedicated attention at the international level. The MI Principles, adopted by the UN General Assembly in 1991, was one of the results of the 'Decade for Disabled People' from 1983 to 1992 and the appointment of two special rapporteurs on human rights abuses and welfare in the context of disability.[24] The principles have been praised as 'the first step in providing a global set of minimal standards for protecting persons with mental illness and improving mental healthcare'.[25] The principles are phrased as 'the most comprehensive international human rights standards' for the group and 'a critical global step in recognizing mental disability rights issues within the human rights arena'.[26] The MI Principles are particularly worth reviewing here, as they have formed the basis of many other international standards or guidance of mental health and human rights. These standards and guides include the World Health Organisation's 'Ten Basic Principles of Mental Health Care Law' and subsequently the 'Resource Book on Mental Health, Human Rights and Legislation'.[27] More importantly, the principles represent a classic 'necessary but safeguarded' approach to involuntary mental health interventions adopted by the international human rights law prior to the CRPD, as will be discussed below.

The Principles represent a combination and compromise of both liberal values and beneficent (or arguably paternalistic) values.[28] Liberal values are evident in many principles. For example, every patient in a mental health facility has the right to 'recognition everywhere as a person before the law',[29] and '[a]ll persons with a mental illness, or who are being treated as such persons, shall be treated with humanity and respect for the inherent dignity of the human person'.[30] Discrimination on the grounds of mental illness shall be prohibited.[31] Besides, the MI Principles also prohibit using medication as 'a punishment or for the convenience of others'[32], exploited labour,[33] sterilisation[34] and psycho-surgery or other irreversible treatments on involuntary patients,[35] and places a restriction on the uses of seclusion and restraint.[36] More evidently, Principle 9 provides that 'treatment

24 Ibid., 37.
25 Maingay et al. (n 23), 19.
26 Michael Perlin and Eva Szeli, 'Mental Health Law and Human Rights: Evolution and Contemporary Challenges' in Michael Dudley, Derrick Silove, Fran Gale (eds.) *Mental Health and Human Rights: Vision, Praxis, and Courage* (Oxford University Press 2013), 80.
27 Brendan Kelly, Mental Illness, Human Rights and the Law (Royal College of Psychiatrists 2016) 28.
28 Eric Rosenthal and Leonard S Rubenstein, 'International Human Rights Advocacy under the "Principles for the Protection of Persons with Mental Illness"' (1993) 16 *International Journal of Law and Psychiatry* 257.
29 MI Principles, principle 13 para 1(a).
30 Ibid., Principle 1 para 2.
31 Ibid., Principle 1 para 4.
32 Ibid., Principle 10 para 1.
33 Ibid., Principle 13 para 4.
34 Ibid., Principle 11 para 12.
35 Ibid., Principle 11 para 14.
36 Ibid., Principle 11 para 11.

should be directed towards preserving and enhancing personal autonomy'.[37] All these principles are encouraging, especially considering its historical background of how persons with mental health issues were treated at that time, as discussed above in the previous subsection.

At the same time, the beneficent values are also explicitly endorsed, stressing on providing high-quality services. The title of the MI Principles contains the wording of 'for the Improvement in Mental Health Care'. Principle 1 starts with '[a]ll persons shall have the right to the best available mental health care, which shall be part of the health and social system'.[38] To achieve this goal of providing better care, the Principles also require investment of resource into mental health facilities, including qualified professional staff and adequate supply of medication,[39] personalised treatment or care plan[40] that is appropriate to one's health needs[41] and cultural background.[42]

These two sets of values are clearly interrelated.[43] Such interrelation reflects on the principle of 'least restrictive or intrusive treatment',[44] individualised care plan involving the discussion with the person and under review,[45] and the requirement of the therapeutic or diagnostic purpose of medication,[46] for example. After all, the freedom from institutionalisation is usually based on adequate access to high quality and non-coercive service in the community.[47] Nevertheless, the two sets of values are also in conflict, and the MI Principles 'resolve them in a manner that favours paternalistic state coercion exercised through the actions of professionals over individual autonomy'.[48] For example, Principle 11 on consent to treatment has been subjected to heated criticism, being seen as a retreat rather than the enhancement of the right to consent or refuse treatment.[49] The most evident reflection of such a retreat is that, with the authorisation of an independent authority, a person having mental capacity under detention could be forced to

37 Ibid., Principle 9.
38 Ibid., Principle 1 para 1.
39 Ibid., Principle 14 para 1.
40 Ibid., Principle 9 para 2.
41 Ibid., Principle 8 para 1 and principle 9 para 1.
42 Ibid., Principle 7 para 3.
43 Rosenthal and Rubenstein (n 28), 261.
44 MI Principles, principle 9 para 1.
45 Ibid., Principle 9 para 3.
46 Ibid., Principle 10 para 1.
47 However, it is also worth noting that some community-based measures could also be a venue in which the professional coercive power extends from institutions to the community. See, generally, Simon Lawton-Smith, John Dawson and Tom Burns, 'Community Treatment Orders Are Not a Good Thing' (2008) 193 *The British Journal of Psychiatry* 96.
48 Rosenthal and Rubenstein (n 28), 262.
49 More on the discussion, particularly on the weak protection towards persons who is considered to lack mental capacity but does not resist treatment, see Caroline Gendreau, 'The Rights of Psychiatric Patients in the Light of the Principles Announced by the United Nations: A Recognition of the Right to Consent to Treatment?' (1997) 20 *International Journal of Law and Psychiatry* 259.

receive treatment. It is so if 'the patient *unreasonably* withholds consent for medication' and the proposed medication is considered 'in the best interest of the person's health needs' and necessary to protect the safety of the person or others.[50] This provision is believed to diminish the principle of autonomy completely by 'ceding all decision-making power concerning medication to professionals'.[51]

Similarly, involuntary admission could also be justified. The criteria are the severity of mental illness, 'impaired judgement', and 'failure to admit or retain that person is likely to lead to a serious deterioration in his or her condition or will prevent the giving of appropriate treatment that can only be given by admission to a mental health facility in accordance with the principle of the least restrictive alternative'.[52] Although the principle of 'least restrictive alternative' is in place, the scope of 'prevent the giving of appropriate treatment that can only be given by admission to a mental health facility' is still broad. This provision may inspire the legislators of the MHL, as will be discussed in Chapter 4. Another problematic provision is that the person's informed consent would not be necessary if his or her 'personal representative empowered by law', for example a guardian under the MHL, gives the informed consent.[53] In relation to the substantive provisions of detention and consent to treatment, the principles 'remove patients' rights rather than reinforce them'.[54]

The procedural safeguards of depriving one's decision-making authority and liberty are considered to be 'elaborate'.[55] The safeguards include fair hearing, judicial or other independent and impartial review body, access to counsel, periodic review, and a right to appeal.[56] The focus on procedural safeguards is on its face laudable, reflecting an awareness of due process against a serious threat to personal liberty and integrity. Nevertheless, the combination of the strong procedural safeguards and the weak substantive respect for autonomy appears to be 'a sham', merely justifying 'coercion in the name of treatment'.[57] This concern has been proved a reality in many places in the world.[58] It is worth noting here, however, that China did not follow these principles of procedural safeguards in enacting its first national MHL two decades later, as will be discussed in Chapter 4.

50 MI Principles, Principle 11 para 6. Emphasis added.
51 Rosenthal and Rubenstein (n 28), 265.
52 MI Principles, Principle 16 para 1(b).
53 Ibid, Principle 11 para 7.
54 TW Harding, 'Human rights law in the field of mental health: a critical review' (2000) 399 *Acta Psychiatric Scandinavica Supplement* 24, 24.
55 Rosenthal and Rubenstein (n 28), 266.
56 More, see MI Principles, Principle 17, 18.
57 Rosenthal and Rubenstein (n 28), 267.
58 For example, in Ireland and the US. See, generally, Darius Whelan, 'Protecting Rights in Mental Health Law: The Relationship between the Courts and Mental Health Tribunals' in Mary Donnelly and Murray Claire (eds), *Ethical and Legal Debates in Irish Healthcare: Confronting Complexities* (Manchester University Press 2016); and Michael L Perlin, '"Salvation" or a "Lethal Dose"? Attitudes and Advocacy in Right to Refuse Treatment Cases' (2004) 4 *Journal of Forensic Psychology Practice* 51.

It raises a question of enforcement of the MI Principles, that were intended to form the 'minimal United Nations standards for the protection of fundamental freedoms and human and legal rights of persons with mental illness'.[59]

The implementation is unsatisfactory because the MI Principles are not the same status as a treaty or convention, which means the states do not have a legal obligation to follow.[60] No implementation mechanism is set up on this basis,[61] making the weak protection even more toothless. That said, the MI Principles have, arguably, great significance in interpreting other binding law, including the ECHR[62] and domestic constitutional and human rights law.[63] The Principles also provide a set of international standards for the rights of persons with mental health issues that could be a powerful tool in human rights monitoring process[64] and could be utilised by international human rights NGOs, survivor groups and Disabled People's Organisations in their advocacy.[65] These indirect effects of promoting human rights for persons with mental health issues have been less successful in China, for political-legal factors that will be explained in Chapter 3.

The World Network of Users and Survivors of Psychiatry (WNUSP), an international advocacy group for the human rights of persons with mental health issues, criticised the MI Principles for the evident endorsement of psychiatric paternalism in both detention and involuntary treatment. The WNUSP articulates the endorsement to the lack of participation or consultation of mental health service users and survivors in the drafting process.[66] It argues that, if the adequate participation had been in place, 'the Principles would have been quite different and would have a greater level of credibility'.[67] Disabled People's International, a pan-disability organisation, was found to be the only NGO from a disability rights perspective that participated in the drafting negotiations and upheld the value of autonomy.[68]

To summarise, the MI Principles represent a recognition of the 'necessary but safeguarded' approach to the involuntary mental health interventions at the UN level. The drafters made innovative efforts to provide guidance on the regulation of mental health services and promotion of human rights and due process in the mental health institutions by adopting a number of encouraging principles. For this book, however, the very basis of the principles, including the endorsement of involuntary measures, sees the refusal of treatment or failure of giving informed

59 UN, Report of the Working Group on the Principles for the Protection of Persons with Mental Illness and for the Improvement of Mental Health Care, U.N. Doc. E/CN.4/1991/39 (1991), para 2–3, as cited in Gostin and Gable (n 20), 43.
60 Rosenthal and Rubenstein (n 28) 268.
61 Harding (n 54).
62 Rosenthal and Rubenstein (n 28), 272–279.
63 Gendreau (n 49), 266.
64 Gostin and Gable (n 20), 43–44.
65 Maingay et al. (n 23).
66 Melinda Jones, 'Can International Law Improve Mental Health? Some Thoughts on the Proposed Convention on the Rights of People with Disabilities' (2005) 28 *International Journal of Law and Psychiatry* 183, 203.
67 Ibid.
68 Gendreau (n 49), 269.

consent as an obstacle to accessing treatment and restoring one's mental health. Thus, the involuntary measures should be subject to safeguards to prevent abuse, but they are necessary and even desirable under certain circumstances. This mindset is critical in understanding the core spirit of the MHL. As will be elaborated in Chapters 3 and 4, the MHL arguably only follows the 'necessary' part and omits the 'safeguarded' part, against the background that policy priority in China is to increase the treatment rate.[69]

2.2.3 The European Convention on Human Rights and its jurisprudence on involuntary interventions

This subsection presents a brief review of the ECHR and its case law on detention and involuntary treatment for people with mental health issues. The ECHR was adopted by the Council of Europe (CoE), a leading human rights organisation in Europe, in 1950, and the European Court of Human Rights (ECtHR) was founded in 1959 with a mission to apply and interpret the ECHR in cases brought by individuals against the Member States of the CoE.[70] This subsection will reveal that, although procedural safeguards are required to prevent arbitrariness, involuntary mental health interventions are in principal permitted under the ECHR and its case law. It represents the position of 'necessary but safeguarded' towards involuntary measures in the mental health setting, just like the MI Principles as discussed above.

Although China is not a Member State of the CoE and, hence, the ECHR and its case law do not apply to China, this mechanism still merits consideration for two main reasons. First, the ECtHR jurisprudence represents a 'due process of law' approach to the regulation of involuntary mental health interventions, which plays an important role in facilitating mental health law reforms in its Member States, like the UK and Ireland.[71] Second, the case law involves Member States of considerable diversity in terms of ideological history, the rule of law, and economic development, from Russia to Malta, which arguably provides a better reference to China than the mental health law of any particular country.[72]

Before moving to the review of the relevant provisions and case law, it is worth noting that CoE also gives recommendations to its Member States in relation to mental health law and human rights. From the 1970s, the CoE has adopted a series of recommendations, for example Recommendation 818 (1977) on the Situation of the mentally ill,[73] Recommendation No. R (83) 2 on the legal protection of persons suffering from mental disorder placed as involuntary

69 Chapter 3, Section 2.

70 See, generally, CoE < www.coe.int/en/web/portal/home > accessed 1 July 2021.

71 Brown (n 17).

72 CoE '46 Member States' < www.coe.int/en/web/portal/47-members-states > accessed 5 July 2021.

73 CoE Parliamentary Assembly, 'Recommendation 818 on Situation of the mentally ill' (1977).

patients,[74] urging its Member States to turn their focus on rights protection in mental health settings and transfer the authority from psychiatric professional to courts.[75] However, many requirements provided by these recommendations are significantly similar to the ones from the MI Principles. For example, the least restrictive measures[76] and procedural safeguards[77] appear in both the MI Principles and the CoE recommendations. Therefore, the legally binding force and the nature of constantly developing make the ECHR and its case law a 'front-runner' in human rights protection.[78]

The ECtHR has developed a body of case law on mental health detention and treatment. The basis of these cases includes Article 3 on the prohibition of torture, inhuman or degrading treatment, Article 5 on the right to liberty and security, Article 6 the right to a fair trial, Article 8 on the right to respect for private and family life.[79] The book does not seek to make an original contribution to the literature of the ECHR and mental health laws. It only aims to suggest the principal position of the ECHR and its relevant case law towards mental health detention and involuntary treatment, as a typical position before the adoption of the CRPD. Hence, guided by the secondary resources written by scholars in this particular field, the subsection briefly reviews the ECHR Articles and the relevant case law under the following categories.

2.2.3.1 Lawfulness of involuntary detention

Article 5(1) forms the legal ground of deprivation of liberty from people with mental health issues. It reads:

> Everyone has the right to liberty and security of person. No one shall be deprived of his liberty save in the following cases and in accordance with a procedure prescribed by law:
>
> ...
>
> (e) the lawful detention of persons for the prevention of the spreading of infectious diseases, of persons of *unsound mind*, alcoholics or drug addicts or vagrants.[80]

74 CoE Committee of Ministers, 'Recommendation No. R (83) 2 of the Committee of Ministers to Member States concerning the legal protection of persons suffering from mental disorders placed as involuntary patients' (1983).
75 Brown (n 17).
76 CoE Parliamentary Assembly (n 73), para 15.
77 Ibid; CoE Committee of Ministers (n 74), art 8.
78 Kelly (n 27), 15. Also, see Penelope Weller, 'The Convention on the Rights of Persons with Disabilities and the Social Model of Health: New Perspectives' (2011) *Journal of Mental Health Law* 74.
79 ECHR, art 3, 5, 6, and 8.
80 Ibid., art 5. Emphasis added.

The ECHR itself does not define the 'persons of unsound mind', an out-of-date term that represents 'old prejudices' in respect of persons with mental health issues.[81] The criteria for detention on this basis, however, has been clarified in a number of cases. The court held in *Winterwerp v the Netherlands*, to justify a deprivation of liberty for a person of 'unsound mind', a psychiatric diagnosis should be made on the basis of 'objective medical expertise', a 'true' mental disorder of 'a kind or degree warranting compulsory confinement', and 'the validity of continued confinement depends upon the persistence of such a disorder'.[82] The court saw mental disorders as 'constantly evolving with medical science' and, therefore, did not adopt any precise definition.[83] Flynn observes that there exists 'a wide margin of appreciation by the court to determine who is a person of unsound mind'.[84] Nevertheless, to prevent abuse as a form of unjustified social control, the court provided that the detention on the ground of 'unsound mind' cannot be used when the person's 'views or behaviour deviate from the norms prevailing in a particular society'.[85] In another case, the court held:

> The detention of an individual is such a serious measure that it is only justified where other, less severe measures have been considered and found to be insufficient to safeguard the individual or public interest which might require that the person concerned be detained. That means that it does not suffice that the deprivation of liberty is executed in conformity with national law but it must also be necessary in the circumstances.[86]

Article 5(1) requires that the deprivation of liberty should be 'in accordance with a procedure prescribed by law'.[87] The ECtHR has interpreted that the detention of persons with mental health issues must not be decided arbitrarily.[88] In determining arbitrariness, the case law suggests that the domestic law prescribing detention must comply with the provisions of the ECHR[89] and also be accessible and precise to ensure foreseeability in the application.[90]

81 Jonathan Bindman, Samantha Maingay and George Szmukler, 'The Human Rights Act and Mental Health Legislation' (2003) 182 *British Journal of Psychiatry* 91, 91.
82 *Winterwerp v the Netherlands* (1979) 2 EHRR 387, para 39. More cases see, for example, *Witold Litwa v Poland* (2001) 33 EHRR 387, para 68.
83 Ibid.
84 Eilionóir Flynn, 'Disability, Deprivation of Liberty and Human Rights Norms: Reconciling European and International Approaches' (2017) 2016 *International Journal of Mental Health and Capacity Law* 75, 76.
85 *Winterwerp v the Netherlands* (1979) 2 EHRR 387, para 37.
86 *Witold Litwa v Poland* (2001) 33 EHRR 387, para 78.
87 ECHR, art 5.
88 *Winterwerp v the Netherlands* (1979) 2 EHRR 387, para 39; *Kawka v Poland* App No 2587/94 (ECHR, 9 January 2001), para 48; *Amuur v France* (1996) 22 EHRR 533, para 42.
89 *Plesó v Hungary* App No 41242/08 (ECHR, 17 January 2012), para 59.
90 *Kawka v Poland* App No 2587/94 (ECHR, 9 January 2001), para 46. Also, see *H.L. v United Kingdoms*, App No 45508/99 (ECHR, 5 October 2004), para 114.

Lastly, to guarantee the lawfulness of the detention on this basis, states must ensure the detention is imposed in a therapeutic environment where the detainee could receive appropriate medical attention.[91]

2.2.3.2 Independent and periodical review

Article 5(4) of the ECHR forms the basis of the independent and periodical review of the detention.

> Everyone who is deprived of his liberty by arrest or detention shall be entitled to take proceedings by which the lawfulness of his detention shall be decided speedily by a court and his release ordered if the detention is not lawful.[92]

The term 'court' has been interpreted broadly, as long as it is considered to have: 'independence from the executive; independence from the parties to the case; and a judicial character'.[93] Therefore, regardless the review body is named as a court or a mental health tribunal, it should have the authority to find the detention in question invalid or unlawful and order release, rather than being advisory only.[94] The ECtHR jurisprudence has also established that, considering the significance of detention of persons with mental health issues, the requirement of impartiality provided in Article 6 on the right to a fair trial is also applicable to detentions on the ground of 'unsound mind'. If a psychiatrist involved with the procedure of a patient before the review, he or she should not sit in the court, or tribunal, in order to ensure independence and impartiality.[95]

Another requirement by Article 5(4) is that the review must be speedy. The ECtHR has further interpreted this requirement, finding periodic reviews should be in place to ensure the liberty of persons in detention is not restricted unnecessarily when the detention is no longer justified.[96] As will be addressed in Chapter 4, the MHL adopts a similar substantive requirement, albeit absent the requirement for periodic independent review as a procedural safeguard.

Article 5 also applies to cases in which deprivation of liberty based on 'unsound mind' occurs outside of psychiatric institutions. In *Stanev v Bulgaria*, the plaintiff was under guardianship and legal representative authorised his institutionalisation in a social care home. The Court found the government breached Article 5, thereby 'broadening the scope of locations' where deprivation of liberty can occur.[97]

91 *Aerts v Belgium* (1998) 29 EHRR 50, para 49.
92 ECHR, art 5(4).
93 Bartlett, Lewis and Thorold (n 14), 62.
94 *X v United Kingdom* (1981) 4 EHRR 188, para 61.
95 *DN v Switzerland* (2003) 37 EHRR 21, para 42–56.
96 *Winterwerp v the Netherlands* (1979) 2 EHRR 387, para 55. Also, see Brown (n 17) for a review of case law about how often the periodic review should take place.
97 *Stanev v Bulgaria* (2012) 55 EHRR 22; Flynn (n 84), 78.

2.2.3.3 Involuntary treatment and informed consent

As suggested above, the ECHR has a strong focus in preventing arbitrary detention and requires procedural safeguards in the case law. On the other hand, ECHR and the case law only provide 'weak protection' to involuntary treatment that usually occurs during detention in mental health settings.[98]

Although not directly addressed in the ECHR, the ECtHR has gradually developed precedents from case law on this issue, by adopting a broad interpretation of Article 3 on inhuman or degrading treatment and Article 8 on private life. Article 3 provides that '[n]o one shall be subjected to torture or to inhuman or degrading treatment or punishment'. In *Herczegfalvy v Austria*, the ECtHR stressed that persons with mental health issues detained in mental health facilities are protected by this provision and established two requirements for involuntary treatment. The treatment must be 'to preserve the physical and mental health of the patient'; and, the patient must be 'entirely incapable' of deciding on the acceptance of refusal of the treatment.[99] Although involuntary treatment can constitute inhuman and degrading treatment, such finding is difficult to achieve:

> Individuals who are detained in secure psychiatric institutions who have been deemed unable to consent to medical care, or who can be subject to treatment for a 'mental disorder' under the terms of their detention, face great challenges if they are to establish that involuntary treatment breaches Article 3 ECHR. Such treatment will not breach Article 3 if it is found to be therapeutically necessary.[100]

The wide margin of appreciation on 'therapeutic necessity' has been criticised for not taking account of alternative less intrusive or restrictive interventions.[101] An example used to suggest the unreasonableness of the wide margin of appreciation is the delivery of electro-convulsive treatment, which can be administered with a lower likelihood of causing injuries under anaesthetic and with muscle relaxants.[102] The court could reasonably adopt a more substantive approach in considering 'whether the treatment was administered in a humane way or indeed, in accordance with the wishes of the patient, who may have been willing to consent to the treatment in one form, but not in another'.[103]

Article 8 provides for the right to respect for private and family life is also relevant here, which reads:

98 Lisa Waddington and Bernadette McSherry, 'Exceptions and Exclusions: The Right to Informed Consent for Medical Treatment of People with Psychosocial Disabilities in Europe' (2016) 23 *European Journal of Health Law* 1.

99 *Herczegfalvy v Austria* (1993) 15 EHRR 437, para 82

100 Waddington and McSherry (n 98), 15.

101 Anete Erdmane, 'Liberty behind Closed Doors-Involuntary Placement and Medical Treatment in Psychiatric Institutions from the Human Rights Perspective' (2010) 4 *Vienna Online Journal on International Constitutional Law* 90.

102 Waddington and McSherry (n 98), 15.

103 Ibid.

> 1. Everyone has the right to respect for his private and family life, his home and his correspondence.
> 2. There shall be no interference by a public authority with the exercise of this right except such as is in accordance with the law and is necessary in a democratic society in the interests of national security, public safety or the economic well-being of the country, for the prevention of disorder or crime, for the protection of health or morals, or for the protection of the rights and freedoms of others.[104]

On this basis, the ECtHR has established case law in which involuntary treatment amounts to an unjustified interference in one's private life as protected by Article 8. The Court stressed in *Storck v Germany* that 'even a minor interference with the physical integrity of an individual must be regarded as an interference with the right to respect for private life under Article 8 if it is carried out against one's will'.[105] However, the general prohibition of involuntary treatment seems only to apply to persons who are considered as having mental capacity.[106] This is largely because Article 8(2) provides justifications to the restrictions of the right, including interference by a public authority that is 'in accordance with the law' and 'for the protection of health or morals, or for the protection of the rights and freedoms of others'.[107] The application of this justification has been concluded as

> if the domestic law provides for sufficient safeguards, including the review of treatment at appropriate intervals, and if the treatment is regarded as necessary and serving the legitimate aim of protecting the health of the patient or the rights and freedoms of others, such treatment can be imposed without consent.[108]

2.2.3.4 A summary

This subsection reveals that the ECHR and its case law allow mental health detention and involuntary treatment in principle, given procedural safeguards and therapeutic necessity are in place. Compared to the growing jurisprudence on procedural safeguards for the deprivation of liberty on the ground of 'unsound mind', the ECtHR appears to grant the Member States a wider margin of appreciation in regulating involuntary treatment. Although involuntary treatment could constitute an unjustified interference in one's private life, such finding is difficult to achieve.

2.2.4 Section summary

This section illustrates how international human rights instruments prior to the CRPD address detention and involuntary treatment imposed on persons with

104 ECHR, art 8.
105 *Storck v Germany*, App No 61603/00 (ECHR, 16 June 2005), para 143.
106 Waddington and McSherry (n 98), 19.
107 ECHR, art 8(2).
108 Waddington and McSherry (n 98), 19.

mental health issues. In principle, involuntary interventions are permissible under certain circumstances and should be safeguarded by due process of law. In other words, the position of international human rights law before the CRPD on involuntary mental health interventions is 'necessary but safeguarded'. This position is argued to be based on the presumption that limitation to personal liberty, integrity and autonomy of persons with mental health issues is justified and necessary, and 'the issue was determining the bounds of permitted compulsion'.[109] On this basis, the MI Principles intended to raise the awareness of good quality mental health services, promoting voluntariness and individualised care plan while endorsing detention and involuntary treatment as necessary measures to 'facilitate' accessing care. The case law produced by the ECtHR is another typical reflection of such efforts in developing a human rights protection regime in line with the 'necessary but safeguarded' approach. However, having such a regime may simply reinforce systems of coercion due to the margin of appreciation of states.

In contrast to this 'necessary but safeguarded' approach, the CRPD has raised fundamental challenges to this very presumption and the legality of involuntary mental health interventions. Although this approach has not been altered in its case law, the ECtHR has suggested a growing, but still fragmented, awareness in citing the CRPD in its judgments.[110] The next section will turn to discuss the CRPD and its application to involuntary mental health interventions in more depth.

2.3 The Convention and the 'Paradigm Shift'

The CRPD is the first international human rights convention in the 21st century and 'represents the culmination of two and a half decades of development in international human rights law aimed at addressing human rights violations experienced by people with disabilities'.[111] After the ratification by its 20th States Parties, the CRPD entered into force on 3 May 2008. This section will closely examine the CRPD provisions that are relevant to mental health detention and involuntary treatment.[112]

Before proceeding to the details of these provisions, this section will briefly introduce the CRPD as a whole. It will be followed by an examination of UN

109 Peter Bartlett, 'The United Nations Convention on the Rights of Persons with Disabilities and Mental Health Law' (2012) 75 *The Modern Law Review* 752, 753.

110 Oliver Lewis, 'Council of Europe' in Lisa Waddington and Anna Lawson (eds), *The UN Convention on the Rights of Persons with Disabilities in Practice: A Comparative Analysis of the Role of Courts* (Oxford University Press 2018). Also, see Andrea Broderick, 'The United Nations Convention on the Rights of Persons with Disabilities and the European Convention on Human Rights: A Tale of Two Halves or a Potentially Unified Vision of Human Rights?' (2018) 7 *Cambridge International Law Journal* 199.

111 Gooding (n 14), 46.

112 For a comprehensive introduction to the CRPD, see Shivaun Quinlivan, 'The United Nations Convention on the Rights of Persons with Disabilities: An Introduction' (2012) 13 *ERA Forum* 71.

human rights bodies' interpretations of the CRPD's new requirement on involuntary mental health interventions and how the practice has upheld.

2.3.1 An introduction to the Convention

Similar to the ineffectiveness of the generic protection for persons with mental health issues, under the international human rights law prior to the CRPD, the broader community of persons with disabilities have not been generally considered to be the holders or subjects of human rights.[113] The 'default setting for considering disability' has been 'a mixture of charity, paternalism and social policy' that usually only aim to maintain persons with disabilities, not supporting their full and meaningful participation.[114] This approach is not only the result of resource limitation, for example, nearly 80 per cent of the 650 million persons with disabilities are living in the developing countries; it has also been argued to be underpinned by a perception that sees disability as 'eroding' human existence.[115]

To this background, and after years of difficult advocacy and negotiations, the CRPD sets out a human rights agenda of addressing the global issue of disability. In this human rights agenda of disability, the CRPD requires its States Parties to treat persons with disabilities as '"subject" with full legal personhood', rather than as '"object" to be managed and cared for'.[116] Drawing on the importance of positive measures of promoting substantive equality and the interdependence of all human rights, the CRPD forces people to rethink, more fundamentally, 'when or whether the difference requires separate, special treatment' that is usually done by creating segregation in the name of protection.[117]

The purpose of the CRPD is set out in Article 1: 'to promote, protect and ensure the full and equal enjoyment of all human rights and fundamental freedoms by all persons with disabilities, and to promote respect for their inherent dignity'.[118] Without adopting an explicit definition of disability, Article 1 provides a *de facto* definition:

> Persons with disabilities *include* those who have *long-term* physical, *mental*, intellectual or sensory impairments which in interaction with various barriers may hinder their full and effective participation in society on an equal basis with others.[119]

The text of Article 1 adopts the term 'mental impairments', clearly referring to people with mental health issues. However, since 'long term' is included, Kelly raises a question whether all persons with mental disorders fit the definition, since

113 Quinn (n 19), 89.
114 Ibid.
115 Ibid., 90.
116 Ibid., 90. Also, see Degener (n 16).
117 Quinn (n 19), 92.
118 CRPD, art 1.
119 Ibid. Emphasis added.

'many disorders are not "long term"'.[120] A common response to this question relies on the term of 'include', which implies the CRPD does not mean to exclude any individual or group, and Preamble paragraph (e) that recognises disability as 'an evolving concept' and focuses on the 'interaction' between persons with impairments and various social barriers.[121]

As a 'hybrid convention' that contains not only all the relevant substantive rights and also the philosophy of non-discrimination and inclusive equality[122], the broad range of rights could be broadly categorised into the following kinds: (a) the rights that protect the person, (b) the rights that 'restore autonomy, choice and independence', (c) the rights of participation, (d) liberty rights and (e) economic, social and cultural rights.[123] Regardless of the academic debate where the CRPD creates any new human rights,[124] the CRPD does include some rights that are not found in existing human rights conventions, for example the right to living independently and being included in the community.[125] It targets the issue of institutionalisation, a particular problem to persons with disabilities that requires 'national investment in community-based living options'.[126]

These rights are also governed by a set of general principles set out in Article 3, including:

a Respect for inherent dignity, individual autonomy including the freedom to make one's own choices, and independence of persons;
b Non-discrimination;
c Full and effective participation and inclusion in society;
d Respect for difference and acceptance of persons with disabilities as part of human diversity and humanity;
e Equality of opportunity;
f Accessibility;
g Equality between men and women;
h Respect for the evolving capacities of children with disabilities and respect for the right of children with disabilities to preserve their identities.[127]

With all the specific rights and principles, in particular the emphasis on individual autonomy and full and effective participation and inclusion in society, the CRPD aims to shift the old paradigm that persons with disabilities are

120 Kelly (n 27), 30.
121 Rosemary Kayess and Phillip French, 'Out of Darkness into Light? Introducing the Convention on the Rights of Persons with Disabilities' (2008) 8 *Human Rights Law Review* 1.
122 CRPD Committee, 'General comment No. 6 (2018) on equality and non-discrimination' (26 April 2018), CRPD/C/GC/6.
123 Quinn (n 19), 99–111.
124 Kayess and French (n 121), 32.
125 Ibid, art 19.
126 Kayess and French (n 121), 29.
127 CRPD, art 3. Emphasis added.

objects of social welfare to a human rights model under which persons with disabilities are 'subjects of rights' and 'active members of society'.[128] The next sub-section will elaborate on the reflection of this paradigm shift in mental health laws.

The CRPD is also special and innovative in other respects: the highly participatory drafting process,[129] the stronger monitoring function of the CRPD Committee,[130] and the 'transformative vision for fostering change at the domestic level'.[131] First, the CRPD is widely agreed to be 'the most participatory international legal instrument', and 'those typically subject to the human rights violations in question took a leading role in its development'.[132] The leading role played by the WNUSP in shaping a number of relevant provisions to involuntary intervention is well documented.[133] Second, the monitoring mechanism required by the CRPD is expected to 'reconfigure the structure and process of human rights oversight'.[134] The innovations include the creation of the periodic Conference of States Parties to exchange the experience of implementation and the CRPD Committee's mandate of receiving collective complaints and consulting Disabled People's Organisations (DPOs).[135] Third, the focus of fostering domestic change is explicit in Article 33 and Article 4. In addition to the requirement in regard to domestic implementation monitoring mechanism,[136] Article 33 requires States Parties to establish 'one or more focal points' within government and 'give due consideration to the establishment or designation of a coordination mechanism',[137] urging States Parties to have a coordinated framework to make changes at the domestic level.[138] This mandate is supported by Article 4(3)

128 Kayess and French (n 121), 3. Also, see Degener (n16).
129 Gooding (n 16).
130 Michael Ashley Stein and Janet E Lord, 'Monitoring the Convention on the Rights of Persons with Disabilities: Innovations, Lost Opportunities, and Future Potential' (2010) 32 *Human Rights Quarterly* 689.
131 Janet E Lord and Michael Ashely Stein, 'The Domestic Incorporation of Human Rights Law and the United Nations Convention on the Rights of Persons with Disabilities' (2008) 83 *Washington Law Review* 449.
132 Gooding (n 14), 49.
133 Cliona De Bhailis and Eilionóir Flynn, 'Recognising Legal Capacity: Commentary and Analysis of Article 12 CRPD' (2017) 13 *International Journal of Law in Context* 6. Also, see Tina Minkowitz, 'CRPD Advocacy by the World Network of Users and Survivors of Psychiatry: The Emergence of an User/Survivor Perspective in Human Rights' (Social Science Research Network 2012) SSRN Scholarly Paper ID 2326668 < papers.ssrn.com/abstract=2326668 > accessed 1 July 2021.
134 Stein and Lord (n 129), 690.
135 Ibid., 696–697.
136 CRPD, Art 33(2).
137 CRPD, Art 33(1).
138 Gerard Quinn, 'Resisting The "Temptation of Elegance": Can The Convention On The Rights Of Persons With Disabilities Socialise States To Right Behaviour?', *The UN Convention on the Rights of Persons with Disabilities: European and Scandinavian perspectives* (Brill 2009).

that requires persons with disabilities should be involved 'in the development and implementation of legislation and policies to implement the present Convention, and in other decision-making processes concerning issues relating to persons with disabilities'.[139]

2.3.2 Provisions relevant to involuntary mental health interventions

Article 14(1) of the CRPD requires States Parties to ensure that persons with disabilities enjoy the right to liberty and security on an equal basis with others and 'that the existence of a disability shall in no case justify a deprivation of liberty'.[140] Although involuntary mental health detention is not explicitly mentioned, Flynn argues it 'must be read to prohibit all deprivations of liberty where the existence of disability is a factor in justifying the detention'.[141] It means any criterion of deprivation of liberty that takes disability into account is considered arbitrary and, therefore, impermissible.[142] According to this strict reading, a combination of disability and dangerousness or necessity for treatment, which is widely adopted by most mental health laws in the world, is not permitted by the CRPD.[143]

In regards to involuntary treatment and informed consent, the CRPD provides in Article 25 that States Parties 'recognise that persons with disabilities have the right to the enjoyment of the highest attainable standard of health without discrimination on the basis of disability' and

> [r]equire health professionals to provide care of the same quality to persons with disabilities as to others, *including on the basis of free and informed consent* by, *inter alia*, raising awareness of the human rights, dignity, autonomy and needs of persons with disabilities through training and the promulgation of ethical standards for public and private health care.[144]

It is significant in the sense that informed consent is explicitly required as an element of the right to health in international human rights law.

Article 15 and Article 17 are also relevant here. Article 15 provides that '[n]o one shall be subjected to torture or to cruel, inhuman or degrading treatment or punishment'.[145] Article 17 provides that '[e]very person with disabilities has a right to respect for his or her physical and mental integrity on an equal basis with others'.[146]

139 CRPD, Art 4(3).
140 Ibid., Art 14.
141 Flynn (n 48), 81.
142 CRPD Committee, 'Guidelines on article 14 of the Convention on the Rights of Persons with Disabilities The right to liberty and security of persons with disabilities' (September 2015), para 13.
143 Ibid.
144 CRPD, art 25. Emphasis added.
145 CRPD, art 15.
146 CRPD, art 17.

Treatments without the informed consent of persons with disabilities, especially those intrusive and irreversible medical treatments, may violate the right to integrity and the right to freedom from torture or cruel, inhuman or degrading treatment.[147]

Most importantly, Article 12 provides the core of the 'paradigm shift' that underpins all these provisions. Article 12 requires States Parties to 'recognise that persons with disabilities enjoy legal capacity on an equal basis with others in all aspects of life' and to provide access to support in exercising their legal capacity.[148]

The CRPD Committee, the monitoring body set up in accordance with Article 34, elaborates the close connection between Article 12 and above articles addressing involuntary detention and treatment in the General Comment No.1 on Article 12 Equal recognition before the law:

> The denial of the legal capacity of persons with disabilities and their detention in institutions against their will, either without their consent or with the consent of a substitute decision-maker, is an ongoing problem. This practice constitutes arbitrary deprivation of liberty and violates Articles 12 and 14 of the Convention. States parties must refrain from such practices and establish a mechanism to review cases whereby persons with disabilities have been placed in a residential setting without their specific consent.[149]

The General Comment continues to provide that:

> States Parties have an obligation to require all health and medical professionals (including psychiatric professionals) to obtain the free and informed consent of persons with disabilities prior to any treatment. In conjunction with the right to legal capacity on an equal basis with others, States parties have an obligation not to permit substitute decision-makers to provide consent on behalf of persons with disabilities. All health and medical personnel should ensure appropriate consultation that directly engages the person with disabilities.[150]

Acknowledging that '[f]orced treatment is a particular problem for persons with psychosocial, intellectual and other cognitive disabilities', the CRPD Committee also requires States Parties to abolish law and policy allowing or perpetrating forced treatment that violates all the rights proscribed by Article 12, 15, 16 and 17.[151]

147 Valentina Della Fina, Rachele Cera and Giuseppe Palmisano, *The United Nations Convention on the Rights of Persons with Disabilities: A Commentary* (Springer 2017), 307–337.
148 CRPD, art 12 (2)(3).
149 CRPD Committee, 'General Comment No 1: Article 12: Equal Recognition Before the Law' (11 April 2014) UN Doc CRPD/C/GC/1, para 40.
150 Ibid., para 41.
151 Ibid., para 42.

The position of abolishing involuntary mental health interventions, with other forms of substituted decision-making, has been repeated by the Guidelines on Article 14 of the Convention on the Rights of Persons with Disabilities – The right to liberty and security of persons with disabilities.[152] The CRPD Committee has also continued recommending States Parties to do so in its Concluding Observations, among which the recommendation to China is quoted at the beginning of Chapter 1.

Moreover, this seemingly absolutist approach has also been accepted by some other UN human rights bodies. The most recent report by the Special Rapporteur on the rights of persons with disabilities urges States Parties to abolish '[m]ental health legislation, as long as it authorizes and regulates the involuntary deprivation of liberty and forced treatment of persons based on an actual or perceived impairment (i.e. diagnosis of "mental health condition" or "mental disorder")'.[153] The Special Rapporteur on torture and other cruel, inhuman or degrading treatment or punishment also calls to

> [i]mpose an absolute ban on all forced and non-consensual medical interventions against persons with disabilities, including the non-consensual administration of psychosurgery, electroshock and mind-altering drugs such as neuroleptics, the use of restraint and solitary confinement, for both long- and short-term application.[154]

The UN Working Group on Arbitrary Detention also adopted its report in 2015, referring to States' obligation to prohibit involuntary mental health interventions.[155]

However, not all UN human rights bodies adopt the approach of abolition. The Human Rights Committee states in its General Comment No. 35 that

> [t]he existence of a disability shall not *in itself* justify a deprivation of liberty but rather any deprivation of liberty must be necessary and proportionate, for the purpose of protecting the individual in question from serious harm or preventing injury to others. It must be applied only as a measure of last resort and for the shortest appropriate period of time, and must be accompanied by adequate procedural and substantive safeguards established by law.[156]

152 CRPD Committee (n 142).

153 Human Rights Council, 'Report of the Special Rapporteur on the rights of persons with disabilities' (11 January 2019) A/HRC/40/54, para 64.

154 Human Rights Council, 'Report of the Special Rapporteur on torture and other cruel, inhuman or degrading treatment or punishment' (1 February 2013) A/HRC/22/53, para 81.

155 Working Group on Arbitrary Detention, 'United Nations Basic Principles and Guidelines on the right of anyone deprived of their liberty to bring proceedings before a court' (4 May 2015) WGAD/CRP.1/2015, para 56.

156 Human Rights Committee, General comment No. 35 Article 9 (Liberty and security of person) (16 December 2014) CCPR/C/GC/35, para 19. Emphasis added.

Flynn points out that the Guidelines on CRPD Article 14 and the report of the UN Working Group on Arbitrary Detention are published later than the Human Rights Committee General Comment No. 35, which may solve the technical problem of the application of human rights law discrepancy between different interpretations.[157] The obvious gap of different understanding among different UN human rights bodies reflects the controversy of the requirement of abolition. The division of attitudes may also reflect on the potential sectional interests. As the next section will suggest, the groups of users and survivors of psychiatry have invested enormous efforts in advocating that the UN bodies accept the approach of abolition,[158] whilst the governments of most, if not all, States Parties and psychiatrists strongly oppose abolition.

2.3.3 Section summary

As explained above, the relevant CRPD provisions and the interpretations provided by the CRPD Committee represent a seemingly extreme standard regarding involuntary mental health interventions. Compared to the human rights mechanism prior to the CRPD under which, given certain conditions are met, such interventions are subject to safeguards but still permissible, the CRPD approach requires an overall abolition.

The different positions presented by the CRPD approach and the approach of the ECHR or the Human Rights Committee suggest the tension among different stakeholders. The next section will examine the major criticism about the CRPD approach and how scholars with different backgrounds attempt to reconcile the opposing viewpoints.

2.4 Criticism of the Convention's Approach and Possible Steps Forward

Section 2.3 above reveals the revolutionary 'paradigm shift' proposed by the CRPD and this section considers the criticism of the shift and the efforts to find a middle ground. As will be suggested below, the conflict between people for and against the so-called radical and unrealistic approach is in fact limited to the necessity of maintaining the involuntary mental health interventions as a last resort. Nevertheless, the consensus is clear that the access to less restrictive measures should be increased and support should be in place in the community, in other words maximising the autonomy of persons with mental health issues in the decision-making of mental health treatment. In doing so, the section attempts to argue that the significance of the debate is not about whether a piece of law providing involuntary mental health interventions as a last resort is CRPD-compliant, since the answer given by the CRPD Committee is a clear no. The importance of such work, however, is to learn from the consensus which could potentially benefit further research and facilitate meaningful changes in law reform and practice.

As briefly mentioned earlier, a number of States Parties issued declarations, understandings and reservations when they ratified the CRPD even before the publication of the General Comment No. 1.[159] Australia declared its understanding that 'the Convention allows for compulsory assistance or treatment of persons, including measures taken for the treatment of mental disability, where such treatment is necessary, as a last resort and subject to safeguards'.[160] When the Committee was calling for comments and contribution to the draft of the General Comment No.1, a number of States Parties to the CRPD, civil society organisations and academic institutions submitted their statement, many of which had critical views.[161] For example, the Federal Government of Germany[162] and the Essex Autonomy Project[163] explicitly disagree that all forms of substituted decision-making, which means one's decision is made by someone else, should be abolished.

The controversy over the CRPD approach during the drafting negotiations is well documented.[164] De Bhailís and Flynn observe that the literature on Article 12 after the General Comment No. 1 has turned its focus to 'either plotting its practical implementation or criticising the Committee's interpretations and providing alternatives'.[165] For example, the Netherlands made a number of declarations about involuntary interventions upon its ratification in 2016. The Dutch government declared its understanding that 'the Convention allows for compulsory care or treatment of persons, including measures to treat mental illnesses, when circumstances render treatment of this kind necessary as a last resort, and the treatment is subject to legal safeguards'.[166] It also interprets Article 12 as 'restricting substitute decision-making arrangements to cases where such measures are necessary, as a last resort and subject to safeguards'.[167]

Given these critical attitudes, it is particularly worth noting that the CRPD requirement of abolishing involuntary mental health interventions does not imply

159 See 'Declarations and Reservations of the CRPD' < https://treaties.un.org/Pages/ViewDetails.aspx?src=TREATY&mtdsg_no=IV-15&chapter=4&lang=_en&clang=_en > accessed 1 July 2021.

160 Ibid.

161 See the submission from Norway, Law Society of Scotland, and Essex Autonomy Project for example < www.ohchr.org/en/hrbodies/crpd/pages/dgcarticles12and9.aspx > access 1 July 2021.

162 Federal Republic of Germany, *German Statement on the Draft General Comment on Article 12 CRPD* (20 February 2014) < www.ohchr.org/Documents/HRBodies/CRPD/GC/FederalRepublicOfGermanyArt12.pdf > accessed 1 July 2021.

163 Wayne Martin et al., *Response to the Committee's Draft General Comment on Article 12 of the UN Convention on the Rights of Persons with Disabilities* (21 February 2014) < www.ohchr.org/Documents/HRBodies/CRPD/GC/EAPArt12.doc > accessed 1 July 2021.

164 Amita Dhanda, 'Legal Capacity in the Disability Rights Convention: Stranglehold of the Past or Lodestar for the Future' (2006) 34 *Syracuse Journal of International Law and Commerce* 429. See also Fina, Cera and Palmisano (n 146), 263–280.

165 De Bhailís and Flynn (n 133).

166 'Declarations and Reservations of the CRPD' (n 127).

167 Ibid.

that people in crisis should be abandoned and left without treatment or support. On the contrary, the CRPD Committee stressed that supported decision-making, a set of alternative and non-coercive decision-making support, should be invested in and made available and accessible to people in need, and its application in mental health laws have attracted increasing attention from both academia and policymakers.[168] In other words, under the new regime endorsed by the CRPD Committee, the States Parties have an obligation to do more, not less. As this section will suggest below, the confidence in the effectiveness of these alternative and non-coercive measures holds the key to the debate.

This section firstly considers the major criticisms. Subsequently, it will examine the different proposals of how to work with the CRPD and the controversy around it, in order to facilitate meaningful reforms in mental health services and law.

2.4.1 Criticism of the Convention's approach

From the declarations, understandings and reservations quoted earlier in this section, it appears that the States Parties recognise the value of supported decision-making arrangements and the necessity of reducing involuntary interventions in mental health service. The persistence of maintaining involuntary interventions and substituted decision-making measures as the 'last resort' is arguably because the States Parties, as well as many scholars, find the non-coercive paradigm impractical and unrealistic.

Acknowledging the purpose of the CRPD in maximising autonomy, Dute argues that an overall abolition of substituted decision-making, including involuntary mental health intervention, is 'definitely a step too far'.[169] This judgement is based on the 'obvious' reality to Dute that there are always people unable to exercise legal rights 'even with the most comprehensive support'.[170] Dute believes that to abolish substituted decision-making will lead to 'unworkable situations, especially in healthcare, where complicated and sometimes far-reaching decisions must be made'.[171]

Critical commentators like Dute often base their doubts on the effectiveness of supported decision-making arrangements. The so-called 'hard cases' are usually raised to illustrate difficulties in applying supported decision-making in real life and the necessity of keeping substituted decision-making usually on the basis of 'Best Interest Principle'.[172] A typical 'hard case' may be a person in a coma but a

168 Piers Gooding, 'Supported Decision-Making: A Rights-Based Disability Concept and Its Implications for Mental Health Law' (2013) 20 *Psychiatry, Psychology and Law* 431.

169 Joseph Dute, 'Should Substituted Decision-Making Be Abolished?' (2015) 22 *European Journal of Health Law* 315, 318.

170 Ibid.

171 Ibid.

172 The Best Interest Principle is usually adopted when a substitute decision-maker is appointed for the person concerned to make decision for him or her on the basis of what the substitute decision-maker believe as the best interest of the person. For example, see 'Mental Capacity Act Code of Practice' < www.gov.uk/government/up

medical decision is urgently needed.[173] Admittedly, the General Comment No.1 contains a solution to this scenario: 'the "best interpretation of will and preferences" must replace the "best interests" determinations'.[174] When informed consent is impossible to get from the person concerned, or his or her expressed will and preference conflict with each other, an external person should be appointed to achieve the best interpretation of the will and preference of the person concerned. This best interpretation should form the basis for a decision in that situation and is subject to safeguards prescribed in CRPD Article 12.

However, New Zealand states in its submission to the draft of General Comment No. 1 that 'it is conceivable that effective supports in this context will be *indistinguishable* from substitute decision making', which essentially questions how the best interpretation of one's wills and preferences differs from the principle of best interest in practice.[175] The Law Society of Scotland also shared the same doubt. It questioned the difference between the 'best interpretation of will and preferences' and the substituted judgement of 'the choice or decision which, it is believed, the adult would have arrived at if able to make and communicate a choice or decision in the matter in question'.[176]

To some commentators, abolishing involuntary interventions is not only unrealistic but also undesirable. Dute argues that the over-emphasis on autonomy will go against the principle of protecting vulnerable people 'against the consequences of irresponsible decisions they may take and against possible abuse by others'.[177] Freeman and colleagues argue that the CRPD Committee's interpretation 'threatens to undermine critical rights for persons with mental disabilities, including the enjoyment of the highest attainable standard of health, access to justice, the right to liberty, and the right to life' and will also worsen the social stigma and discrimination against people with mental health issues.[178] World Psychiatry, an official publication of the World Psychiatric Association, also published an editorial, calling the CRPD 'a problem child of international human rights law' that will hurt 'the very people it purports to help'.[179]

loads/system/uploads/attachment_data/file/224660/Mental_Capacity_Act_code_of_practice.pdf > accessed 1 July 2021.

173 Piers Gooding, 'Navigating the "Flashing Amber Lights" of the Right to Legal Capacity in the United Nations Convention on the Rights of Persons with Disabilities: Responding to Major Concerns' (2015) 15 Human Rights Law Review 45.

174 CRPD Committee (n 118), para 21.

175 New Zealand, *Submission to the CRPD Committee on the Draft General Comment on Article 12 CRPD* (11 March 2014) < www.ohchr.org/Documents/HRBodies/CRPD/GC/NewZealand_art12.doc > 1 July 2021. Emphasis added.

176 Law Society of Scotland, *Submission to the CRPD Committee on the Draft General Comment on Article 12 CRPD* (November 2013) < www.ohchr.org/Documents/HRBodies/CRPD/GC/LawSocietyOfScotlandArt12.doc > accessed 1 July 2021.

177 Dute (n 169).

178 Melvyn Colin Freeman et al., 'Reversing Hard Won Victories in the Name of Human Rights: A Critique of the General Comment on Article 12 of the UN Convention on the Rights of Persons with Disabilities' (2015) 2 *The Lancet Psychiatry* 844.

179 Paul S Appelbaum, 'Saving the UN Convention on the Rights of Persons with Disabilities – from Itself' (2019) 18 *World Psychiatry* 1, 1.

In addition to the concerns above, the claimed radical position of abolition, as required by the CRPD Committee, appears to its critics to be deterring law reforms in the States Parties of the CRPD. Freeman and his colleagues write that the States are now 'facing intense pressure to implement far reaching changes that challenge fundamental principles of mental health care and treatment hitherto widely accepted as reflecting a human rights perspective'.[180] However, even under this 'intense pressure' Dawson observes no evidence that States Parties are following the Committee's 'more radical suggestions' in mental health law reforms and, therefore, a 'more realistic interpretation' should be adopted to guide future reform.[181]

2.4.2 Searching for the middle ground

Facing the heated debate around the legitimacy of involuntary interventions and substituted decision-making, States Parties and scholars working in this field have sought to find a middle ground. A conceivable middle ground could address the concerns of both sides of supporting and opposing the CRPD requirement, thereby facilitating progressive reforms in law, policy and practice.

Some scholars have attempted to reconcile the tension by putting the CRPD's new requirement into the development history of mental health law and policy. Gooding observes that the functions of mental health laws in the common-law tradition have remained unchanged:[182] protecting the public from the potential harm from people with mental health issues, obtaining access to the services these people need, and safeguarding user's civil rights.[183] In the light of this account of continuity and changes in the development of mental health laws, instead of denying the necessity, the CRPD merely requires an alternative arrangement to the coercive services in the pre-CRPD regime, namely supported decision-making.[184] Therefore, as discussed in the last sub-section on criticism towards the CRPD, the problem largely lies in the effectiveness of these non-coercive measures perceived by policy and lawmakers.

For example, Dute believes the practice of Personal Ombudsman in Sweden, a well-known non-coercive practice in mental health, and similar arguably CRPD-compliant arrangements are 'expensive and time-consuming' and impossible to be applied widely.[185] A determination of the effectiveness and feasibility of these arrangements are beyond the scope of this study.[186] However, it is worth noting that,

180 Ibid.
181 Dawson (n 3).
182 Gooding (n 16).
183 Brenda Hale, 'Justice and Equality in Mental Health Law: The European Experience' (2007) 30 *International Journal of Law and Psychiatry* 18.
184 See, generally, Gooding (n 16).
185 Dute (n 169).
186 There has emerged research that examines the effectiveness of non-coercive alternative mental health services, see Piers Gooding and Bernadette McSherry, 'Alternatives to Compulsory Detention and Treatment and Coercive Practices in Mental Health Settings' (2018) 26 *Journal of Law and Medicine* 300.

in his review of the history of mental health laws, Gooding refers to the resistance to informed consent among medical professionals and scholars in the past, drawing on its similarity with the objecting comments to the CRPD nowadays. Gooding quotes Beauchamp, a leading U.S. scholar in informed consent ethics and law, who observes that in the mid-1970s '[p]hysicians saw the demands of informed consent as impossible to fulfil, at least in some cases, inconsistent with good practice care'.[187]

Another effort of this kind is to develop a system that could provide necessary intervention in emergency situations to save lives but is delinked to any disability specific criteria. Some scholars argue for a moderate approach to making existing law and policy CRPD-compliant. For example, the Essex Autonomy Project, an interdisciplinary research team based in the University of Essex (UK), argues that the Mental Capacity Act 2005 (MCA) of England and Wales could become CRPD-compliance with certain minor amendments.[188] They argue that the functional test, a method of identifying mental capacity, becomes CRPD-compliant if the scope of application extends to everyone from the original disability-specific group of persons who lack mental capacity 'because of an impairment of, or a disturbance in the functioning of, the mind or brain'.[189] Against the interpretation offered in the General Comment No. 1, they believe the amended version will free the MCA from the accusation of direct discrimination, as the amended standard is for everyone with and without disability and therefore 'on an equal basis with others' as suggested by the CRPD Article 12.[190] Similar reasoning is also adopted in the proposal of fusing legislation of mental health and capacity law. For example, Dawson's proposal of 'more realistic interpretation' reflects the understanding that using mental capacity as the basis for substituted decision-making is disability-neutral and therefore CRPD-compliant.[191] This approach echoes the proposal of the functional approach of legal capacity,[192] which is rebutted by the General Comment No.1.

However, there are other scholars who believe the moderate approach is insufficient[193] and, therefore, propose more comprehensive legal reforms.[194] Relying on

187 Tom L Beauchamp, 'Informed Consent: Its History, Meaning, and Present Challenges' (2011) 20 *Cambridge Quarterly of Healthcare Ethics* 515, 516.

188 Wayne Martin et al. 'Achieving CRPD Compliance' (Essex Autonomy Project 2014) < repository.essex.ac.uk/13624/1/EAP-Position-Paper-FINAL-copy.pdf > accessed 1 July 2021.

189 Ibid.

190 Ibid.

191 Dawson (n 3).

192 Mary Keys, 'Legal Capacity Law Reform in Europe: An Urgent Challenge' in Gerard Quinn and Lisa Waddington (eds), *European Yearbook of Disability Law*, vol 1 (Intersentia 2009).

193 Amita Dhanda, 'Universal Legal Capacity as a Universal Human Right' in Michael Dudley, Derrick Silove and Fran Gale (eds), *Mental Health and Human Rights* (Oxford University Press 2012).

194 Piers Gooding and Eilionóir Flynn, 'Querying the Call to Introduce Mental Capacity Testing to Mental Health Law: Does the Doctrine of Necessity Provide an Alternative?' (2015) 4 *Laws* 245. Eilionoir Flynn, 'Mental (in)Capacity or Legal Capacity: A Human Rights Analysis of the Proposed Fusion of Mental Health and Mental Capacity Law in Northern Ireland' (2013) 64 *Northern Ireland Legal Quarterly* 485.

the position held by the CRPD Committee in the General Comment No.1 that the functional test is discriminatory in nature, Flynn and Arstein-Kerslake argue that it should be possible to develop a truly disability-neutral basis for intervention.[195] For example, state intervention should be 'situation specific' and only permitted in cases of 'imminent and grave harm', rather than population specific and far-reaching in every aspect of life.[196]

Lastly, there are also proposals that the access, quality and regulation over voluntary mental health service should be improved even when the involuntary approach is still in place. The Special Rapporteur on the right of everyone to the enjoyment of the highest attainable standard of physical and mental health published a comprehensive report in 2017, analysing the power imbalance in the traditional biomedical mental health services.[197] Instead of following many other UN human rights bodies that call for abolishing involuntary interventions overall, it adopts a pragmatic approach to giving recommendations. The report recommends states and other relevant stakeholders to explore and scale up investment in non-coercive alternative service models, to redirect resources that used to be put in institutional care into community-based care, and to invest in psychosocial services to empower users and respect their autonomy.[198] In short, the Special Rapporteur only recommends states to '[t]ake targeted, concrete measures to *radically reduce* medical coercion and *facilitate the move* towards an end to all forced psychiatric treatment and confinement'.[199]

Similarly, McSherry also proposes a shift of focus into voluntary provisions that could potentially gain access to mental health service and aid the enjoyment of the highest attainable standard of mental health.[200] This proposal is based on the context in Australia, and also in many other developed countries, that most service users are voluntary, the definition of which may be in question, but mental health laws only focus on involuntary measures.[201] McSherry writes:

> If mental health laws shift the focus more towards voluntary admission and treatment rather than focusing solely on involuntary admission and treatment, then there is at least a possibility that adequate resourcing of services and a reduction in counter-therapeutic coercive practices may follow.[202]

195 Eilionóir Flynn and Anna Arstein-Kerslake, 'State Intervention in the Lives of People with Disabilities: The Case for a Disability-Neutral Framework' (2017) 13 *International Journal of Law in Context* 39.

196 Ibid.

197 Human Rights Council, 'Report of the Special Rapporteur on the right of everyone to the enjoyment of the highest attainable standard of physical and mental health' (28 March 2017) A/HRC/35/21.

198 Ibid.

199 Ibid., para 95(f). Emphasis added.

200 Bernadettte McSherry, 'The Right of Access to Mental Health Care: Voluntary Treatment and the Role of Law' in Bernadette McSherry and Penelope Weller (ed), *Rethinking Rights-Based Mental Health Laws* (Hart Publishing 2010).

201 Ibid.

202 Ibid., 395.

As will be discussed in Chapter 4, the MHL appears to follow this proposal of promoting voluntary services without abolishing involuntary measures.

2.4.3 Section summary

This section addresses the main criticism of the 'radical' and 'unrealistic' interpretation of CRPD in relation to involuntary mental health interventions and substituted decision-making. It also reviews the efforts in reconciling the opposing positions of the debate. The section suggests that one of the most fundamental disagreements may rest on the effectiveness and feasibility of non-coercive measures, which takes time to build an evidence-based case for. The mindset of practitioners and policy and lawmakers also takes time to change. Relying on the report of the Special Rapporteur on the right to health, the section then addresses what States Parties could do, before the final abolition of involuntary mental health interventions as required by the CRPD Committee.

The point of this section is that a clear consensus of developing non-coercive services and reducing the reliance on involuntary measures is evident, given the enormous criticism towards the CRPD approach. Accordingly, since they point to the same direction of maximising autonomy and developing non-coercive services, the scholarly attempts of finding a middle ground merit serious consideration, for the purpose of assessing the MHL.

2.5 Chapter Conclusion

This chapter has reviewed the 'necessary but safeguarded' approach in regulating coercive services in the MI Principles and ECHR case law, the 'radical and unrealistic' requirement of freedom from involuntary mental health interventions provided by the CRPD, and the tension between the two. As addressed earlier, the position of abolishing involuntary mental health interventions and substituted decision-making overall is hotly contested: it has been strongly welcomed and promoted by certain groups, for example UN human rights bodies[203] and survivor groups,[204] but equally strongly opposed by medical professionals and scholars.[205] Given the polarised perspectives, the reality is that no State Party has achieved CRPD-compliance in this regard. However, as argued in this chapter we need to move beyond the narrow focus on the permissibility of the involuntary interventions.

Nevertheless, an important consensus is still identifiable: States Parties should maximise the autonomy of persons with mental health issues and avoid coercive

203 See Chapter 2, Section 2.3.2.

204 See, for example, Tina Minkowitz, 'Why Mental Health Laws Contravene the CRPD– An Application of Article 14 with Implications for the Obligations of States Parties' (2011) Available at SSRN 1928600 < papers.ssrn.com/sol3/papers.cfm?abstract_id=1928600 > accessed 1 July 2021; and Minkowitz (n 23).

205 See, for example, Paul Appelbaum, 'Protecting the Rights of Persons with Disabilities: An International Convention and its Problems' (2016) 4 *Psychiatric Services* 366.

interventions where possible, by increasing the access to non-coercive, community-based mental health services and exploring alternative forms of support. This consensus is critical to this book, as it serves as a guide in assessing whether the mental health law reform in China has taken a step closer to the requirements of the CRPD. Before examining the relevant law reform in China in Chapter 4, the next chapter will provide the context necessary to understand mental health services and the legal system of China.

3 Background

Mental Health Services and the Legal System in China

3.1 Chapter Introduction

This chapter seeks to provide the background of China's mental health services and the broader political-legal system in general that situates the Mental Health Law (MHL).[1] This background is essential in understanding the purpose of the MHL and the policy priority in mental health. Due to the complexity of both the mental health services and legal system in China, this chapter will highlight a list of critical features.

The chapter starts with some basic information about China and a brief history of its mental health system. It is followed by a discussion of seven interrelated features of the planning and delivery of the services. Then, it provides an overview of China's political-legal framework, indicating its emphasis on maintaining political stability and the marginalisation of human rights protection.

3.2 Basic Information and Mental Health Services in China

China is an Eastern Asian country, with a population of around 1.4 billion and a territory of 9.6 million square kilometres.[2] Apart from Hong Kong Special Administrative Region (SAR), Macao SAR, and Taiwan,[3] which have their own mental health services systems and legal systems, respectively, this book addresses the law and practice in the remaining thirty-one provinces, centrally administered municipalities, and autonomous regions of minorities. Despite years of rapid

1 Mental Health Law of the People's Republic of China (passed by the Standing Committee of the National People's Congress on 26 October 2012, entered into force on 1 May 2013) (MHL).

2 Central Intelligence Agency (CIA), 'China' (*The World Factbook*) < www.cia.gov/the-world-factbook/countries/china/ > accessed 1 July 2021.

3 To justify the inclusion of Taiwan in this statement, the European Union states that it 'pursues a "One China" policy and recognises the government of the People's Republic of China as the sole legal government of China' and 'supports the peaceful resolution of differences between Taiwan and the People's Republic of China'. See European Economic and Trade Office in Taiwan, 'Taiwan and the EU' <https://eeas.europa.eu/delegations/taiwan_en/2000/Taiwan%20and%20the%20EU> accessed 1 July 2021.

DOI: 10.4324/9781003212034-3

economic growth, China is still a developing country with the GDP per capita of 16,117 US dollars estimated in 2019 (ranked 106th globally),[4] and there exist enormous gaps between the economic and social development in coastal (eastern) and inland (western) regions.[5]

Due to reasons unknown to the public, there is no recent, accurate and authoritative statistical data revealing how many people have mental health issues in China.[6] A widely cited survey in China indicates that there are 'over 170 million adults suffering from at least one type of mental disorder in China' and 16 million people have severe mental illness.[7]

The distribution of mental health resources is an example of the gaps in economic and social development. Thirty-seven western and rural counties or regions, which are home of over 40 million people and contributing one-third of the country's territory, have no access to a psychiatric bed at all.[8] On the other hand, Shanghai, an eastern port and national economic centre, have about 20,000 psychiatric beds for 24 million people.[9]

Albeit there is some visibility of traditional Chinese medicine in the formal health care system, the mental health system is primarily of western or modern style.[10] Historical documents report that China had policies on addressing madness related issues in the Tang dynasty (around 618–917 A.D.).[11] Unsurprisingly, however, the arrangements were more charity-based rather than medical.[12] China 'embraced' the western system in 1897 when an American missionary built the first psychiatric hospital in Guangzhou, an important port city and one of the first

4 CIA (n 2).

5 See, generally, Yehua Dennis Wei, *Regional Development in China: States, Globalization and Inequality* (Routledge 2013).

6 Yu-Tao Xiang et al., 'Mental Health in China: Challenges and Progress' (2012) 380 *The Lancet* 1715, 1716.

7 Jiwei Qian, 'Mental Health Care in China: Providing Services for under-Treated Patients' (2012) 15 *The Journal of Mental Health Policy and Economics* 179, 179. See also, generally, Michael R Phillips et al., 'Prevalence, Treatment, and Associated Disability of Mental Disorders in Four Provinces in China during 2001–05: An Epidemiological Survey' (2009) 373 *The Lancet* 2041. A recent study finds that 16.6% of 32,552 participants have mental disorders in their lifetime before the interview. See Yueqin Huang et al., 'Prevalence of Mental Disorders in China: A Cross-Sectional Epidemiological Study' (2019) 6 *The Lancet Psychiatry* 211. Besides, a Lancet editorial wrote in 2015 that '[a]n estimated 173 million adults in China have mental health disorders, of whom 4.3 million are registered as having severe mental health problems'. See *The Lancet*, 'Mental Health in China: What Will Be Achieved by 2020?' (2015) 385 *The Lancet* 2548, 2548.

8 Keqing Li, 'The review and prospect of China's mental health work' (2012) 29 (2) *Medical Research and Education* 1, 6.

9 Ibid.

10 For a detailed account, see Kam-Shing Yip, 'An Historical Review of the Mental Health Services in the People's Republic of China' (2005) 51 *International Journal of Social Psychiatry* 106.

11 Jin Liu et al., 'Mental health system in China: history, recent service reform and future challenges' (2011) 10 *World Psychiatry* 210.

12 Ibid.

cities where foreigners were allowed to do business in China.[13] However, that period of history was not the best time for modern psychiatry to grow in China: the Qing dynasty was overthrown by the revolution by which the Republic of China was founded in 1911; warlords were competing with each other (1916–1928); Japan invaded China (1937–1945), as a part of World War II; and the civil war between the Communist Party and the Nationalist Party (1927–1949).[14] By 1 October 1949, when the People's Republic of China[15] was founded, there were around one hundred psychiatrists and one thousand beds in psychiatric hospitals, providing services to over four hundred million people in the country.[16]

The development of mental health services did not accelerate immediately after the decades of war and the foundation of the People's Republic of China. Indeed, more psychiatric hospitals have been built, and the idea of community mental health service was raised and promoted in the first National Mental Health Meeting in 1958.[17] The Great Leap Forward (1958–1960) and the Cultural Revolution (1966–1976), however, stopped most social development projects in the country. According to a review article on mental health services and resources in China, the total number of psychiatric hospitals in 1965 dropped to only 55% of the number in 1961.[18] When the Cultural Revolution ended, the opening and reform towards a market economy (1978 onwards) became the new national policy priority and altered communist China fundamentally. It provided a relatively stable political and social environment for mental health services to develop.[19] On the other hand, the sharp, and arguably unprepared, transformation into a market economy cut most of the healthcare service providers from full public funding and pushed hospitals to make profits for self-sustaining.[20] As will be discussed further in Chapter 6, this had a substantive impact on the practice of mental health services. Chinese psychiatry has not only vast coercive powers over service users but also a financial motivation to fill the wards.

Under the new era, a set of stable mental health policies became possible. The second National Mental Health Meeting in 1986 brought an initial policy paper that set out to develop and guide mental health work.[21] After decades without a settled national policy on mental health, the Ministry of Health,[22] the Ministry of

13 Ibid.

14 See, generally, Immanuel Chung-yueh Hsü, *The Rise of Modern China* (Oxford University Press 2000).

15 'People's Republic of China' will only be used where indicates the particular regime; 'China' will be used in other occasions.

16 Liu et al. (n 11).

17 Ibid.

18 Keqing Li et al., 'Mental health services in China: A review of delivery and policy issues in 1949–2009' (2012) 26 (5) *China Mental Health Journal* 321, 323.

19 See, generally, Liu et al. (n 11) and Li et al. (n 18).

20 Li et al. (n 18), 324.

21 The Ministry of Health, the Ministry of Civil Affairs, and the Ministry of Public Security, Opinions on Strengthening Mental Health Work *(1987)*.

22 For consistency and clarity, 'the Ministry of Health' will be used throughout this book to refers to the branch of China's central government that is in charge of (mental) health-related work, whose official name has changed several times during the

Public Security, the Ministry of Civil Affairs, and China Disabled Persons' Federation published the first National Mental Health Plan 2002–2010.[23] Two years later, the Opinions on Further Strengthening Mental Health Work was carried out jointly by more Ministries.[24] These policy documents set the foundation for more policies afterwards, including the Guidelines for National Mental Health Work 2008–2015[25] and the National Mental Health Work Plan 2015–2020.[26]

However, mental health services and policies in China is a complicated field, involving various considerations, stakeholders, and constraints. For the book, a complete account is impossible and unnecessary. Instead, this chapter will present a selection of interrelated features of mental health policies and services system in China, providing a context in which the MHL applies.

3.2.1 Western psychiatry as an incomplete or biased importation

As mentioned earlier, the current mental health system in China is Western in style. Chinese traditional medicine could earn some visibility in policy and practice. For example, there is usually a department of Chinese medicine in each big hospital, and there are also specialised Chinese medicine hospitals which may have a psychiatric department.[27] In particular, during political movements like the Cultural Revolution when half of the hospitals were damaged or closed, Chinese

decades. The current name is 'National Health Commission of the People's Republic of China', changed from 'National Health and Family Planning Commission of the People's Republic of China' in 2018.

23 The Ministry of Health, the Ministry of Civil Affairs, the Ministry of Public Security, and China Disabled People's Federation, National Mental Health Plan 2002–2010.

24 The Ministry of Health, the Ministry of Education, the Ministry of Public Security, the Ministry of Civil Affairs, the Ministry of Justice, the Ministry of Finance, and China Disabled People's Federation, Opinions on Further Strengthening Mental Health Work (2004).

25 The Ministry of Health, the Publicity Department of the Central Committee of the Communist Party of China, National Development and Reform Commission, the Ministry of Education, the Ministry of Public Security, the Ministry of Civil Affairs, the Ministry of Justice, the Ministry of Finance, the Ministry of Personnel, the Ministry of Labour and Social Security, the Ministry of Culture, National Food and Drug Administration, All China Federation of Trade Unions, Central Committee of the Chinese Communist Youth League, All China Women's Federation, China Disabled People's Federation, and the Office of National Working Commission on Ageing, Guidelines for National Mental Health Work 2008–2015 (Guidelines 2008–2015).

26 The Ministry of Health, Central Comprehensive Management Office, National Development and Reform Commission, the Ministry of Education, the Ministry of Public Security, the Ministry of Civil Affairs, the Ministry of Justice, the Ministry of Finance, the Ministry of Labour and Social Security, and China Disabled People's Federation, National Mental Health Work Plan 2015–2020 (National Mental Health Work Plan 2015–2020).

27 For example, the National Mental Health Work Plan 2015–2020 calls on providing psychiatric trainings for practitioners of Chinese medicine, involving Chinese medicine practitioners into psychiatric diagnosis, treatment and research, and developing psychiatric department in Chinese medicine hospitals.

medicine became more popular among the general public and was endorsed by the government.[28] Research reveals that, before the introduction of Western psychiatry, Chinese healers understood and diagnosed mental issues by a set of original ideas and terminology.[29]

That said, the Western and modern psychiatry dominates the mainstream mental health service in China.[30] In 1897, a western missionary and doctor built the first psychiatric hospital in China.[31] The first generation of Chinese psychiatrists were also trained by their Western colleagues in China dating back to 1931.[32] Institutional treatments, the 'alien forms grafted onto Chinese society rather than an indigenous product', has become the most important form of mental health services one can get in China.[33]

However, psychiatry in China differs from its Western counterparts, in that the psycho-social consideration of mental illness has been mostly absent. It is partly because social science subjects in higher education were banned in the mid-1950s.[34] Psychology, sociology, anthropology or social work were no longer taught or researched in universities for being 'too Western'.[35] Instead, under the political influence of the Soviet Union at that time, 'Pavlovian theory, ideological indoctrination, and work therapy were widely employed'.[36]

To some extent, the biological approach is believed to be a form of self-protection for mental health professionals. Under that period of ideological struggling with the West, mental illness was conceptualised by the communist/socialist world as a result of capitalism on the exploited.[37] 'Capitalism drives people mad'.[38] It is not difficult to understand that the Chinese psychiatrists, who also suffered from continuous political movements themselves, prefer a biological approach in explaining and treating mental health issues.

Since the Chinese leadership set aside ideological revolution and shifted to focus on economic development in the 1980s, this scenario started to change. To better cope with the stress coming along with economic growth and modernity, the

28 Yip (n 10).

29 See, generally, Xiehe Liu, 'Psychiatry in Traditional Chinese Medicine' (1981) 138 *The British Journal of Psychiatry* 429.

30 See, generally, Yip (n 10); Zhi-hua Pan, 'Preliminary Study of Psychiatry History in China and the Western Countries' (2013) 1 Disability Research 59; Veronica Pearson, *Mental Health Care in China: State Policies, Professional Services and Family Responsibilities* (Royal College of Psychiatrists 1995), 28.

31 Pan (n 30), 62.

32 Ibid.

33 Veronica Pearson, 'The Chinese Equation in Mental Health Policy and Practice: Order plus Control Equal Stability' (1996) 19 *International Journal of Law and Psychiatry* 437, 439.

34 Ibid.

35 Ibid, 440.

36 William L Parry-Jones, 'Psychiatry in the People's Republic of China' (1986) 148 *The British Journal of Psychiatry* 632, 634; on the Soviet Union's influence on Chinese psychiatry in the history, see Pearson (n 33), 440 and Pan (n 30), 62.

37 Qian (n 7), 13.

38 Pearson (n 33), 440.

government supported the teaching and practice of psychology.[39] Pilot projects on community service were undertaken and promoted in all versions of the National Mental Health Work Plan.[40] Social workers are integrated into the mental health team in some regions.[41] However, these are very recent developments. The biomedical model is still dominant in the mental health system without competing and effective alternative approaches to understanding and coping with mental distress.[42]

3.2.2 Addressing under-treated patients as the policy priority

Research shows that 'undersupply of the mental health service is the most pivotal issue for policy-makers' in China.[43] All versions of the National Mental Health Work Plan and other relevant policy documents reflect this concern. For example, the baseline for the treatment rate of schizophrenia set in the Guidelines 2008–2015 is 15% to 30%, and the aim is 60% in 2010 and 80% in 2015.[44] The policy goal of promoting treatment is crucial in understanding service providers' attitudes about service users' right to decision-making and autonomy. Under this policy goal, refusing treatment is more likely to be seen as a barrier to accessing treatment and, therefore, coercion is necessary to facilitate treatment.

Psychiatric research supports this policy priority. As more recent data is unavailable, a study published in 2009 reveals that during 2001 to 2004 91.8% of people with a diagnosis of mental disorders and 27.6% of people with a diagnosis of psychotic disorders never sought help in China.[45] Another study, based on the data from World Health Organisation (WHO) world mental health surveys, reveals that the treatment rate of common mental disorders (including anxiety disorder, emotional disorder, substance use disorder but excluding schizophrenia) was only 11.3%.[46]

39 See, generally, Jie Yang, *Mental Health in China: Change, Tradition, and Therapeutic Governance* (John Wiley & Sons 2017).
40 Liu et al. (n 11).
41 Ibid; also, see Bo Chen and Shiyuan Huang, 'Promoting the autonomy of persons with mental disabilities through social worker's intervention: a qualitative study guided by the Convention on the Rights of Persons with Disabilities' in Wanhong Zhang (eds) *Disability Rights Studies in China* (Social Science Academic Press, Beijing 2014) 120.
42 Zhiying Ma, 'In the name of love and medicine? Understanding the experience of female psychiatric inmates from the perspective of rights' in Wanhong Zhang (eds) *Disability Rights Studies in China* (Social Science Academic Press, Beijing 2014) 224, 225. Also, see Pearson (n 29), 22–28.
43 Qian (n 7), 2.
44 Guidelines 2008–2015.
45 Liu et al. (n 11), 211. More general information, see Phillips et al. (n 7).
46 Ming-Yuan Zhang 'Challenge to mental health services in China: thinking from World Mental Health Surveys' (2006) Vol 26 (4) *Journal of Shanghai Jiaotong University* (Medical Science) 329.

One of the underlying reasons for the low treatment rate is the different attitudes toward mental illness before and after the 1980s. As mentioned earlier, in the decades of political movements, diagnosis and treatment of mental illness were under obvious political influence. From 1964 to 1976, people with mental health issues were seen as having wrong or problematic political attitudes.[47] Accordingly, political education, particularly the thoughts of Chairman Mao, rather than psychiatric drugs were prescribed to many people.[48]

When China entered a new era that economic development prevails and a medical view of mental health re-emerges, the broken mental health system was unable to cope with the increased needs, whose existence had been denied or unrecognised before.[49] Interestingly, as the economic development and social stability becomes the most important national project, the development of mental health services has to justify itself by associating with the country's social agenda. For example, the Guidelines 2008–2015 starts with '[m]ental health work relates to the health of people and social stability and is important to the social and economic development and the building of harmonious socialist society'.[50] The similar wording is also adopted in many other policies, like the National Mental Health Work Plan 2002–2010.[51]

Another reason for the low treatment rate is believed to be the under-supply of mental health services and inadequate resources. Research reports that the cost of mental illness contributes 13% of the total burden of disease globally.[52] In the case of China, a study estimates that the total disability-adjusted life of the common psychiatric conditions was about 254 million years in 2011 and accounted for 2,681 billion RMB (approximately 356 million euros) loss in gross domestic product.[53] By contrast, the mental health workforce in China is unable to address this huge burden. As mentioned earlier, psychiatrists (16,103) and psychiatric nurses (24,793) in more than 500 psychiatric hospitals are the primary professionals in China's mental health service.[54] The number of clinical psychologists and social workers is unknown but remarked as 'few' by a policy paper which also clearly states there was no occupational therapist at least in 2011.[55] Taking its enormous population into account, China's workforce (1.24 psychiatrists, 1.91 psychiatric nurses, and 10 psychiatric beds every 100,000 population) is considerably lower

47 Yip (n 10) 108–109. Interestingly, a few decades later, people with problematic political attitudes were deemed to have mental illnesses. See Yip (n 10) 112.
48 Ibid., 108.
49 See, generally, Yang (n 39).
50 Guidelines 2008–2015.
51 National Mental Health Work Plan 2002–2010.
52 Murali Thyloth, Hemendra Singh and Vyjayanthi Subramanian, 'Increasing Burden of Mental Illnesses across the Globe: Current Status' (2016) 32 *Indian Journal of Social Psychiatry* 254.
53 Liu et al. (n 11), 211. The conditions include unipolar depressive disorder, bipolar disorder, schizophrenia, alcohol use disorders, Alzheimer's and other dementias, drug use disorders, post-traumatic stress disorder, obsessive-compulsive disorder, panic disorder, and insomnia.
54 Ibid.
55 Ibid.

than the average level of the world (4.15 psychiatrist, 12.97 psychiatric nurses, and 43.6 psychiatric beds every 100,000 population).[56]

Inadequate investment is argued to be a direct reason for the under-supply of service. Citing data from the WHO, research in 2011 reports that only 2.35 of the total health budget went to mental health services.[57] As the public funding to health is mainly the responsibility of local governments, whose financial capacity varies from region to region, the problem of inadequate investment is worsened in the underdeveloped areas. An authoritative policy paper acknowledges that in some western regions 'the existing national mental health policies become just well-written documents'.[58]

3.2.3 Lack of coordination among different categories of service providers

While the inadequate investment is echoed in most studies about China's mental health system, lack of coordination receives less attention. For historical reasons, the Ministries of Health, Public Security and Civil Affairs have developed their service system respectively, acting as the primary workforce in mental health. The actual statistics, however, are more complicated and largely unknown to the public.[59] A study refers to a monograph by a leading psychiatric institution in China that in 1990 there were

> 473 psychiatric institutions under the Ministry of Public Health, 190 under the Ministry of Civil Affairs, 81 under the Ministry of Industry and Mining, 23 under the Ministry of Public Security, 24 run by the People's Liberation Army, and 12 under local collectives.[60]

However, Pearson doubts that this list is complete as she has visited 'at least one psychiatric hospital run by the railway ministry'.[61]

The division of work among the three main Ministries is less clear than it should be. Psychiatric hospitals under the Ministry of Health are supposed to provide mainstream mental health treatment to the public. Psychiatric hospitals under the Ministry of Civil Affairs, however, are supposed to be less medical and relieve the burden from the Ministry of Health by taking patients who occupy the beds for unnecessary length.[62] These may include chronic patients and so-called 'three have-nots' patients: no home, no job, and no accommodation.[63] A study in 1994 reveals that about 33%

56 Ibid.
57 Ibid.
58 Ibid., 214.
59 Pearson (n 33), 445.
60 Ibid. Pearson makes the reference to 'a monograph by the Psychological Medicine Research Centre of the West China University of Medical Sciences (1990)'. No further reference information is provided.
61 Ibid.
62 Ibid., 446.
63 Yip (n 10) 111. There exists different translation of the 'three have-nots', however the key message is that they have no means of support. See ibid.

of patients with a diagnosis of a mental disorder were taken care of in psychiatric hospitals run by the Ministry of Civil Affairs.[64]

Hospitals under the Ministry of Public Security (known as Ankang Hospitals nationwide) have a direct tie with the police. However, they do not only deal with patients who have committed criminal offences, diverted from the judicial system, but they also accept patients with less severe violence, who are usually addressed by civil commitment systems.[65] The police, however, also have a duty to monitor the mentally ill in the community and determine whether they are harmful or dangerous to others or public order.[66] The various versions of the National Mental Health Work Plans, or policy documents of a similar nature,[67] and the local mental health regulations grant police the power of taking people with (suspected) mental illness to Ankang Hospitals that are managed by the police without adequate external oversight.[68] This has left room for abuse. The police had the powers to determine whether a person with mental health issues is dangerous, to take the person for assessment to a mental health facility, to decide compulsory treatment in the Ankang Hospitals, and to run the Ankang Hospitals.[69]

This situation remained unchanged until 2012 when China reformed its Criminal Procedure Law. Under the new rules, whether a person who committed a criminal offence should be diverted to the Compulsory Psychiatric Institutions (the new name of the Ankang Hospitals) is now decided by the courts, no longer by the police.[70] The MHL also introduces some degree of safeguards to prevent the abuse from police, which will be discussed in Chapter 4. The point here, however, is that the boundaries between facilities of a different nature are not always clear. Most mental health facilities in China could be social caring, medical, and violence preventive at the same time but run by different governmental departments with different rules. It raises a question of whether mental health services in China are delivered and monitored in a clear-cut or legally precise manner.

The lack of coordination among the three main Ministries also reflects on the assertion by some commentators that no one is taking responsibility for planning and control for decades. The first attempt to coordinate among different Ministries (and departments at local levels) dates back to 1958 when national policy

64 Weicai Tian et al., 'A Brief History of the Development of Rehabilitative Services in China' (1994) 165 *The British Journal of Psychiatry* 19.

65 Pearson (n 33) 446.

66 Veronica Pearson, 'Law, Rights, and Psychiatry in the People's Republic of China' (1992) 15 (4) *International Journal of Law and Psychiatry* 409.

67 For example, the National Mental Health Work Plan 2002–2010 requires local police, among other government officials, regularly visit and monitor 'unstable patients', 'address the risk or trigger' promptly, commit these dangerous or risky patients 'smoothly'.

68 Chapter 4.4.2.

69 See, generally, Robin Munro, 'The Ankang: China's Special Psychiatric Hospitals' (2006) 1 *Journal of Comparative Law* 41.

70 The Criminal Procedural Law of the People's Republic of China (adopted in 1979, amended in 2018), Part 5 Chapter 4.

urges all levels of local governments to establish the so-called 'three persons leading groups' consisting of leaders from each department.[71] More Ministries have been involved in the coordination framework. The first National Mental Health Work Plan 2002–2010 sets duties to more than ten Ministries and government branches at the national level.[72] Moreover, the Guidelines 2008–2015 were co-issued by even more central government/Communist Party of China (CPC) bodies, namely the Ministry of Health, the Publicity Department of the Central Committee of the CPC, National Development and Reform Commission, the Ministry of Education, the Ministry of Public Security, the Ministry of Civil Affairs, the Ministry of Justice, the Ministry of Finance, the Ministry of Personnel, the Ministry of Labour and Social Security, the Ministry of Culture, National Food and Drug Administration, All-China Federation of Trade Unions, Central Committee of the Chinese Communist Youth League, All China Women's Federation, China Disabled People's Federation, and the Office of National Working Commission on Ageing. The intention to enhance the coordination at the national level was well reflected on the long list of co-issuing bodies. The 'politics' behind the scene is also complicated and generally unknown.[73]

The implementation plan and standard, however, is left to the local governments to deliver 'according to local situations', as various versions of National Mental Health Work Plans put it.[74] It is undoubtedly reasonable to take the reality of different regions into account, as China is enormously diverse regarding population, culture, and economy. Under the institutional mechanism of implementation, however, the old pattern is likely to last in which any progress largely depends on individual entrepreneurship, specific timing and environment. The development of community service serves as a good example.

3.2.4 Long road to community services

Community mental health services in China is a complex topic itself and with many inconsistencies and paradoxes. On the one hand, institutionalisation has not been an issue in China for long. A study in 2005 further asserts that 'large-scale institutionalisation of people with mental illness has been avoided or relatively uncommon in China; the innovative, community mental health service in China may stimulate new approaches to de-institutionalisation in the West'.[75] As mentioned in earlier subsections, the dominant voice in relevant research and policy emphasises that too few rather than too many patients receive treatment in mental health facilities.

71 Pearson (n 33), 446.
72 National Mental Health Work Plan 2002–2010.
73 For example, there is a widely known 'rumour' that a leading psychiatrist, also an early drafter of the MHL, said the message from the Ministry of Finance was clear that no extra fund was available to improve the system after the MHL.
74 For example, the Opinions on Strengthening Mental Health Work (1987) urges provincial governments to 'carry [the opinions] out according to the local situation'.
75 Mao-Sheng Ran et al., *Family-Based Mental Health Care in Rural China* (Hong Kong University Press 2005), 4.

Paradoxically, when greater awareness of mental health has been raised and government funding has increased, there has emerged a movement of building new institutions or expanding the existing institutions. Data from 2004 reveals that there were 557 psychiatric hospitals (among which 359 had 100 beds or more and 44 had 500 beds or more), and 1.0 beds in psychiatric hospitals every 10,000 population.[76] Another piece of research in 2016 reports that the number of psychiatric hospitals increased to 728 (with 323 beds per hospital on average) and psychiatric beds per 10,000 population rose to 1.7.[77] A policy paper reveals that 15 billion RMB (approximately 2 billion euros) would had been spent to construct 550 new psychiatric hospitals around 2013–2014.[78] It is important to note that, the data used above comes from different sources, as such there may exist some overlapping numbers or inconsistent methods of calculation. This section, therefore, does not aim to provide an accurate description of how many psychiatric hospitals or beds there are, but only to identify the clear direction to institutionalisation. Given the policy priority of treating the untreated patients, a certain level of capacity buildings for service provision in specialised institutions is not unforeseeable. The problem, however, is that community services have failed to receive equal attention and funding as that invested in large-scale psychiatric hospitals.

Community mental health services have a special status. For decades, psychiatrists and policymakers have acknowledged its importance, but the reality remains that for most Chinese people 'the only form of service patients and their family could receive is the institutionalised treatment and care'.[79] Community service was encouraged by the government as early in 1958 by the Five-Year Plan for Mental Health (1958–1962)[80] and emphasised again in Opinions on Strengthening Mental Health Work (1987). Yet, nearly 60 years later, the National Mental Health Work Plan 2015–2020 admits that 'the community rehabilitation system for mental disorders has not been built'.[81]

In addition to the financial factor that always matters, some other reasons may also contribute to the underdevelopment of community-based services. For example, there may also exist lack of coordination, as the community service is usually conceptualised as community rehabilitation and responsible by the Disabled People's Federation at different levels, while psychiatric hospitals and the Ministry of Health deal with treatment. As mentioned earlier, the boundary is not always clear. Psychiatric hospitals are running their own rehabilitation programmes within hospitals too, and, therefore, conflicts of interest may arise preventing

76 Liu et al. (n 11) 211. Also, see World Health Organization Department of Mental Health and Substance Abuse and others, Mental Health Atlas 2005 (World Health Organization 2005), 133.

77 Vikram Patel et al., 'The Magnitude of and Health System Responses to the Mental Health Treatment Gap in Adults in India and China' (2016) 388 *The Lancet* 3074, 3077.

78 Liu et al. (n 11), 210.

79 Ma (n 42), 225.

80 Ran et al. (n 75). The original policy document is out of reach.

81 National Mental Health Work Plan 2015–2020, Section 1.

hospitals from transferring people back into the community with proper services.[82] As a result, some new community programmes have emerged. A recent example is the Clubhouses for people with mental illness, which aim to provide a safe place for members/users and help them 'regain a normal life'.[83] At least seven Clubhouses are operating in China, thanks to the enormous endeavour of founders and precious support from local governments. Nevertheless, the process of nationwide spread has been very slow.[84]

The understaffing in the community, in particular the professionals from non-medical expertise, may also explain the difficulties associated with community service. It has been addressed earlier that the biomedical model dominates Chinese psychiatry, as subjects providing a social understanding of mental health were banned from higher education. Another result of the ban is that there are very few professionals in social work or psychology who can work with psychiatrists, in hospital or community.[85] Therefore the community service programmes have to rely on village doctors or even members of neighbourhood/village councils who have very limited awareness of mental health but high sensitivity to social stability.[86] Since there is no alternative, it is observed that most community services 'are directed toward ensuring the patients comply with antipsychotic drug treatment and do not pose a threat to the public order'.[87] In this context, the popular ideas that 'if someone is seriously mentally ill then the proper thing is for that person to receive hospital treatment'[88] and 'mental hospitals [are] the sole solution and not just one component of mental health services'[89] have been reinforced when someone is deemed as out of control and sent away.

The '686 Program' starting from 2005 (named after the number of initial funds 6.86 million RMB, approximately 1 million euro) was designed to change the landscape of community mental health service. The background of this project is noteworthy in that many people with mental health problems, especially those in underdeveloped regions, were locked up at home by their families who have no social or public support.[90] It partly explains the idea above 'if someone is seriously mentally ill, then the proper thing is for that person to receive hospital treatment'.

Compared to just locking them at home, the 686 Program made progress in 2005 and onwards so people with mental health problems could get some

82 Pearson (n 33), 448.
83 Cathaleene Macias et al., 'What Is a Clubhouse? Report on the ICCD 1996 Survey of USA Clubhouses' (1999) 35 *Community Mental Health Journal* 181, 181.
84 Yuxi Tan et al., 'The application of Clubhouse Model in community mental health rehabilitation' (2018) 45 (1) *Journal of International Psychiatry* 114, 116.
85 Liu et al. (n 11), 211.
86 Pearson (n 33), 448.
87 Ran et al. (n 75), 18.
88 Pearson (n 33), 448.
89 Ran et al. (n 75), 16.
90 Hong Ma et al., 'An important pathway of mental health service reform in China: introduction of 686 Program' (2011) 25 (10) *Chinese Mental Health Journal* 725.

treatment in specialised hospitals with some subsidies from the government.[91] In contrast to western societies which have a long history of rethinking psychiatry and general community service systems, the 686 Program started from a thin foundation, establishing 60 demonstration sites in the beginning and later becoming a standard model for local governments nationwide.[92] The crucial components include having built a database of people with serious mental illness, expanding the access to service in hospitals into the community (primarily follow-up service though), and providing training. Most importantly, the Program

> promoted a more comprehensive approach to the treatment of mental illnesses, an approach that is more integrated, that includes multifunctional treatment teams, that is less focused on symptoms and more focused on functioning, and that pays less attention to patients' disabilities and more attention to enhancing their strengths.[93]

The program has received applause, being expected to 'provide useful models for the development of mental health policies in other countries with limited mental health personnel'.[94] A list of legitimate concerns may also be raised, some of which will be discussed below. However, the commitment and action to develop community service that works in China's reality deserve cautious acknowledgement. After all, like an observer from the United States comments, '[m]odels relevant for the development of mental health services in low-resource settings are unlikely to come from North America, Europe or Australia'.[95]

3.2.5 Financial factors

As addressed above, more public investment goes to psychiatric hospitals rather than community service. But this does not necessarily mean that hospitalised care has become accessible. Because the insurance policies and local governments' financial abilities differ hugely from one place to another, a detailed examination is impossible and also out of the scope of this book. The key message here is that, although insurance coverage is improving, treatment in psychiatric hospitals is still expensive for most Chinese people.[96]

As a commentator puts it, '[a] Western outsider might simply assume from what he or she knew of socialism that China would provide health care free to all

91 The economic/financial factor is also relevant here but will be discussed in the next subsection.
92 Ma et al. (90).
93 Ibid, 727–728.
94 Byron J. Good and Mary-Jo DelVecchio Good, 'Significance of the 686 Program for China and for global mental health' (2012) 24 (3) *Shanghai Archives of Psychiatry* 175, 175.
95 Ibid.
96 See Li et al. (n 18), 324.

her citizens. This has never been the case'.[97] The fact is, many years after the foundation of the socialist regime, only public employees could enjoy generous health insurance that covers all medical cost; people in the countryside, however, only had some policies as a last resort provided by the village when no other family support was available.[98] This may explain why many families for a long time had no other options but to lock and chain their relatives with severe mental health issues at home.

With the economic reform, most hospitals in China, including psychiatric hospitals, stopped being fully funded by the government and are expected to make profits for self-sustaining.[99] Psychiatric hospitals which have a power of deprivation of liberty now also have a motivation to avoid their beds being unoccupied. It is not hard to imagine the abuses that come along.

The improvement of health insurance, as a result of the economic reform, makes the situation even more complicated. On the one hand, the increased coverage of health insurance does reduce the burden of treatment and care for people with mental health issues. For example, it has been revealed by a study that in 2004 only 26% of the total population had health insurance in China, and one treatment session in a psychiatric hospital usually costs half of the personal income of a year.[100] Thanks to a project promoting health insurance for villagers, the coverage level has risen to 87.2% in 2008 and over 95% in 2012.[101]

It is important to note here that being covered by the public health insurance does not mean the treatment would be free, as there is a mechanism to determine whether and how much the cost could be covered.[102] For example, if everything in a treatment plan is on the approved list, the insurance for villagers would often cover 70% of inpatient treatment but only 50% of outpatient treatment; most community services are not covered by any insurance plan.[103] It is arguable that the insurance policy may encourage or motivate people to choose inpatient treatment rather than outpatient treatment. The increased level of insurance coverage also allows more families to hospitalise people with mental health issues. The book will revisit this point in Chapter 6 that explains the decision-making framework in more detail.

97 Pearson (n 33), 439.
98 Ibid.
99 Ibid.
100 Li (n 8), 6.
101 Jie Feng et al., 'A study on health insurance equality in China through the lens of coverage rate' (2010) 18 *Modern Business* 96, 96.
102 Most private insurance policies do not accept people with mental health issues. It is also a commonly complained issue to many service users and family members in my interviews that before 2005 the system only covered old-fashioned psychiatric drugs with more serious side effects.
103 The State Council Information Office of the People's Republic of China, 'Whitepaper on the Development of China's Public Health as an Essential Element of Human Rights' (2017) Section 5.

3.2.6 Family's role

Family plays an important role in mental health care,[104] and China is not an exception in this regard. Still, the relationship between people with mental health issues and their family members in Chinese society have its own characteristics that nevertheless merit explanation. Legal duties of family members and what they could legally do to people with mental health issues will be discussed further in Chapters 4–6. This subsection addresses a general cultural and social perspective.

In the Chinese tradition, mental health issues associate with negative meanings. Being mentally ill entails violence, shame, or punishment resulting from one's ancestors' misconduct.[105] This set of traditional beliefs still shape the mindset of many, if not most, Chinese people.[106] In both urban and rural regions, the lack of community services leaves no choice for family members who bear most, if not all, responsibilities of care. The traditional Confucian values of family self-reliance and lifelong interdependence have further reinforced this family-oriented care model.

This family-oriented model, which applies to all services not just the care of people with mental health issues, has also been acknowledged by Chinese law, and the government only provides a public system for those without family support. For example, it is a moral rule known as 'filial piety' and a legal duty that adults in China are expected to take care of their elderly family members, phrased as 'raise a son for security when getting old'.[107] In the context of the One-Child Policy,[108] it is common that, if the first child has a disability, including severe mental health issues, the couple would be permitted to have a second birth. They do so with a hope that the new child would take care of the family, particularly the older sibling with disabilities.[109] Otherwise, parents have to use their usually meagre pension to support children with disabilities, phrased as 'the elderly feed the disabled'.[110]

104 For example, see Mary Donnelly and Claire Murray, 'The Role of Family in Mental Health Law: A Framework for Transformation' 26.

105 Ran et al. (n 75), 25.

106 See, generally, Chow S Lam et al., 'Chinese Lay Theory and Mental Illness Stigma: Implications for Research and Practices' (2010) 76 *Journal of Rehabilitation*; Alexandria 35.

107 Ran et al. (n 75), 27–29.

108 In October 2015, China's one-child policy, implemented for 30 years from 1979 was replaced by a universal two-child policy. See Junsen Zhang, 'The Evolution of China's One-Child Policy and Its Effects on Family Outcomes' (2017) 31 *Journal of Economic Perspectives* 141. It has been transformed into a three-child policy with even looser sanctions in 2021. See BBC 'China NPC: Three-child policy formally passed into law' *BBC News* (London, 20 August 2021) < www.bbc.com/news/world-asia-china-58277473 > accessed 24 August 2021.

109 See, generally, Ran et al. (n 75); Zhiying Ma, 'An Iron Cage of Civilization? Missionary Psychiatry, the Chinese Family and a Colonial Dialect of Enlightenment' in Howard Chiang (eds) *Psychiatry and Chinese History* (Routledge 2014). Also, see Kun Li, 'A Research on the Issues of Two Subsidy Systems for the Disabled People through Perspective of Policy Implementation' (2014) 4 *Disability Research* 48.

110 Ibid.

More importantly, from the lens of traditional political thought, the social recognition and even the meaningfulness of Chinese people is based on the fulfilment of the role within the family, and the notion of self or self-identity lies on the family rather than the individual.[111] Therefore, since mental illness is perceived as damaging a person's social functioning and the notion of self, other parties in society, particularly psychiatrists, take family members as the legitimate agent in expressing needs and describing conditions on behalf of the person concerned.[112] Internally, however, family members should 'control' and 'direct' the lives of people with mental health issues.[113] It may be in tension with the liberal understanding of self and the emphasis on the patient-state relationship of the mental health laws in the West.[114] Nevertheless, the collective notion of self may also have a theoretical potential of being closer to the relational autonomy[115], which is arguably promoted by the United Nations Convention on the Rights of Persons with Disabilities.[116]

The history of communist governance adds another layer of complexity to the situation. Before China's economic reform of the market to open up to globalisation, people's lives had been tied closely with the state, either through their employers, mostly government or state-owned factories, or through collective communes in villages. Putting political abuse of psychiatry aside, under the totalitarian system, a person could only be treated in hospital and covered by health insurance with approval from employers or other forms of government/Party officials.[117] Although public control has largely retreated from people's private lives in the market economy, the power of governments, especially in underdeveloped areas, is still arbitrary. The professionalism of psychiatry is not strong enough to refuse an order from the government to detain someone. A large number of cases were revealed by media that 'petitioners'[118] were sent to psychiatric hospitals by the local government to silence

111 See, generally, Xiaotong Fei, *From the Soil: The Foundations of Chinese Society* (University of California Press 1992).
112 Ma (n 109).
113 Ran et al. (n 75), 9.
114 Donnelly and Murray (n 104).
115 Lucy Series, 'Relationships, Autonomy and Legal Capacity: Mental Capacity and Support Paradigms' (2015) 40 *International Journal of Law and Psychiatry* 80.
116 UN Convention on the Rights of Persons with Disabilities (adopted 24 January 2007, entered into force 3 May 2008) A/RES/61/106 (CRPD).
117 Chunyan Ding, 'Family Members' Informed Consent to Medical Treatment for Competent Patients in China' (2010) 8 *China: An International Journal* 139.
118 This term has a particular meaning in China, referring people going to higher levels of governments and accusing local officials of corruption or any other misconduct, usually associated with protest individually or in groups. It is generally ineffective as an institution. But in many cases petitioners could have a better position in bargaining with local government by petitioning or threatening to go, as the local officials' promotion opportunity may be affected if petitioners from their responsible region are recorded by governments of higher levels. See, generally, Carl F Minzner, 'Xinfang: An Alternative to Formal Chinese Legal Institutions' (2006) 42 *Stanford Journal of International Law* 103.

or punish them.[119] As people with mental health issues are perceived as being dangerous, untrustworthy, and incapable of self-protection, a substituted decision-maker and caregiver is always necessary. Unless government or psychiatry earn people's trust by any means, family members remain the only safe and right choice as substituted decision-makers, advocates, and protectors.[120]

The presumption of no conflict of interest among family members is argued to influence or underpin the MHL.[121] A more realistic interpretation, however, may be that the legislators were clear that, with the current social reality and resources, family members are the least wrong choice in caring for people with mental health problems and ensuring the social stability at the same time. This arrangement is conceptualised as the 'domestic citizenship': family monitor individual's mental health, decide when an individual is harmful to oneself, and therefore become the substituted decision-maker with knowledge and guidelines provided by psychiatry and the government.[122] It has become so not only because of Chinese collective tradition or the lack of a public social care system but also the current fear of the old totalitarian society.[123]

3.2.7 Emphasis on social stability

Social stability appears to be a common theme in all the topics considered above. Psychiatrists have used the large number of undertreated patients and their perceived harm or risk to disturb social stability in advocating for their professional status and public investment.[124] Since funding is never adequate, all national policies prioritise a treatment and management (or monitoring) system for people with severe mental disorders who are believed to be inherently dangerous.[125] As mentioned above, the Ministry of Public Security developed its psychiatric hospitals nationwide to address this particular issue without judicial oversight until 2012.[126]

119 Chunyan Ding, 'Involuntary Detention and Treatment of the Mentally Ill: China's 2012 Mental Health Law' (2014) 37 *International Journal of Law and Psychiatry* 581.

120 Zhiying Ma, 'Biopolitics of intimacy: family responsibility and mental health law-making' (2014) 40 (3) *The Ideological Front* 42.

121 Ibid 43–45; Ding (n 119), 585.

122 Ma (n 120), 48. Also, see Veena Das and Renu Addlakha, 'Disability and Domestic Citizenship: Voice, Gender, and the Making of the Subject' (2001) 13 *Public Culture* 511.

123 Ma (n 120).

124 See, for example, Yue-qin Huang, 'Status quo and challenge of mental health in China' (2011) 4 (9) *Chinese Journal of Health Policy* 5, 6–8.

125 See, for example, National Mental Health Work Plan 2015–2020, Section 1, which requires the governments of all levels to formally include the treatment and management of people with severe mental disorders into their budget for basic health care programmes but only ask for or encourage support for other disadvantaged groups with mental health needs.

126 Pearson (n 33) 445.

The workforce at the community level is also more sensitive to social stability than providing decent care, and hospitals and local officers teach family members about how to control people with mental health problems at home with rare real social support.[127] Pearson comments

> [Chinese policy on community service] is framed in ways that emphasise the need to control the patient, rather than the familiar Western rhetoric couched in terms of providing the most normal living conditions, increasing senses of self-worth and value, and improving quality of life. It may be that the goals are similar but the Chinese are more honest in stating them![128]

What matters, however, is how the very reasonable concerns about social stability could be balanced and restricted by any procedure and other equally legitimate concerns. For example, as will be explored in Chapter 4 on the MHL, there is no independent mechanism determining involuntary detention or any voice other than psychiatry or government talking about the connection between mental health problems and violence in more detail.

It is a particularly important issue in the Chinese context that, unlike in some countries, the professionalisation of psychiatry, relatively free media, or social movements may bear the role of checks and balances in protecting society.[129] Public authority in China is so powerful that all other stakeholders have to follow the public agenda. The focus on social stability in various public policies not only reinforces the stereotype that people with mental health issues are dangerous among the general public but also influences the attitudes of psychiatrists. As will be explored in Chapter 5, which draws insights from qualitative interviews, psychiatrists in China often justify coercive institutional care by referring to the extreme crimes committed by people with mental health issues. Their social images have become invisible 'bombs' among people in the society, and harm can only be avoided through segregated institutions, psychiatric drugs, and long-term social monitoring or surveillance.[130] Under this public pressure, psychiatrists see themselves more responsible for protecting society than providing care to their patients.

Against this background, which has always been particularly sensitive to social stability, the autonomy and consent of people with mental health issues have become very vulnerable.

127 Ran et al. (n 75), 18–24.

128 Pearson (n 33), 452.

129 See, generally, Nick Crossley, *Contesting Psychiatry: Social Movements in Mental Health* (Routledge 2006).

130 Many new reports and even law journals consider people with (severe) mental health issues as 'booms that blow any time' and calls on enhanced commitment and monitoring. For example, see Junyu Bian, 'They are bombs that blow any time: experts' interpretation on crimes committed by the mentally ill' (2009) 13 *Law and Life*, 8.

3.2.8 Section summary

This section provides an overview of mental health services and policy development in China. It matters because this is the reality to which China's MHL applies. Because of the long period of wars and political movements, there were only a few trained mental health professionals in China and the governments of different regions had no intention or resource to develop their community services. After the reform into a market economy, the government prioritised the problem of untreated patients as a major threat to social stability and economic growth, thereby promoting policies that control people with mental health issues, through their families at home or in institutions. In recent years, with the growing financial ability of the Chinese government and the enactment of the MHL, the investment into mental health work has increased. However, as there is no voice advocating against the expansion of psychiatry, most public investments go into the construction of segregated psychiatric hospitals.

All these interrelated themes are crucial in understanding the MHL and the practice in decision-making, as they affect people's attitudes, external pressure, and whether any alternative is available.

3.3 China's Legal System and Relevant Features

China's legal system is a complicated topic and is deeply embedded in Chinese history and politics. A Chinese law expert from the United States remarks that

> Any account of the legal system of the People's Republic of China must be prefaced by a warning of the need to distinguish between the formal system and what actually happens. Such a gap is of course present in some degree in all countries, but in many areas it is particularly broad in China.[131]

The primary purpose of this section, accordingly, is to provide the 'formal' framework in which the MHL and other related norms operate. It will also draw a picture of 'what actually happens' about China's legal system that assists with the analysis in later chapters on the MHL.

3.3.1 An overview of the current legal-political landscape

When the People's Republic of China was founded in 1949, there was a vacuum of law as all the laws made by the predecessor government were abolished.[132] However, the official perception, as well as mainstream attitude among the general public, was that a formal legal system was 'unnecessary'.[133] Several reasons may

131 Donald Clarke, 'The Chinese legal system in 1500 words' (2005) available at < donaldclarke.net/public/ChineseLegalSystem.html > accessed 15 July 2021.

132 Ibid.

133 Jingjing Liu, 'Overview of the Chinese Legal System' (2012) *The Environmental Law Reporter* (China Update) <https://elr.info/sites/default/files/china_update_premiere_issue.pdf> accessed 1 July 2021.

contribute to this attitude.[134] First, there is a lack of motivation to enact laws that restrict the authority of the CPC, since the Party took power by the victory of a civil war.[135] Second, the legislative and juridical bodies were not functioning well, due to decades of war and political movements.[136] Third, the planned economy had a low need for a comprehensive and formal legal system, as business disputes, for example, were normally solved by government, 'without reference to legal rights and duties'.[137]

Building a modern legal system had not become a priority until China transformed into a market economy in 1978. The demand for some degree of the rule of law was particularly urgent when China started the negotiation for its membership of the World Trade Organisation.[138] The institutional components of legal systems such as the courts and lawyers resumed operating and acquired official support and acknowledgement. Massive efforts have been put into legal transplantation from the West.[139] The clauses of 'respect for human rights' and 'ruling the country in accordance with the law' have been amended into the Constitution of the People's Republic of China in 2004, and 'building a socialist country of law' has been prescribed as a national goal.[140]

Under the current constitutional framework, the People's Republic of China is a unitary state in which the National People's Congress (NPC) is vested with the highest powers.[141] The NPC also exercises the national legislative power, issuing laws which are binding nationwide.[142] Its supremacy in state power also reflects on the constitutional arrangement that the President of the Supreme People's Court, the Procurator General of the Supreme People's Procuratorate, and the Premier as the head of State Council, which is the highest executive body, are all elected and appointed by the NPC.[143] The NPC has around 3,000 deputies (the term adopted by the Constitution for delegates or people's representatives) who are not elected by popular vote but elected by the people's congresses at the provincial level.[144] The deputies of provincial people's congresses, however, are also

134 Clarke (n 131).
135 Ibid.
136 Ibid.
137 Ibid.
138 Liu (n 133).
139 Ibid.
140 Constitution of the People Republic of China (adopted in 1982, amended in 2018) (Constitution), art 5, 33.
141 Constitution, art 57.
142 Ibid, Art 58.
143 Ibid., Art 62. However, it is worth noting and widely acknowledged that the real power is occupied by the Standing Committee of the Politburo of the CPC whose status of leadership is written in the Constitution. Most of the heads of government bodies are CPC members and every public sector has CPC committees that control the decision-making.
144 Ibid., Art 59. The Election Law of the National People's Congress and People's Congresses at Different Levels of the People's Republic of China provides how the number of NPC deputies are calculated.

indirectly elected by that of lower levels, and only the people's congresses at the lowest level consist of directly-elected delegates.[145]

Holding such great power, including amending the Constitution and supervising its implementation, enacting and amending laws, and deciding on the 'questions of war and peace', its deputies convene regularly only once a year.[146] The Standing Committee of the NPC (SCNPC), composed of 175 standing deputies elected by the NPC, is therefore established as a permanent body, who exercises the powers to interpret the Constitution, to enact, amend and interpret laws, and to supervise the work of the State Council and the Supreme People's Court.[147]

The State Council, the National Supervision Commission, the Supreme People's Court, and the Supreme People's Procuratorate are all responsible to the NPC and the SCNPC.[148] The State Council, divided into ministries and commissions, is the executive branch of the central authority.[149] It also has the power to enact administrative regulations which are binding nationwide as laws, while the ministries and commissions can enact departmental rules within their scope of management.[150] The Supreme People's Court is the highest judicial organ,[151] with a special power to issue judicial interpretations. The content of these judicial interpretations, however, often go beyond the scope of just interpretation of the law but are in fact making new norms that are applicable in courts.[152] The National Supervision Commission's constitutional status has been established in 2018 by a constitutional amendment. It serves as the highest supervision body over all Party members and public officials, which reflects the fact that the internal mechanisms of the CPC have deeply intertwined with the national ones.[153]

To summarise, the Chinese constitutional structure, in which all powers flow from the NPC, was conceptualised as 'vertical and horizontal centralism'.[154] However, it does not mean there is no tension between the governments of different levels or between departments of different sectors. Provinces, centrally-administered municipalities, autonomous regions of minorities, as well as a selection of other municipalities meeting certain standards, also enjoy the power to enact local regulations.[155]Chapter 4 will address the issue that seven municipalities had their mental health regulations before the MHL.

145 Constitution, Art 97.
146 Ibid., Art 61, 62.
147 Ibid., Art 64–67.
148 Ibid., Art 92, 126, 130, 138.
149 Ibid., Art 85.
150 Ibid., Art 89–90.
151 Ibid., Art 132.
152 See, generally, Li Wei, 'Judicial Interpretation in China' (1997) 5 *Willamette Journal of International Law and Dispute Resolution* 87.
153 See, generally, Jinting Deng, 'The National Supervision Commission: A New Anti-Corruption Model in China' (2018) 52 *International Journal of Law, Crime and Justice* 58.
154 Clarke (n 131).
155 Constitution, Art 100.

One of the examples of local-central and inter-departmental tensions is the complexity of different sources of norms. In addition to international human rights conventions that are not directly applicable in Chinese courts, there are the Constitution, national laws enacted by the NPC and the SCNPC, administrative regulations enacted by the State Council, departmental rules enacted by relevant ministries and commissions, judicial interpretations issued by the Supreme People's Court, and local regulations enacted by local peoples' congresses and their standing committees. As the rights of people with mental health issues are possibly affected by the various sources of norms, how to solve the inevitable conflicts in mental health-related cases will serve as the first issue of further consideration below.

3.3.2 Unsolved conflict of norms

How to categorise China's legal system is a debated question.[156] For the purpose of identifying legal sources, China is closer to civil law countries where codified statutes are the primary sources of law.[157] Although the Supreme People's Court publishes cases in its law reports as guides to lower courts nationwide. As a principle, however, the cases decided by Chinese courts are not binding on future cases and are in general not cited in judgments.[158] However, this does not make it easier to understand the hierarchy of written norms and their conflicts in China.

Clarke observes that different institutions at various levels 'are capable of issuing documents and rules purporting to be binding on various parties to varying degrees' but 'there appears to be no institution with the will and the capacity to resolve such conflicts authoritatively' when the norms are in conflict.[159]

The Legislation Law might be expected to assist in solving this problem by bringing about a hierarchy of norms, at least in theory. The hierarchy of norms is as follows:

- Constitution
- Laws (by the NPC and SCNPC)
- Administrative Regulations (by the State Council)
- Local People's Congress Regulations (by local people's congresses and their standing committees at the provincial level and a selection of municipalities granted with regulation-making power)
- Government Rules (by local governments at the provincial level) and Departmental Rules (by central-level ministries, commissions, and agencies directly under the State Council)[160]

156 See, generally, Buyun Li, 'Several questions about legal family and the application of case law in China' (1990) 1 *China Legal Science* 13.
157 Clarke (n 131).
158 See, generally, Jerome Alan Cohen, 'Chinese Common Law? Guiding Cases and Judicial Reform' 129 *Harvard Law Review* 2213.
159 Clarke (n 131).
160 The Legislation Law of the People's Republic of China (adopted in 2000, amended in 2015) (Legislation Law), Art 87–90.

The Legislation Law also provides that certain issues could only be addressed by laws, including state sovereignty, crimes and criminal sanctions, deprivation of liberty, and fundamental civil institutions (for example, guardianship law and marriage law), being conceptualised as 'the principle of legal reservation'.[161] The clause of deprivation of liberty echoes the protection provided by the Constitution which states that '[f]reedom of the citizens of the People's Republic of China is inviolable'.[162]

Before the enactment of the MHL, however, there were seven municipalities which had enacted their mental health regulations that authorised detention and involuntary treatment, as will be discussed in Chapter 4. The Shanghai Mental Health Regulation is the earliest of them, passed in 2001 and amended in 2014, shortly after the MHL's entry into force. The constitutionality of these mental health regulations may be reasonably questioned, since they involved provisions on deprivation of liberty that must be addressed by law. However, there has been no official procedure initiated by the judiciary or legislature to examine whether they contravene the Legislation Law or the Constitution in respect to the legal reservation of deprivation of liberty.

Conflicts of norms may also occur between laws and departmental rules. For example, as will be explored further in Chapter 4, considering an adult's decision-making in civil affairs, like entering a contract and making a donation, is critical to everyone's life. The Civil Procedure Law sets out procedures that one's capacity for civil conduct, a term of mental capacity adopted by Chinese law, must be declared by a court.[163] It is a procedural requirement explicitly provided by national law. What is followed in practice, however, are many departmental rules issued by the Ministry of Health, allowing relatives of mental health service users to act as the *de facto* substituted decision-makers without undergoing any proceedings before a court. For example, there has existed a general practice in Chinese psychiatry that 'the discharge must be completed by the family member who decided on the detention for treatment in the first place'.[164] Most mental health facilities ignore the safeguard provided by the Civil Procedure Law. No mechanism has been initiated to ensure the national law prevails over some departmental rules either.

This situation may be attributed to the fact that, unlike countries with some forms of judicial review, judges or courts in China do not have the power to rule on the constitutionality of laws, regulations or other forms of norms.[165] The

161 Ibid., Art 8.

162 Constitution Art 37.

163 The Civil Procedure Law of the People's Republic of China (adopted in 1991, amended in 2017) (Civil Procedure Law) Chapter 15 Section 4 Art 170–173.

164 Xuetao Huang, Jiajia Liu, and Xiaohu Liu, The Involuntary Commitment System in China: A Legal Analysis <blog.sina.com.cn/s/blog_66b9e1f30100m2h1.html> accessed 1 July 2021.

165 See, generally, Guobin Zhu, 'Constitutional Review in China: An Unaccomplished Project or a Mirage' (2009) 43 *Suffolk University Law Review* 625.

SCNPC has the power to monitor the implementation of the Constitution[166] but has not undertaken any formal review, actively or upon application.[167]

3.3.3 (Overly) politicised human rights

Another observation of China's legal system is that human rights have not been a central position in law-related activities. The fact that respect and protection of human rights were amended into the Constitution in 2004 is phrased as landmark progress.[168] Given the fact that China has not developed a functional mechanism of judicial review, the human rights provision is mostly declarative rather than applicable in courts.[169]

It is also rare that any domestic issue would be conceptualised as a human rights issue by the government or the media in China. However, the white papers of human rights development in China are published by a publicity (or official news) agency which also publishes human rights records in the United States.[170] This arguably reflects the perception of seeing human rights primarily as a weapon in foreign relations.

One possible explanation of this situation is that the Chinese government has adopted the 'human rights language' as a defensive move against the human rights attacks from the West.[171] The government increasingly supported human rights research in the 1990s, when international criticism on human rights violations in China became a 'regular occurrence'.[172] The defensive mindset well reflects on the first Chinese Human Rights White Paper in 1991, which wrote:

> China is opposed to interfering in other countries' internal affairs on the pretext of human rights and has made unremitting efforts to eliminate various abnormal phenomena and strengthen international cooperation in the field of human rights.... Using the human rights issue for the political purpose of imposing the ideology of one country on another is no longer a question of human rights, but a manifestation of power politics in the form of interference in the internal affairs of other countries. Such abnormal practice in international human rights activities must be eliminated.[173]

166 Constitution, Art 67 (1).

167 There have been debates about whether there exists *de facto* judicial review in China. See, generally, Yongkun Zhou, 'On the Judicial Review under the System of People's Congress' (2006) *3 Jiangsu Social Science* 120.

168 Qianhong Qin and Junmin Chen, 'The Rational Thought about Human Right Written in the Constitution' (2004) 19 (3) *Legal Forum* 7.

169 See, generally, Qianfan Zhang, 'On the selective application of the Constitution' (2012) 24 (5) *Peking University Law Journal* 887.

170 For example, see State Council Information Office of the People's Republic of China, 'Human Rights Record of the United States in 2016' (2017) <www.xinhuanet.com/english/china/2017-03/09/c_136115481.htm> accessed 1 July 2021.

171 James D Seymour, 'Human Rights in Chinese Foreign Relations' in Samuel S Kim eds *China and the World* (Routledge 2018).

172 Pitman Potter, *China's Legal System* (Polity Press 2014), 42.

173 State Council Information Office of the People's Republic of China, 'Human Rights in China' (1991) <www.china.org.cn/e-white/7/7-L.htm> accessed 1 July 2021.

This is not to deny the existence of 'Human Rights Diplomacy' in which human rights are a part of bargaining, negotiation, and diplomacy among states.[174] Instead, the point here is that the communicational, educational, and constructive aspects of the international human rights law have been marginalised in Chinese society and excluded from domestic legal practice.

In addition to the political reasons, historical legal tradition and current legal-political structure in China are also relevant to the non-emphasis of human rights. In the long imperial history, traditional Chinese law centred on 'state concerns' and 'dealt with private matters only incidentally'.[175] Law was seen primarily as an instrument for the state to protect and advance its interests, for example, to ensure officials followed the law or to increase government efficiency.[176] Protecting individual rights from public power was not a major concern or even believed not necessary at all.[177] Although China has experienced a rapid period of legal transplantation from European and American law, it has been argued that 'law in the PRC today serves primarily as an instrument of rule for the Communist Party of China'.[178] Accordingly, its first and foremost aim is to protect the leadership of the CPC, and other priorities include supporting economic development and safeguarding other collective interests.[179] Under this structure, it is not difficult to understand that human rights, often arose by individuals to challenge the authority, are discouraged by the Party/State in addressing domestic issues.

3.3.4 Rule of law with 'Chinese Characteristics'

Article 5 of the Constitution requires the government to 'govern the country according to law' and build 'a socialist country under rule of law'.[180] However, the instrumentalist approach of law adopted by the Party/State above reflects the reality that the legal system in China is not an autonomous institution independent from the Party but under its total control and leadership, which raises doubts about whether there exists any rule of law in China.[181] A theoretical review of the rule of law in China is beyond the scope of this book. For the purpose of this book, as it may have an impact on cases involving people with mental health

174 See, generally, Barbara Keys, 'Congress, Kissinger, and the Origins of Human Rights Diplomacy' (2010) 34 *Diplomatic History* 823.

175 Clarke (n 131).

176 Ibid.

177 Jingjing Liu notes that '[t]here was a notion in traditional Chinese culture that there could not possibly be any substantial conflict between the interests of the state and the interests of its individual citizens, and therefore it was unnecessary to protect individual rights against abuse by public power'. Liu (n 133), 7.

178 Poter (n 172), 2.

179 Ibid.

180 Constitution, Art 5.

181 See, generally, Ronald C Keith, 'China's Struggle for the Rule of Law' in Ronald C Keith eds, *China's Struggle for the Rule of Law* (Palgrave Macmillan UK 1994).

issues, it is noteworthy that even the daily practice of courts is deeply embedded in the Party/State's overall agenda of social control.

As with all other government bodies in China, there are Party committees within the courts at all levels, taking the leadership of every aspect of their daily work.[182] In addition to this, political-legal committees, consisting of the heads of police, court and prosecutor at the same level, are set in the Party's branches in every county, municipality, province and the nation.[183] The purposes of the political-legal committees include coordinating among different bodies on complicated or controversial cases, providing guidance, unifying the thoughts and actions among different sectors, and, most importantly, ensuring the law-related bodies would implement the Party's 'routine, policy and arrangement'.[184]

Under this political structure, when the Party/State started a movement to prosecute crimes in the 1980s, the NPC quickly passed amendments to the Criminal Procedure Law, shortening the period for appeal from ten days to three days and allowing less time for a defendant to prepare a trial.[185] As part of the governments determined measures to cope with the financial crisis in the 2000s, the judicial system adopted special measures to provide a friendly environment for business, or in their own terms 'serving the bigger picture' and 'promoting the economic and social development'. For example, the courts would be cautious in using measures that would pose a higher financial risk to those important companies in their regions and help them get through difficulties by offering legal advice.[186]

The courts at all levels function mostly in a bureaucratic manner. A so-called 'adjudication committee' is set up to review controversial or complicated cases that have been tried by other judges in that court.[187] The adjudication committees consist of senior judges and court officials, with a mission to ensure those cases would be ruled 'appropriately and correctly'.[188] However, this practice has been criticised heavily. It is not uncommon that judges who try the case and examine the evidence do not make the decision; the decisions are made by a group of judges who do not necessarily have adequate information of the case or expertise in the field of law.[189] The behind-the-scenes style of decision-making also opens

182 See, generally, Ling Li, 'The "Production" of Corruption in China's Courts: Judicial Politics and Decision Making in a One-Party State' (2012) 37 *Law & Social Inquiry* 848.
183 Pitman B Potter, 'The Chinese Legal System: Continuing Commitment to the Primacy of State Power' (1999) 159 *The China Quarterly* 673.
184 Xinhua News Agency < www.gov.cn/zhengce/2019-01/18/content_5359135.htm > accessed 15 July 2021.
185 See, generally, Susan Trevaskes, 'Courts on the Campaign Path in China: Criminal Court Work in the "Yanda 2001" Anti-Crime Campaign' (2002) 42 *Asian Survey* 673.
186 Shengjun Wang, 'Supreme People's Court's Work Report to the National People's Congress' (2009) <www.gov.cn/test/2009-03/17/content_1261386.htm> accessed 1 July 2021.
187 Xin He, 'Black Hole of Responsibility: The Adjudication Committee's Role in a Chinese Court' (2012) 46 *Law & Society Review* 681.
188 Liu (n 133) 6.
189 Ibid.

the door for undue influence in individual cases, especially when the government is involved.[190]

3.3.5 Section summary

This section provides a brief overview of China's legal system. It is part of a centralised political system, closer to the continental European legal tradition than to the common law system, lacking an effective mechanism to solve the conflicts among norms, conservative to human rights claims, and deeply embedded in the Party/State's social agenda. As abstract as it may be, the purpose is to help understand the broader legal context of the MHL and potential influence on its legal practice.

It should now be clear that Chinese courts are not authorised or motivated to hold that some government policies or rules are against the Constitution or the national law. Similarly, as people with mental health issues are often portrayed as threats to public security and social stability, it would not be a surprise that the MHL is interpreted by courts favouring the emphasis on social stability, rather than respecting the autonomy and wishes of people with mental health issues as possible.

3.4 Chapter Conclusion

This Chapter presents an overview of the mental health system and a broader legal context in which the MHL sits. It aims to inform readers that both the service delivery and rights protection for people with mental health issues in China are at an early stage of development. Any praise or criticism should not be isolated from this reality.

More importantly, however, it is worth noting that the full picture provided in this chapter does not aim to justify or defend the *status quo*. On the contrary, the short history of developing coercive and institutional psychiatry could potentially prevent the substantial cost of correcting wrongdoings. The best practices of services and the new advancement of international human rights law in the field of mental health could alter people's mindset and benefit the endeavour on the ground. Drawing the insights provided by the CRPD in particular, as examined in Chapter 2, this study will critically examine the MHL and adult guardianship law in more depth in Chapter 4 and explore the medical and judicial practice in Chapter 5.

190 He (n 186).

4 China's Mental Health Law Reform

A Doctrinal Review

4.1 Chapter Introduction

This chapter explores the current normative framework of mental health detention and treatment under China's first national Mental Health Law (MHL).[1] It argues that the MHL and current adult guardianship law have taken some steps forward, at least in theory, in promoting autonomy and reducing the over-reliance on involuntary inpatient treatment in the Chinese mental health system.

The MHL adopts the voluntary principle for mental health treatment. Compared to its predecessors, the MHL has also narrowed the substantive criteria for involuntary interventions. Meanwhile, the newly amended adult guardianship system has introduced the principle of maximising autonomy, which now governs guardians' actions. These changes are arguably in line with the consensus discussed in Chapter 2 that States Parties to the United Nations Convention on the Rights of Persons with Disabilities[2] must, at very least, maximise the autonomy of persons with mental health issues and promote non-coercive services and support in the community. The changes introduced under the current normative framework, as will be discussed in more detail below, are commendable for moving in the direction of the development of international human rights standards. This chapter will also raise several critical questions of implementation and interpretation.

This chapter starts with a brief overview of the 28-year law-making process. It is followed by an examination of the provisions for decision-making in mental health detention and treatment under the MHL and its predecessors, highlighting the recent changes. The chapter will also examine the adult guardianship law, focusing on its interaction with the MHL.

1 Mental Health Law of the People's Republic of China (passed by the Standing Committee of the National People's Congress on 26 October 2012, entered into force on 1 May 2013) (MHL).

2 UN Convention on the Rights of Persons with Disabilities (adopted 13 December 2006, entered into force 3 May 2008) 2515 UNTS 3 (CRPD).

DOI: 10.4324/9781003212034-4

4.2 The Mental Health Law: 28 Years in the Making

As mentioned in Chapter 3, the regulation of 'mad' people dates back to the Tang dynasty (around 618–917 A.D.).[3] The current MHL, however, is a modern creation, and its law-making history (from 1985 to 2012) is believed to be one of the longest in China.[4] This section provides a brief overview of this process, identifying the critical documents that will be considered in the following sections.

The project of enacting a piece of national mental health legislation began in 1985.[5] At the time, the Ministry of Health commissioned the Departments of Health in Sichuan Province and Hunan Province to host discussions among psychiatric experts, with the mission of receiving their initial scholarly drafts.[6]

A leading psychiatrist in China observed that the process was slow in the 1980s, due to the lack of reference or sample laws governing mental health detention and treatment.[7] Against this background, the World Health Organisation (WHO) offered assistance by hosting workshops on mental health laws from 1987 to 1999.[8] Nevertheless, the government was not accelerating the law-making process in the 1990s.[9] It is partly because mental health was not among the legislative priorities, which were focused on facilitating economic growth.[10] The political movement in 1989 and the national campaign against cults in 1999,[11] whose practitioners claimed to have been detained and treated in psychiatric facilities without due process,[12] may also explain the lack of progress in developing the MHL.

After consideration and consultation for 12 years, the Ministry of Health handed a draft to the State Council in 2007.[13] From 2007 to 2011, the draft was the responsibility of the Legislative Affairs Office of the State Council (LAOSC). During these years, the LAOSC conducted four major consultations with relevant ministries, governments of lower levels, medical facilities, and university scholars, and also sought opinions from international organisations' offices in China, in particular, the WHO.[14] Most, if not all, of these consultations took place behind closed doors.[15] The draft was only open for comments from the general public for the first time in June 2011.[16]

3 Chapter 2, Section 2.
4 *Training Textbook for Healthcare Professionals on the Mental Health Law of the People's Republic of China* (China Legal Publishing House 2013) (*Training Textbook*) 1.
5 Shicheng Zhang and Tao Zhang, 'The process and major contents of the Mental Health Law' (2013) 20 *China Health Law* 4, 4.
6 *Training Textbook* (n 4).
7 Bin Xie, 'The law-making history of the Mental Health Law' (2013) 13 China Hospital CEO 86.
8 Ibid.
9 Ibid.
10 Ibid.
11 Ibid.
12 Sunny Y Lu and Viviana B Galli, 'Psychiatric Abuse of Falun Gong Practitioners in China' (2002) 30 *Journal of the American Academy of Psychiatry and the Law Online* 126.
13 Zhang and Zhang (n 5).
14 Ibid.
15 Ibid.
16 Ibid.

After the State Council's approval in September 2011, the draft entered the Standing Committee of the National People's Congress (SCNPC) for review. The SCNPC reviewed and revised the draft of the MHL three times before it was finally passed on 26 October 2012. It is worth noting that the full text of the draft after the first review was made available to the general public, whilst the other revisions were only available partly via media.[17]

The mental health legislation in common law jurisdictions usually only regulates detention and involuntary treatment. By contrast, the MHL covers broader issues. Its 85 articles are divided into seven chapters, covering a wide range of issues. They include psychological well-being promotion and mental disorder prevention,[18] diagnosis and treatment of mental disorders,[19] rehabilitation of mental disorders,[20] and measures necessary to implement the law such as financial contributions.[21]

Although this research focuses on the provisions for detention and treatment, some other provisions are also broadly relevant. For example, family members' significant decision-making status and responsibility, as will be discussed later, may be seen as reflections of the general principle in Article 21 of the MHL, which requires:

> Household members should care for one another, create a good and amiable home environment and raise awareness of mental disorder prevention; if it is discovered that a household member may have a mental disorder, [others] shall help them to immediately see a doctor, look after their life and take care of them.[22]

The MHL also includes some other provisions that are unlikely to appear in mental health legislation in other jurisdictions. For example, Article 11 provides that the state encourages and supports the training of specialised personnel in mental health, the protection of the legal rights and interests of mental health workers, and the strengthening of the professional mental health workforce.[23] However, Zhao and Dawson rightly point out that many provisions like this 'must be reviewed as largely aspirational'.[24] As the MHL allocates responsibilities for

17 For the draft in full text, see < www.npc.gov.cn/npc/c1481/201110/63b7dc2ae45147e59367d5d71c73f60a.shtml > accessed 1 July 2021; a list of public documents that reveal parts of the other drafts, see < www.npc.gov.cn/wxzl/gongbao/2013-02/25/content_1790870.htm > accessed 1 July 2021.
18 MHL, Chapter 2.
19 Ibid., Chapter 3.
20 Ibid., Chapter 4.
21 Ibid., Chapter 5.
22 Ibid, Art 21. There is no official English translation of the MHL. The translated text in quote is provided by a project that translates Chinese law into English. See China Law Translate, < www.chinalawtranslate.com/en/mental-health-law-of-the-peoples-republic-of-china >, accessed 1 July 2021.
23 MHL, Art 11.
24 Xiju Zhao and John Dawson, 'The New Chinese Mental Health Law' (2014) 21 *Psychiatry, Psychology and Law* 669, 670.

developing and managing mental health services across so many agencies, 'there is the risk that no-one will take responsibility'.[25] After all, clauses like Article 11 lack clarity as to the standard or the legal consequence for failing to fulfil the obligation.[26]

During the 28-year period it took to create the MHL, seven municipal mental health regulations were developed and implemented in seven cities: Shanghai (whose mental health regulation entered into force in 2002), Ningbo (2006), Hangzhou (2007), Beijing (2007), Wuxi (2007), Wuhan (2010), and Shenzhen (2012). These cities are among the most economically and socially developed across China or at least in their regions. These mental health regulations were developed and implemented while the MHL was being drafted; as such they are important in understanding the MHL. This is particularly so in understanding the changes made to the MHL as various drafts were developed. The next section will explore the provisions on mental health detention and involuntary treatment as set out in these municipal regulations and drafts of the MHL.

4.3 Mental Health Detention and Treatment in Municipal Regulations and National Drafts

An essential function of those municipal mental health regulations is to authorise detention and involuntary treatment. As suggested in Chapter 3, the constitutionality of these municipal regulations has been called into question.[27] The regulations authorised the deprivation of liberty; however, according to the Legislation Law, only national law can prescribe on the restrictions of liberty.[28] That said, these regulations have been implemented, and the concerns about their constitutionality over them has never been formally considered by a competent body. Moreover, the Legal Affairs Committee of the SCNPC refers to the provisions of these regulations in its interpretation of the MHL.[29] Therefore, this book considers these municipal mental health regulations are a legitimate source of norms in examining the change introduced by the MHL.

Another subject of consideration in this section are the various drafts of the MHL. The previous section reveals that there are at least five full drafts of the MHL over the course of its 28-year development. Two drafts were produced by the Ministry of Health and the State Council, respectively, and three more drafts were reviewed by the SCNPC. However, only the draft produced by the State Council (LAOSC Draft) and the one for the first SCNPC review (SCNPC Draft) were made available to the general public. Although limited information about other drafts will be incorporated whenever possible, the LAOSC Draft and the SCNPC Draft, together with the seven municipal regulations, form the basis of analysis in this section.

25 Ibid.
26 Xia Li, *Research on the Legal System of Mental Health* (Shanghai Sanlian Bookstore 2016) 25.
27 Chapter 3, Section 3.3.2.
28 Ibid.
29 For example, see Xin Chunying (eds) *The Interpretations of the Mental Health Law of the People's Republic of China* (Law Press China 2013), 127.

This section consists of two parts. The first part will look at the general criteria that directly deprive service users the right to receive information and the right to make decisions. The second part will focus on the evolution of norms on mental health detention and treatment from local regulations to the national drafts. The section aims to suggest that, under the normative framework prior to the MHL, detention and involuntary treatment can be imposed on a person based on psychiatric diagnosis and the family member's decision.

4.3.1 Different thresholds for service users in decision-making

This book considers the prominent role of family members in decision-making in the context of detention and treatment in mental health services. However, it is important to note that in China family members or guardians also play a central role in decision-making in the context of general healthcare.[30] For example, Article 26 of the Medical Practitioners Law says a medical practitioner must truthfully describe the condition to the patient or his or her family member.[31] Therefore, it is important to note that all seven municipal mental health regulations and the MHL provide that the 'patient or family member' has the right to receive information and the right to make decisions. However, the municipal regulations and the MHL adopt different thresholds for service users in enjoying and exercising these rights. As will be discussed below, the right of a service user to make decisions could be denied if it is considered that lacking insight or for other reasons.

The Mental Health Regulation of Shanghai (2002), the first municipal mental health regulation in China, provides a good illustration of the threshold for restricting the right to make decisions and receiving information.[32] Article 36 provided the exercise of the right to information and the right to decision-making should be on the premise that the patient retains insight.[33] The Shanghai Regulation defined 'insight' as the ability to recognise, understand and properly describe one's own abnormal mental state or behaviour.[34]

Clearly, the determination of a service user's insight holds the key to exercising ones' rights. Once determined to lack 'insight' a service user was placed under so-called 'medical monitoring'.[35] The Shanghai Regulation considered medical monitoring as a right or entitlement of a service user when they fully or partially

30 See, generally, Chunyan Ding, 'Family Members' Informed Consent to Medical Treatment for Competent Patients in China' (2010) 8 *China: An International Journal* 139.

31 The Medical Practitioners Law of the People's Republic of China (passed by the SCNPC on 26 June 1998, entered into force on 1 May 1999), art 26. (Medical Practitioners Law).

32 The Mental Health Regulation of Shanghai (the version before amendment according to the MHL was passed on 28 December 2001 by the Standing Committee of Shanghai Municipal People's Congress, entered into force on 7 April 2002) (Shanghai Regulation (2002)).

33 Shanghai Regulation (2002), Art 36.

34 Ibid., Art 47.

35 Ibid., Art 17.

lose insight; for this chapter, however, 'medical monitoring' essentially entails the removal of a series of decision-making rights. The duty of medical monitoring is an onerous obligation for family members, as it combines the roles of substituted decision-maker in mental healthcare and caregiver in daily life. The obligations include provision of care to the service user, to prevent harm to oneself, others or society, to ensure the patient undergoes clinical or inpatient treatment, and to complete the admission and discharge procedures from mental health services.[36] The Shanghai Regulation further explained in Article 30 that when a qualified psychiatrist believed a service user lacked insight, the psychiatrist should propose the medical protective inpatient treatment to the guardian and the guardian must comply.[37] The next subsection will consider the procedure and decision-making governing mental health detention. The point here is that insight serves as a general threshold for service users in enjoying and exercising their right to receive information and make decisions. Similarly, the Mental Health Regulation of Wuxi[38] also adopts insight as the precondition of exercising the right to receive information.[39]

In a similar manner, the Ningbo Regulation,[40] the Hangzhou Regulation,[41] and the Wuhan Regulation[42] adopted 'capacity for civil conduct', a Chinese civil law term to be explained in the section of adult guardianship, as the criterion for denying a service user's decision-making rights; whilst the wording choice of the LAOSC Draft and the SCNPC Draft was 'ability to account for or control one's behaviour'. Regardless how it was expressed in these regulations and drafts, it is clear from the foregoing analysis the voice of service users and right to make decisions is at risk and can be ignored by family members.

As will be discussed in the next section, the thresholds contained in the municipal regulations are removed from the current MHL. The discussion in this subsection help understand the significance of this removal. On the face of it the only limitation imposed on a service user's decision-making in mental health treatment

36 Ibid., Art 19.
37 Ibid., Art 30.
38 The Mental Health Regulation of Wuxi (the version before amendment according to the MHL was passed on 26 July 2007 by the Standing Committee of Wuxi Municipal People's Congress, entered into force on 1 November 2007) (Wuxi Regulation (2007)).
39 Wuxi Regulation (2007), Art 36.
40 The Mental Health Regulation of Ningbo (the version before amendment according to the MHL was passed 29 September 2005 by the Standing Committee of Ningbo Municipal People's Congress, entered into force on 1 April 2006) (Ningbo Regulation).
41 The Mental Health Regulation of Hangzhou (the version before amendment according to the MHL was passed on 27 December 2006 by the Standing Committee of Hangzhou Municipal People's Congress, entered into force on 1 March 2007) (Hangzhou Regulation).
42 The Mental Health Regulation of Wuhan (the version before amendment according to the MHL was passed on 20 November 2008 by the Standing Committee of Wuhan Municipal People's Congress, entered into force on 1 September 2010) (Wuhan Regulation).

is the imposition of detention for involuntary treatment. However, before moving to consider the MHL, the next subsection will consider the changing standards of detention and involuntary treatments under the MHL's predecessors.

4.3.2 *Changing standards of detention and involuntary treatment*

This subsection considers the common themes that emerged from an analysis of the involuntary measures provided for under the municipal mental health regulations. It then makes observations on the changes among various drafts of the MHL. As there is little research that maps how the norms of detention and involuntary treatment evolved from the municipal regulations and the national drafts to the final MHL,[43] the analysis in this subsection seeks to contribute to the literature.

4.3.2.1 *Medical protective admissions and emergency admissions in the municipal regulations*

Under the municipal mental health regulations, there are generally two main kinds of detention and involuntary treatment: medical protective admission and emergency admission.[44] The former refers to admissions that are 'executed by a family member of the mentally ill person who is unable to give informed consent'.[45] The latter refers to admissions 'executed by the police or other government authorities for patients who engage in (non-criminal) dangerous behaviour'.[46]

The different municipal regulations prescribe medical protective admissions differently. For example, the Shanghai Regulation (2002) requires that the close relatives of a suspected mentally ill patient should 'assist' the suspected patient in accessing diagnostic assessment and treatment. The term 'assist' seems not to explicitly authorise close relatives to take the person to the mental health facility against his or her will by force. Its coercive nature, however, is widely accepted in practice.[47] The Shanghai Regulation (2002) also provides that where the qualified psychiatrist considers a service user with full or partial loss of insight should receive inpatient treatment, the guardian must comply with the psychiatrist's proposal. In

43 There is some research work that seeks to review the changing standards of involuntary admission, for example, Yang Shao and Bin Xie, 'Approaches to Involuntary Admission of the Mentally Ill in the People's Republic of China: Changes in Legislation From 2002 to 2012' (2015) 43 *Journal of the American Academy of Psychiatry and the Law* 35. This book does not find their review reliable because their use of concepts is inconsistent and misleading. For clarity, however, this book will not provide a point-to-point response to their work.

44 Shao and Xie (n 43), 36.

45 Ibid.

46 Ibid.

47 It is also widely acknowledged that the staff members of psychiatric facilities often took service users from their home to psychiatric facilities against their will, on the request of family members. See *Training Textbook* (n 4), 107.

this case, the criteria include the need for treatment where there is full or partial lack of insight; and the guardian cannot refuse the so-called 'recommendation'.

By contrast, under the Mental Health Regulation of Beijing (2007)[48] the guardian can decline such a recommendation, by providing a formal explanation for their decision to decline the recommendation,[49] and the criteria does not include the need for treatment, only requiring a diagnosis of 'severe mental illness'. Regardless, this type of admission, which is entirely dependent on the opinions of psychiatrists and guardians, has been the main mechanism for involuntary mental health detention and treatment in China.[50]

Emergency admissions, on the other hand, are not provided by all the municipal regulations. Ningbo, Hangzhou and Wuhan merely provide that 'mentally ill patients who are deemed to pose a danger to others or society can only be detained if the dangerous behaviour constitutes a criminal offence', which shall be initiated by the police.[51] However, China has reformed the procedure for involuntary admission through the criminal justice system in 2012. Under the amended Criminal Procedure Law, courts can only authorise compulsory treatment for those people with mental illness who are deemed to lack capacity for criminal responsibility.[52] While this is an important area, discussion on detention and treatment in the context of the criminal justice system is beyond the scope of this book.

Among the other municipal regulations having provisions on emergency admissions, the Shanghai Regulations (2002) provided that if a person with a (suspected) mental illness poses harm to themselves, others or society, his or her guardian, close relatives, employer, grassroots authorities (such as urban neighbourhood committees and rural villagers committees[53]), or the police should take him or her to a mental health facility.[54] Then the facility was required to appoint at least two qualified psychiatrists to make an initial diagnostic assessment.[55] If the diagnosis found that the person concerned must be detained for observation, the

48 The Mental Health Regulation of Beijing (the version before amendment according to the MHL was passed on 8 December 2006 by the Standing Committee of Beijing Municipal People's Congress, entered into force on 1 March 2007) (Beijing Regulation).
49 Ibid.
50 The national data on the delivery method of mental health treatment is unavailable or unknown to public. Some provincial data indicated, before the enactment of the MHL, at least 60% service users were imposed with involuntary treatment that were decided by family members. See Xin (n 29), 394.
51 Shao and Xie (n 43), 37.
52 The Criminal Procedure Law of the People's Republic of China (adopted in 1979, amended in 2018), Part 5 Chapter 4.
53 Urban neighbourhood committees and rural villagers' committees, elected by the local residents, are not a level of government but autonomous bodies. However, in practice they undertake tasks required by governments and often a last-resort safety net for people without family support in daily life. See, generally, Qingwen Xu, Douglas D Perkins and Julian Chun-Chung Chow, 'Sense of Community, Neighboring, and Social Capital as Predictors of Local Political Participation in China' (2010) 45 *American Journal of Community Psychology* 259.
54 Shanghai Regulation, Art 31.
55 Ibid.

facility detained the person and informed his or her guardian or close relatives.[56] The wording implied that the psychiatrists decided on detention for treatment and family members were only informed about the decision.

However, the role of family members was greater in Shenzhen, Beijing and Wuxi where, if the diagnosis confirms mental disorder, guardians are explicitly required to complete the admission procedure and police served as a last resort given the guardian is uncooperative.[57] In addition, there exists a difference in relation to who has the power to initiate diagnostic assessment (only the police in Shenzhen[58]) and whether 'harm to oneself' is included in the criteria (only harm to others and society in Beijing and Wuxi).[59]

Through the examination above, it has become clear that medical protective admissions do not require potential danger but are entirely dependent on the opinions of mental health professionals and guardians; whereas under emergency admissions, dangerousness would justify detention for diagnostic assessment and the continued detention for treatment still requires guardians' cooperation.

4.3.2.2 Detention and involuntary treatment in two drafts

Under the LAOSC Draft, the first public full draft of the MHL released in June 2011, a service user can visit a mental health facility for diagnostic assessment voluntarily, and family members can also 'take' them for assessment, without clarifying whether coercion could be used.[60] When a person with a (suspected) mental disorder poses harm or dangerousness to themselves, public security, the safety of others or disturbing the public order, a broader range of people are obliged to take the person to a mental health facility for diagnostic assessment.[61] These people include his or her guardian, close relatives, employer,[62] neighbourhood committees or villagers' committees, and, as a last resort, the police.[63] This provision remains unchanged in later drafts and also appears in the final text of the MHL.

By contrast, the standards of detention for treatment have changed considerably in the MHL. The LAOSC Draft appears to consider the mental capacity of a service user in deciding upon detention and involuntary treatment, similar to the fusion model of mental health law and capacity law.[64] The LAOSC Draft, in Article 27, provided that patients should decide on their inpatient treatment for

56 Ibid.
57 Ibid., Art 34; Beijing Regulation, Art 32; Wuxi Regulation, Art 28.
58 Shenzhen Regulation, Art 33.
59 Beijing Regulation, Art 31; Wuxi Regulation, Art 27.
60 LAOSC Draft, Art 24.
61 Ibid., Art 26.
62 Work unit, or Danwei, could refer to any enterprise or firm employing personnel, but it more typically refers to state-owned factories in urban areas. See, generally, Dorothy J Solinger, 'The Chinese Work Unit and Transient Labor in the Transition from Socialism' (1995) 21 *Modern China* 155.
63 LAOSC Draft, Art 26.
64 The 'fusion model' refers to a single legislative scheme governing non-consensual treatment of both 'physical' and 'mental' illnesses, based on determination of

mental disorders autonomously; detention for involuntary treatment can be imposed only when the patient is unable to account for or control his or her behaviour and poses harm or a risk of harm to themselves, public safety, other persons' safety, or public order.[65]

In this draft, when the diagnostic assessment favours inpatient treatment and the standards above are met, the guardian is required to complete the procedure.[66] It implied that the guardian had to approve the detention for treatment and accordingly bear the cost. If a patient or his or her guardian disagrees with the diagnostic assessment, they can apply for a reassessment from the same facility and a certification from an external institute for forensic psychiatry.[67]

The most significant change introduced by the LAOSC Draft is that detention for treatment has to meet the criteria of a diagnosis of mental disorder, the inability to account for or control one's behaviour, and the danger to themselves, public safety, others or the public order. This differs from medical protective admissions that only focus on the inability and emergency admissions that only focus on the harm or danger.

However, the standards of detention for treatment in this draft raised social concerns. The inclusion of 'disturbing public order' as a part of the criteria was criticised as being too vague.[68] It is argued that this approach is particularly open to abuse in the Chinese context, where local governments might force litigants and human rights activists into mental hospitals.[69] The legislators seemed to recognise this concern, and this condition was deleted from the later SCNPC Draft in October 2011.[70]

However, the SCNPC Draft added a more 'problematic' provision in Article 25, which authorises involuntary inpatient treatment if the diagnostic assessment shows the patient has a severe mental disorder and he or she has harmed him or herself, or poses a risk of harm to themselves, or the so called 'one's treatment would be affected adversely if he or she is not hospitalised'.[71]

The SCNPC Draft adopted the term 'severe mental disorder',[72] this being defined as the mental disorders that cause severe social functioning of the patient, damages the patient's ability to fully account for their health condition or objective reality, or damage the patient's ability to take care of their own affairs.[73] It seems reasonable to argue that

incapacity. See, generally, John Dawson and George Szmukler, 'Fusion of Mental Health and Incapacity Legislation' (2006) 188 *The British Journal of Psychiatry* 504.

65 LAOSC Draft, Art 27.

66 Ibid., Art 28.

67 Ibid., Art 29–32.

68 Yu-Tao Xiang et al., 'China's National Mental Health Law: A 26-Year Work in Progress' (2012) 379 *The Lancet* 780, 781.

69 Chunyan Ding, 'Involuntary Detention and Treatment of the Mentally Ill: China's 2012 Mental Health Law' (2014) 37 *International Journal of Law and Psychiatry* 581, 581.

70 Xiju Zhao and John Dawson, 'The New Chinese Mental Health Law' (2014) 21 *Psychiatry, Psychology and Law* 669, 674.

71 SCNPC Draft, Art 25.

72 Ibid., Art 25.

73 Ibid., Art 74.

the change between the two drafts is merely a matter of expression: both approaches are essentially about assessing their own mental capacity.[74]

More importantly, although 'disturbing public order' is deleted, the following criteria for detention where 'one's treatment would be affected adversely if he or she is not hospitalised' was added.[75] The inclusion of this criteria with the lack of a clear definition was criticised as it was considered to bolster the paternalistic impulses of medical practitioners. Some commentators criticised this clause for placing civil liberty under psychiatric authority;[76] whilst others suggested it reflected Chinese values and was necessary from a practical perspective.[77] Nevertheless, this clause was removed from the MHL.

The SCNPC Draft also provided that where a service user is detained for treatment by the guardian on the ground of posing harm or dangerousness to themselves, the service user can challenge the guardian's decision by applying an internal reassessment and external certification.[78] However, this complaint mechanism for service users against family members was deleted in later drafts and was not included in the final MHL. This change may suggest legislators perhaps naively assumed a lack of conflict or divergent views between service users and their family members about inpatient treatment.[79] The next section further analyses these two points above.

4.3.3 Section summary

This section has sought to address a significant gap in the literature on mental health law in China by undertaking a comparative analysis of normative documents on the criteria for involuntary detention before the enactment of the MHL. This section considered various restrictions over service users' autonomy and right to make decisions as provided for in the seven municipal mental health regulations and two main drafts of the MHL. The predecessors of the MHL prescribe different thresholds for allowing service users to enjoy and exercise their decision-making rights (namely the loss of insight or the inability to account for or control one's behaviour). When a service user's right to receive information or give their consent is restricted, family members essentially serve as the primary substituted decision-makers for their relatives.

74 See, generally, John Dawson, 'A Realistic Approach to Assessing Mental Health Laws Compliance with the UNCRPD' (2015) International journal of law and psychiatry 70.
75 SCNPC Draft, Art 25.
76 Shu Wang, 'The Mental Health Law rules patients have right to refuse hospitalisation and access to justice' *Beijing News* (Beijing, 27 October 2012) < news.jcrb.com/jxsw/201210/t20121027_972481.html > accessed 5 July 2021.
77 Mingxu Wang and Ruiping Fan, 'Involuntary Treatment of Mental Disorders and the Coordination of Various Authorities' (2016) 29 (1) *Chinese Medical Ethics* 5, 5.
78 SCNPC Draft, Art 26.
79 Ding (n 69), 585.

This section also considered the criteria for detention for diagnostic assessment and treatment under the regulations that predated the introduction of the MHL. As discussed above, emergency admissions are essentially procedures that authorise detention for diagnostic assessment. It is suggested that the decision for the continued detention for treatment, after the diagnosis, is still most likely decided by family members. Medical protective admissions, on the other hand, are also mostly decided by family members, without any requirement of evident harm or dangerousness to themselves or others. Therefore, except for those detentions that are now addressed by criminal procedures, following medical recommendations, family members were the primary decision-makers for the civil commitment under the municipal mental health regulations.

The detailed analysis of the LAOSC Draft and the SCNPC Draft indicate that the drafters gave serious considerations to pivoting away from this approach. The criteria for detention for diagnostic assessment in the two drafts nevertheless remained at a low threshold. However, the inclusion of the criteria for detention for treatment such as 'disturbing public order' and 'one's treatment would be affected adversely if they are not hospitalised' attracted heated debate, reflecting the tension and controversy during the drafting process of the MHL. The final MHL provides that detention for treatment must meet both a diagnostic threshold and the dangerousness standard. Therefore, at least in theory, the prevalent practice of medical protective admissions should no longer be permissible under the MHL. This will be discussed in greater detail in the next section.

4.4 Decision-making for Detention and Treatment under the Mental Health Law

Following a review of the municipal regulations and the two drafts preceding the MHL, and their impact on the MHL this section substantively considers the main provisions of the MHL. The key messages this section seeks to deliver is that unlike the preceding regulations the MHL no longer places a general limitation over a service user's autonomy and decision-making rights (such as the loss of insight or the capacity for civil conduct). The only exception to the voluntary principle is the detention for involuntary treatment, when a diagnostic threshold and a dangerousness standard has been met. This change in theory, should augment service users' autonomy.

The section starts with a critical examination of the voluntary principle of mental health treatment. It then explores the procedures and standards of different stages of inpatient treatment in mental health facilities. In doing so, this section seeks to identify where the MHL has diverged from the municipal regulations and two drafts. The section also critiques some of the unfortunate vagueness in the MHL's provisions.

4.4.1 The voluntary principle

The MHL provides in Article 30 that inpatient treatment of mental disorders shall be voluntary in principle.[80] However, if the result of the diagnostic assessment indicates that a person has a severe mental disorder, the medical facility may impose inpatient treatment when the person is: (1) self-harming, or having a risk of self-harm; or (2) having behaviours that harmed others, or posing a risk to the safety of others.[81]

As a principle, a voluntary service user can choose or refuse inpatient treatment themselves. Accordingly, they can also request discharge at any time, and medical facilities are required to comply.[82] However, the MHL does not make it clear whether a voluntary service user has the right to refuse treatment during hospitalisation. In theory, his or her right to request discharge 'at any time' serves as a last resort if the service user does not want certain treatments to proceed.[83] Nevertheless, Article 45 provides when persons with mental disorders are unable to complete hospital discharge procedures themselves, these procedures shall be completed by their guardians.[84] How this is determined in practice and whether this provision applies to voluntary service users is unclear.

What is clear, however, is that the MHL does not grant a mental health facility the power to detain a voluntary service user if the facility disagrees with the service user's request for discharge. The MHL provides in Article 44 that when the medical facility considers hospital discharge requested by voluntary service users and guardians inappropriate, the facility shall explain their reasons for opposing discharge to the patient and the guardians; and if the patient or the guardians insist on discharge, the registered physician shall write a detailed record of the discussion about discharge in the medical chart and provide recommendations about the medical management of the patient after discharge.[85]

Similar to its predecessors, the MHL adopts 'patients or guardians' as the persons with the right to receive information. As a general rule, the facility is required to inform the patients or their guardians about the patient's rights and treatment plan, including its methods, goals and potential adverse effects.[86] From a legal perspective, mental health facilities will fulfil their obligations under these provisions by merely informing the guardians.

In addition, the right of guardians may still prevail in certain situations. For example, the MHL requires that a mental health facility must allow service users and their guardians to access and copy their medical record.[87] However, unlike the rule of accessing medical records in general health care, the right of a service

80 MHL, Art 30.
81 Ibid.
82 Ibid., Art 44.
83 Ibid.
84 Ibid., Art 45. The definition of guardian in the MHL will be discussed later this section.
85 Ibid., Art 44.
86 Ibid., Art 37, 39.
87 Ibid., Art 47.

user could be legally restricted, if accessing or copying medical record would be potentially detrimental to their treatment.[88] The MHL does not clarify this standard, but it is very likely to be determined by psychiatrist.[89] By contrast, the guardian's right to access the medical records must be ensured, regardless of any situation.[90]

Despite these shortcomings, the most important change is that a general threshold for a service user in exercising the right to receive information and the right to make decisions is no longer in place. Under the MHL, a voluntary service user is genuinely voluntary in its literal meaning. This is arguably laudable, since the term voluntary may carry more complicated and coercive implications when compared to mental health law in other jurisdictions.[91] Therefore, for voluntary service users, although the subjects of the right to information are still 'patients or (in some provisions, and) guardians', in the spirit of the voluntary principle, restriction on the rights of service users to access information and make decisions must not be easily bypassed. Although the MHL does not explicitly mention mental capacity, or the capacity for civil conduct under Chinese civil law, adult guardianship may still be relevant for voluntary service users. The applicable adult guardianship system in China will be addressed later in this chapter.

As addressed above, the MHL explicitly adopts the voluntary principle and moves away from the approach that using 'insight' or 'capacity for civil conduct' to restrict the right of a service user to receive information and make decisions about admission and treatment. The only limitation over a service user's voluntary decision is the imposition of detention and involuntary treatment, which will be considered further in the next subsection.

4.4.2 Detention and involuntary treatment under the Mental Health Law

This subsection addresses the provisions for detention and involuntary treatment, specifically considering detention for diagnostic assessment, detention for treatment, and discharge.

4.4.2.1 Detention for diagnostic assessment

In addition to voluntary appointment in a mental health facility, Article 28 also says close family members 'may' take a person for a mental health assessment, implying that no one in Chinese society can refuse diagnostic assessment in

88 Ibid.
89 Ibid.
90 Ibid.
91 For example, see, generally, Hope Davidson, 'When Is a Voluntary Patient Not a Voluntary Patient? An Examination of the Degree to Which the Irish Courts Have Sought to Engage with the Jurisprudence of the European Court of Human Rights, in Relation to the Treatment and Detention of Voluntary or "informal" Patients' (2017) 2016 *International Journal of Mental Health and Capacity Law* 38.

circumstance where their mental health is called into question. The MHL relies on family members, not necessarily equipped with any expertise in mental health, to determine the presence of a suspected mental disorder, defined as the disturbances or abnormalities of perception, emotion, thinking or other mental processes.[92] The wording of 'may be taken' implies a certain degree of coercion, for example by threat or deception, is permitted in the process of taking a person with suspected mental disorder to a facility. The implementation of this provision merits further discussion. However, it is reasonable to suggest that the decision to restrict a service user's liberty is at the discretion of a family member, without any meaningful threshold.

When a person with a suspected mental disorder is at risk of harming themselves or others, a broader range of entities, including employers and the police, shall immediately intervene and take the person to a mental health facility for diagnostic assessment.[93] However, there is no clear time restriction for the assessment. Article 29 merely provides that, when receiving persons with suspected mental disorders deemed posing a risk, medical facilities shall hold them, designate a registered psychiatrist for diagnostic assessment immediately who issue a formal diagnostic result promptly.[94]

A 72-hour limit to the diagnostic assessment was included in the SCNPC Draft,[95] which was ultimately removed from the MHL. Nevertheless, both the new ('promptly') and the old ('72-hour') rules apply to persons taken for posing harm or risk to oneself or others.[96] By contrast, for persons without such dangerousness who are taken for assessment by family members, the MHL does not provide any time limit for their diagnostic assessment. This arguably reflects a presumption that no conflict of interest between a service user and the family member would arise.

Even for those detained on the ground of danger to themselves or others, the MHL does not provide any mechanism to substantiate the claimed danger. This means a family member without any expertise in mental health can decide on deprivation of liberty for an unknown period of time, based on a suspected mental disorder where they claim or perceive danger.

4.4.2.2 Detention for treatment

As discussed, detention for treatment, or 'involuntary inpatient treatment' in the language of the MHL, has to meet the diagnostic threshold of a severe mental disorder, of which the definition implies consideration of mental capacity,[97] and the dangerousness standard. Unlike mental health legislation in some jurisdictions, the MHL does not require separate procedures or standards for detention and involuntary treatment. The concept of 'inpatient treatment' suggests a service user

92 MHL, Art 28, 83.
93 Ibid., Art 28.
94 Ibid., Art 29.
95 SCNPC Draft, Art 24.
96 MHL, Art 28.
97 Dawson (n 74).

has no control over future treatment as long as he or she is detained. The only exception to this is provided by Article 43, which requires that the delivery of surgeries that result in loss of function of body organ and experimental clinical treatments must obtain separate written consent from service users.[98] If the service user is regarded as 'unable' to give consent, the consent of guardians can be substituted instead, with internal ethical approval from the facility.[99] Again, this provision implies the consideration of mental capacity, but the MHL does not provide any further clarification on how to determine a service user's ability in this context. There is no literature on how this provision of substituted consent works in practice, which requires further research. However, it seems reasonable to assume that the capacity determination will be more likely to apply to the service users who refuse these proposed interventions than those who comply.

In relation to the decision-maker for detention for treatment, the MHL differentiates service users who are dangerous to themselves from those who are dangerous to others. If a service user having a severe mental disorder is considered to pose harm or dangerousness to others, it will ultimately be made by the facility that receives the service user and carries out the diagnosis.[100] Article 36 provides that if the guardians do not complete the hospital admission procedures, the employer, rural villagers' committee or urban neighbourhood committee completes the hospital admission procedures instead and the medical facility records this situation in the patient's medical chart.[101] In this scenario, the service user or the guardian could only apply for a reassessment and medical certification if they disagree with the decision for detention for treatment.[102]

By contrast, if the service user is dangerous to themselves but poses no dangerousness to others, detention for treatment is up to the guardian.[103] A significant deficit in respect of the service users' rights under the MHL is where a service user disagrees with the diagnosis or the guardian's decision for detention, the MHL does not provide any internal complaint mechanism. In the SCNPC Draft, a service user was entitled to apply for a reassessment and further a medical certification against the psychiatrist and the family member about the initial diagnosis and the detention for treatment.[104] However, this provision was removed from the final text of the MHL. According to the official explanation for this deletion, the legislators thought most service users are not willing to accept inpatient treatment and allowing them to challenge the decision of their guardians would 'raise new problems in practice'.[105] They believed the external mechanism, the right to litigate in courts,[106] would serve as an adequate safeguard.[107]

98 MHL, Art 43.
99 Ibid., Art 43.
100 Ibid., Art 30, 32, 35, 36.
101 Ibid., Art 36.
102 Ibid., Art 32, 35.
103 Ibid., Art 30, 31, 32.
104 SCNPC Draft Art 26.
105 Xin (n 29), 93.
106 MHL Art 82.
107 Xin (n 29), 93.

4.4.2.3 Discharge

The discharge provisions in the MHL have adopted different approaches to decision-making. For detained service users imposing harm or danger on themselves, the guardian can request discharge at any time, and the mental health facility must comply.[108] The facility could only advise why discharge is unwise from a professional perspective.[109] If the advice is not accepted by the guardian, the facility can merely note this in the medical record and discharge the service user.[110]

For those service users detained on the basis of posing a risk to others, a mental health facility may decide when discharge is appropriate; whilst the procedure has to be completed by the service user or, when service users are 'unable' to complete hospital discharge procedures, the guardians.[111] Problematically, the MHL is silent on the determination of such ability. If a service user under detention for treatment is automatically deemed unable to make any treatment decision, their liberty is left to their guardian to decide. This is the case even when the mental health facility believes he or she should be discharged.[112] This provision may cause considerable problems in practice.

4.4.2.4 Cross-cutting issues

Through the discussions above, some cross-cutting issues emerge. Chief amongst these is that under the MHL, both the diagnostic assessment and the inpatient treatment can be voluntarily and involuntarily provided, creating potential complications. In theory, a person can consent to a diagnostic assessment on a voluntary basis but then be detained for treatment, if the diagnostic threshold of a severe mental disorder and the dangerousness standard are met. Therefore, the voluntary diagnostic assessment could be viewed as risky from the service user's perspective. It is also possible that a person could be taken by the family member for diagnostic assessment against their will, but, if no dangerousness is found, they should be able to refuse the inpatient treatment and leave. These hypothetical cases are entirely possible by law.

Another cross-cutting issue is that, like its predecessors, the MHL grants guardians or family members significant decision-making power in respect of detention. Granting the power of deprivation of liberty to another individual is clearly at odds with international human rights law. At very least, considering the significant power imbalance between service users and their guardians, the MHL should provide safeguards that recognise the potential for conflict and prevent abusive use of the MHL by family members. However, the MHL provides in Article 83 that

108 MHL, Art 44.
109 Ibid.
110 Ibid.
111 Ibid., Art 45.
112 Bo Chen, 'Xu v the Hospital and His Guardian – Involuntary Inpatient Treatment' (2018) 2016 *International Journal of Mental Health and Capacity Law* 134.

guardians of persons with mental disorders under the MHL are persons who may assume the role of the guardian as specified in Chinese civil law.[113]

As will be explained in the next section, Chinese civil law provides a list of persons that may assume the role of the guardian, including one's spouse, parents or adult children.[114] Without any formal safeguard or further guidance on how to appoint a guardian, the MHL leaves excessive discretion and significant potential for abuse by both psychiatrists and family members or guardians. Moreover, Article 83 may even bypass the safeguards provided under the adult guardianship system. In order to understand this, a substantive examination of the adult guardianship system will be provided in section 4.5.

4.4.3 Section summary

This section examines the MHL's provisions for detention and treatment decision-making. Compared to the preceding municipal regulations and two drafts, the MHL no longer adopts any general threshold for service users in exercising their decision-making rights, such as insight. The voluntary principle of inpatient treatment is explicitly adopted. The only exception to the voluntary principle is that both a diagnostic threshold of a severe mental disorder and a dangerousness standard must be met. The prevalent 'medical protective admission', which allows family members and psychiatrists to decide on detention for treatment upon medical recommendations without any requirement of dangerousness to oneself or others, is no longer permissible. This can be considered a positive change in the direction of maximising service users' autonomy and their right to make decisions.

Nevertheless, the doctrinal examination of the MHL in this article has identified a number of unanswered questions. The MHL does not provide any guidance on many critical determinations, including dangerousness and the ability to complete the procedures for inpatient treatment or discharge. For example, if the dangerousness threshold is interpreted loosely in practice, anyone with a label of a severe mental disorder could be at risk of detention for treatment. The scope for a loose interpretation could render the voluntary principle meaningless in practice.

Another significant issue is the appointment of guardians, who wield enormous decision-making power over service users. The wording of the MHL seems to imply that every person with a severe mental disorder must have a guardian, which places the rights of service users in significant jeopardy. As will be discussed in the

113 The text of Article 83 refers to The General Principles of Civil Law of the People's Republic of China (passed by the National People's Congress on 12 April 1986, entered into force on 1 July 1987) (GPrinciplesCL (1987)). The GPrinciplesCL (1987) has been partly replaced by the GProvisionsCL (2017), and later the Civil Code of the People's Republic of China (passed by the National People's Congress on 8 May 2020, entered into force on 1 January 2021). For clarity, this article will use 'civil law' as a general term to refer a number of pieces of legislations on torts and civil procedures, as well as GPrinciplesCL (1987), GProvisionsCL (2017), and the Civil Code, unless it is necessary to be specific.

114 GPriciplesCL (1987), Art 17; GProvisionsCL (2017), Art 28.

next section, by Chinese civil law a guardian is only necessary for persons who are declared as having no or limited capacity for civil conduct by a court. The diagnosis of having a severe mental disorder should not entail such a declaration of lack of legal capacity. Moreover, Article 83 appears to bypass the procedure of appointing a guardian, by defining a guardian under the MHL as anyone who may assume the role of the guardian. The next section will address the adult guardianship system in China that has an impact on the MHL.

4.5 Adult Guardianship Law in China

Given the critical role of guardians under the MHL, the grounds and procedure for their appointment necessitate consideration, which has been inadequate in the literature generated on the MHL. This section seeks to deliver three key messages about the adult guardianship law in China, which may have an impact on the decision-making in mental health detention and treatment. First, a guardian has full responsibility for the person, including caring, bearing the cost of living of the person, and tort liability should the person cause injury to a third party or their property. Second, the current adult guardianship law requires a consideration of mental capacity in decision-making of the person under guardianship, and, on this basis, a guardian's decision-making power should be limited accordingly. Third, the procedural safeguards for a guardian's appointment may not apply to persons subject to the MHL. This section considers these points in turn and highlights a number of key changes introduced by the Civil Code that enters into force in 2021.

4.5.1 The duties and rights of a guardian

In China's civil law, a guardian's primary duty is to act as the legal agent, or translated as agent *ad litem* in some documents, of the person under guardianship in civil relationships.[115] For example, a person under full guardianship could not independently sign a valid contract with their landlord. This 'civil conduct', the term adopted by Chinese civil law, of entering into a contract must be represented by the guardian as their legal agent.

The Civil Code provides that a guardian's duties also include protecting the personal rights, property rights, and other rightful interest of the person under guardianship.[116] By official interpretations, the duties also include protecting the person's health, looking after the person's life, managing the person's property, representing the person in civil conduct, managing and educating the person, and representing the person in lawsuits if the person's rights and interests are violated.[117]

115 Civil Code, Art 23, 24.
116 Ibid., Art 34.
117 The Opinions on Implementing the General Principle of Civil Law of the People's Republic of China (adopted by the adjudication committee of the Supreme People's Court of People's Republic of China, entered into force on 26 January 1988, referred as 'Opinions on GPriciplesCL 1987' hereafter), art 10. The judicial explanations on

Moreover, a guardian is liable where the person causes injury to a third part or their property.[118] Thus, the role of guardian under the civil law is much wider than that of a substitute decision maker; they play a much greater role as a caregiver and potential liability bearer. Accordingly, the guardian carries a significant 'burden' as the holders of the decision-making power, and, therefore, Civil Code Article 34 protects guardians' rights in fulfilling their duty of guardianship.[119] Reading this provision with the relevant provisions above, the rights in fulfilling the duty of guardianship include the right of representing the person in civil affairs. In practice this means, for example, deciding on where they live or what is the best way to take care of the person.[120] In some jurisdictions, there is a growing awareness that the deprivation of liberty of persons under guardianship violates human rights.[121] However, this emerging understanding of international human rights law has not been reflected in domestic Chinese law yet.

4.5.2 Criteria of adult guardianship

Carrying significant powers and duties, the criteria of establishing guardianship is a critically important issue. It is asserted by the civil law that every natural person has equal status in having rights,[122] and adults are persons with full capacity for civil conduct and can exercise civil conduct independently.[123] However, the civil law also provides that an adult who is unable to account for his own conduct shall be a person with no capacity for civil conduct and shall be represented by their guardians in civil activities.[124] Similarly, a person with limited capacity for civil conduct refers to 'an adult who is unable to fully account for his own conduct'.[125] In the latter scenario, a person with limited capacity could make decisions independently in activities that are purely beneficial or appropriate to the capacity of the person.[126] Otherwise, the civil conduct concerned requires the guardian's approval to become valid in law.[127]

Therefore, the imposition of guardianship depends on the determination of one's capacity for civil conduct, or in other words, the ability to 'account for his own conduct'. According to official interpretations, the consideration includes the

the legal implementation, like the Opinions on GPrinciplesCL (1987), is considered as a source of law in a legal case in front of the court.

118 Civil Code, Art 1188.
119 Ibid., Art 34.
120 Chen (n 112).
121 Eilionóir Flynn, Mónica Pinilla-Rocancio and María Gómez-Carrillo de Castro, 'Disability-Specific Forms of Deprivation of Liberty' < www.nuigalway.ie/media/centrefordisabilitylawandpolicy/files/DoL-Report-Final.pdf > accessed 1 July 2021.
122 Civil Code, Art 14.
123 Ibid., Art 18.
124 Ibid., Art 21.
125 Ibid., Art 22.
126 Ibid.
127 Ibid.

degree of relevance of the conduct with the person's own life,[128] whether the person is able to understand the conduct and foresee the consequence,[129] and the extent to which the person has the ability of judgement and self-protection.[130]

These standards are critical to the division of decision-making rights between guardians and the person under guardianship, which is highly relevant to the MHL's operation. The civil law emphasises that guardians should maximise the respect for the person's true will and not intervene where the persons are capable of deciding.[131] In the latest development, the Civil Code even includes a positive duty that the guardian is obliged to actively promote and assist the person in participating activities appropriate to their capacity for civil conduct.[132] Although the principle of best interests is still in place, the clause of 'maximum respect' is arguably the most crucial progress in adult guardianship law reform in China in recent decades.

On the other hand, the threshold for the imposition of guardianship has been reduced after the civil law reform. The scope of persons under adult guardianship has been extended from 'the mentally ill' as provided for in the GPrinciplesCL (1987) (including people with dementia or intellectual disabilities)[133] to all adults in the GProvisionsCL (2017) and then the Civil Code. The precondition of mental illness has been removed, and loss of the capacity for civil conduct becomes applicable to any adult person. The expanded scope implies a popular but increasingly sceptical belief that adult guardianship is a form of protection for vulnerable people and deserves promotion in use.[134] This paternalistic attitude helps explain why the procedural safeguards are mostly overlooked in practice.[135]

4.5.3 Appointment of a guardian

As discussed above, determination of the full or partial loss of the capacity for civil conduct is the precondition for the imposition of guardianship.[136] The determination, and the declaration, are made by a court. The Civil Code provides any person who shares interests with the adult concerned may apply to a court for a declaration that the person is a person without or with limited capacity for civil conduct.[137] Accordingly, the Civil Procedure Law[138] sets out more detailed provisions on procedural matters.

128 Opinions on GPrinciplesCL (1987), Art 4.
129 Ibid.
130 Ibid., Art 5.
131 Civil Code, Art 35.
132 Ibid.
133 Opinions on GPrinciplesCL (1987), Art 5.
134 For example, Japan introduced a new law to promote the implementation of adult guardianship system. See 'The adult guardianship system' *The Japan Times* (11 February 2017) < www.japantimes.co.jp/opinion/2017/02/11/editorials/adult-guardianship-system/#.XBp1-M_7T6B > accessed 1 July 2021.
135 *Training Textbook* (n 4), 17.
136 Civil Code, Art 21, 22.
137 Ibid., 24.

When a court declares the status of no or limited capacity for civil conduct, the guardian's role should be assumed by (a) spouse, (b) parents or adult children, (c) other close relatives, or (d) other individuals or entities who are willing to act as the guardian with the approval from the villagers' committee or neighbourhood committee.[139] These persons and entities who may assume the role of guardian can negotiate and jointly agree on appointing one of them as the guardian.[140] Otherwise, the law makes it clear that the priority is automatically given in the order from (a) to (d).[141] If there is disagreement about who should assume the role of the guardian, the villagers' committee or the neighbourhood committee can appoint any eligible person under categories (a) to (d).[142]

Under the Civil Code, an application can be lodged directly to the court if any relevant party prefers a court to make the decision about the appointment of the guardian as opposed to the villagers'/neighbourhood committee.[143] By contrast, the GPrinciplesCL (1987) only allows a court's intervention after the villagers'/neighbourhood committee makes an appointment but someone still disagrees.[144] Also, as a back-up plan, if a person declared as having no or limited capacity has no one from (a) to (d), the department of civil affairs in the local government or the applicable villagers'/neighbourhood committee will take up the role of guardian.[145] According to the provisions discussed above, family members and friends remain the primary pool from which guardians are appointed.

Another change from the GPrinciplesCL (1987) to the Civil Code is that the new law introduces a 'power of attorney' clause. A person having full capacity for civil conduct could negotiate with his or her close relatives, or other eligible individuals or entities, about who will be the guardian, and a record of the decision is made in writing.[146] The role of a guardian commences when the person partially or fully loses their capacity for civil conduct.[147] It is only applicable to the decision as to who will assume the role of the guardian. The Civil Code does not provide more guidance on whether the person can make specific advanced decisions or wishes, or whether these advanced decisions are binding.

Since the full or partial loss of capacity for civil conduct forms the basis for the necessity of guardianship, when a person's capacity is considered to be restored, the guardianship arrangement expires.[148] Other conditions of expiry include where the guardian loses their ability to act as the guardian, death of the person or the guardian, and other necessary causes as decided by the court.[149]

139 Civil Code, Art 28.
140 Ibid., Art 30.
141 Ibid., Art 28.
142 Ibid., Art 31.
143 Ibid.
144 GPrinciplesCL (1987), Art 17.
145 Civil Code, Art 32.
146 Ibid., Art 33.
147 Ibid.
148 Ibid., Art 39.
149 Ibid.

4.5.4 Safeguards

This subsection explores how a person under guardianship, or other relevant parties, can challenge the guardian's decisions or the status of guardianship overall, as a safeguard to the person's autonomy.

As addressed above, a court's declaration of loss of the capacity for civil conduct is the precondition of guardianship. Accordingly, the ultimate way to 'escape' from guardianship is to apply to the court for another declaration of restoring one's capacity.[150] Both the person under guardianship and the guardian can initiate the procedures, as articulated in the Civil Procedure Law.[151]

As there is no other public sector body that has the authority to monitor guardianship, an application to the court is the only complaint mechanism available. The court can revoke the guardian's role and appoint another guardian under certain situations, following the application by relevant parties. The situations include when the guardian (a) engages in any behaviour that severely damages the person's health, (b) fails to fulfil the duty or refuses to commission the duty to others when unable to fulfil to duty, or (c) engages in any other behaviour that violates the person's rights and interests.[152] Category (c) could be broadly interpreted and is potentially powerful in cases where guardians ignore or override the person's will in the context of mental health treatment.

4.5.5 Section summary

This section addresses the adult guardianship system, highlighting the positive changes introduced by recent law reform. However, it has been identified that guardianship and substituted decision-making as a form of protection remains the prevalent idea. The state is reinforcing its reliance on family members as the primary caregivers and liability bearers. At the same time, deprivation of liberty is explicitly allowed under the name of 'best interests' and fulfilling a guardian's duty. Persons under guardianship could not access other forms of oversight or remedy other than changing a guardian or ending guardianship through the courts. Without any form of supported decision-making arrangement, this all-or-nothing approach to guardianship serves as the biggest threat to any possible positive human rights informed interpretation of the law.

Nevertheless, aspects of the law reform are positive. The concept of 'person having limited capacity for civil conduct' is promising. It creates the potential for a service user, even under guardianship, to exercise their legal capacity in those activities that are 'appropriate' to their capacity for civil conduct. The newly adopted principle of 'maximum respect' for the will of persons under guardianship also requires the guardian to empower the person in engaging in civil activities as much as possible.

150 Ibid., Art 24.
151 CPL, Art 190.
152 Civil Code, Art 36.

As discussed, the MHL has provisions that implies mental capacity and adult guardianship law plays a critical role in determining mental capacity and protects autonomy from undue intervention. However, this interplay may be legally ignored given the MHL defines the guardian in the context of mental health treatment as the persons who are eligible of assuming the role of the guardian, as provided in the Civil Law. Although it requires further observation from practice about whether and how the adult guardianship law, particularly the appointment procedures and safeguards above, serves as sources of balancing the dominant decision-making power granted to guardians, this chapter argues for promoting consideration of and research into adult guardianship law wherever the MHL is the subject of inquiry.

4.6 Chapter Conclusion

This chapter provides a comprehensive account of the provisions relevant to mental health detention and involuntary treatment. It does so by reviewing the municipal mental health regulations and national drafts before the enactment of the MHL. It also highlights the major changes introduced by the recent reform in both the MHL and the Civil Law.

Under the MHL, the only exception to the voluntary principle is that inpatient treatment must meet both a diagnostic threshold of a severe mental disorder and a dangerousness standard to oneself or others. It is a significant change in the law, compared to the dominant practice of medical protective admissions, which does not require any dangerousness and is supported by the predecessors to the MHL. The MHL does not adopt any general threshold for a service user in exercising his or her right to information and decision-making, (moving away from the old paradigm that relies on insight or capacity for civil conduct). This is laudable for moving in the direction of maximising the respect for service users' autonomy and decision-making rights.

There are a number of potential pitfalls that give cause for concern. The guardians and mental health facilities are still vested with the authority of imposing detention and involuntary treatment. Very little guidance on the determination of severe mental disorders and dangerousness are provided for in the MHL. This is especially vulnerable to abuse, as there is no independent oversight.

The reform of the adult guardianship law reflects another mixed package of provisions. The law reform has introduced the principle of 'maximum respect' for the wishes of persons under guardianship. It also obliges a guardian to actively support the person in engaging in civil affairs as independently as possible. On the other hand, the concept of 'a person having limited capacity for civil conduct' and the procedural requirement of declaring one's capacity has been long established before the law reform but has rarely been followed in practice. This general ignorance raises a doubt as to what extent the positive law reform can be translated into practice. Not to mention that the MHL potentially bypasses the safeguards of guardianship by the special definition of guardian.[153]

153 MHL, Art 82.

This chapter has critically engaged with recent law reform, identifying that at least in theory there is an opportunity for better respect for service users' decision-making rights in mental health treatment. However, to understand the impact of this law reform in practice, it is necessary to move beyond a doctrinal examination of the law. It also requires evidence from the ground. The next chapter will provide this evidence through a qualitative study and an analysis of the courts' judgments.

5 Law in Action

Medical Practice and Judicial Response

5.1 Chapter Introduction

Chapter 4 highlighted the necessity of collecting evidence on the ground. In order to have a full picture of mental health law reform in China, this chapter presents the research relating to the practice of treatment decision-making under the Mental Health law (MHL).[1] On this basis, the chapter suggests that mental health law reform in China, which is supposed to promote the voluntary principle and maximise the autonomy of service users, seems not to have been well translated into practice.

The evidence collected includes 26 semi-structured interviews with different stakeholders in 2017 (see Table 5.1). The participants consist of seven former service users who have experience of detention and involuntary treatment, nine psychiatrists, eight lawyers or NGO workers who have experience of MHL-related cases, and two community or social workers in the field. The purpose of these qualitative interviews, most of which lasted approximately one hour, is to gain an in-depth understanding of the daily practice of mental health treatment decision-making. This chapter will report the main findings according to the chronological order of the mental health treatment in China, from admission for diagnostic assessment to discharge. The limitations of the qualitative interviews are the small sample of participants, compared to the population of persons with mental health issues and the number of psychiatrists in China, and the unsuccessful attempt to include family members in the research.

Nevertheless, such limitations are justifiable. First, this study does not claim statistical representation through a national survey. Instead, these interviews provide a deep understanding of what is happening in their daily practice and their concerns beneath the surface, serving as a baseline study of larger scale in the future. Second, every effort was made to prevent the findings from being overly influenced by biased opinions. Also, interviews with each group of participants only stopped when participants kept giving essentially the same answers. Third, to reach those findings, the study triangulates various sources of information, including a comprehensive analysis of all the courts' judgments over the five-year period of enactment of the MHL.

1 Mental Health Law of the People's Republic of China (passed by the Standing Committee of the National People's Congress on 26 October 2012, entered into force on 1 May 2013) (MHL).

DOI: 10.4324/9781003212034-5

Table 5.1 Interview participants code

Interview time	*Location of participants*	*Code*
17 March 2017	Hangzhou, Zhejiang Province	A-service user
30 March 2017	Shenzhen, Guangdong Prov.	B-service user
10 April 2017	Changsha, Hunan Prov.	C-service user
11 April 2017	Luoyuan, Fujian Prov.	D-service user
12 April 2017, afternoon	Changsha, Hunan Prov.	E-service user
14 April 2017, afternoon	Changsha, Hunan Prov.	F-service user
16 April 2017	Wuhan, Hubei Prov.	G-service user
15 February 2017	Xi'an, Shaanxi Prov.	H-psychiatrist
16 February 2017	Weinan, Shaanxi Prov.	I-psychiatrist
27 February 2017	Shanghai	J-psychiatrist
08 March 2017	Fuzhou, Fujian Prov.	K-psychiatrist
13 March 2017, afternoon	Suzhou, Jiangsu Prov.	L-psychiatrist
13 March 2017, evening	Suzhou, Jiangsu Prov.	M-psychiatrist
14 March 2017, morning	Suzhou, Jiangsu Prov.	N-psychiatrist
14 March 2017, afternoon	Suzhou, Jiangsu Prov.	O-psychiatrist
15 March 2017	Suzhou, Jiangsu Prov.	P-psychiatrist
03 March 2017	Shanghai	Q-lawyer/NGO
28 March 2017	Shenzhen, Guangdong Prov.	R-lawyer/NGO
1 April 2017, afternoon	Shenzhen, Guangdong Prov.	S-lawyer/NGO
1 April 2017, evening	Shenzhen, Guangdong Prov.	T-lawyer/NGO
2 April 2017	Shenzhen, Guangdong Prov.	U-lawyer/NGO
14 April 2017, morning	Zhengzhou, Henan Prov.	V-lawyer/NGO
15 April 2017	Guangzhou, Guangdong Prov.	W-lawyer/NGO
27 April 2017	Beijing	X-lawyer/NGO
02 March 2017	Shanghai	Y-social worker
12 April 2017, morning	Changsha, Hunan Prov.	Z-social worker

The book collected hundreds of judgments of the MHL-related cases decided by the Chinese courts in the first five years since the MHL's entry into force on 1 May 2013. By undertaking the analysis of the judgements, the findings presented in this chapter are not only about the medical practice of the treatment decision-making but also the judicial response from the courts. There are 225 judgments collected from the 'China Judgments Online' (see Table 5.2). 'China Judgments Online' is the official online platform on which the courts' judgments nationwide are released to the public in China.[2] The courts' rulings are not legally binding to

2 During the preparation of the book, the author intended to collect the judgments released on the website in the more recent years. However, millions judgment were removed from the database in June 2021. See Echo Xie 'Millions of court rulings removed from official Chinese database' *South China Morning Post* (Hong Kong, 26

Table 5.2 Information of collected judgments

Criteria	*Number of judgments*
All the collected judgments in which the MHL is mentioned in the full texts	225
The judgments in which the MHL is mentioned in the full texts, but the issue is irrelevant to treatment decision-making	67
The judgments in which the MHL is mentioned in the full texts and the issue is broadly about treatment decision-making, but the courts did not rule on the basis of the MHL or give sufficient legal reasoning for analysis	132
The referenced judgments in which the MHL is mentioned in the full texts, the issue is about treatment decision-making, and the courts rule on the basis of the MHL	26

future cases to be ruled by lower courts. In other words, the findings based on the collected courts' judgments suggest how the MHL is interpreted and applied, but does not create precedent, as in the common law legal system.

The chapter begins with an overall description of both voluntary and involuntary procedures, providing a rough overview of the general differences. The exploration of the different stages of the procedures will also be considered in more detail. It also raises the necessity of a further explanation of the findings presented in this chapter.

5.2 An Overview of Voluntary and Involuntary Tracks

As discussed in Chapter 4, the MHL adopts a voluntary principle in mental health treatment. The only exception is the detention for involuntary treatment that requires a diagnostic threshold of 'a severe mental disorder' and the existence of harm or dangerousness to oneself or others.[3] However, without adopting the term 'involuntary' or 'compulsory' expressively, the MHL does not provide a clear-cut and separate procedure for voluntary and involuntary service users, respectively. Instead, the MHL provides a set of mixed and vague rules that apply to both voluntary and involuntary service users. Therefore, it is helpful to provide an overview of how the voluntary or involuntary procedures operate in practice, before proceeding to break them down into different stages.

Most participating psychiatrists in this research state that, in their practice, there are many more involuntary users than voluntary ones.[4] The status of being voluntary or involuntary, however, depends on various conditions. They include

June 2021) < www.scmp.com/news/china/politics/article/3138830/millions-court-rulings-removed-official-chinese-database > accessed 15 July 2021. Considering the criteria and result of the removal from this platform are unclear to the public, the author has decided to keep the research as it was in 2019, to maintain the accuracy and consistency of the research in the book.

3 MHL, Art 30.

4 Interviews with H-psychiatrist, J-psychiatrist, K-psychiatrist, N-psychiatrist.

severity or category of mental illness, whether a person seeks help on his or her own or is taken to a medical facility, whether service users are complying with admission, and the existence of insight.[5] Meanwhile, the dangerousness standards, as provided by the MHL, is merely a part of the consideration.[6] A participating psychiatrist in this study provided a vivid description of typical processes for a voluntary service user:

> By voluntary, we mean patients seek help by themselves. Normally you need to finish some preliminary procedures first, for example registration with our hospital. Then I will carry out my assessment, by which I have a diagnosis for your condition. If I think your condition is not too bad and it is okay to take medication at home, it is possible to do that. But, if I think your condition meets some degree of severity, so just clinical treatment may not be enough and it is better for you to accept inpatient and comprehensive treatment, I will propose inpatient treatment. Some patients accept because they feel the pain. Of course, there are also patients who do not listen and say they do not want to do inpatient treatment and prefer medication at home, it is okay too.[7]

Most involuntary service users are taken by their family members,[8] which is also confirmed by an official training textbook of the MHL.[9] The psychiatrists also provide in this regard:

> Involuntary patients are mostly taken by family members and do not cooperate with assessment and inpatient treatment at all. So, their family members will describe his condition and what he has done. You know what people with severe mental illness at crisis could do. Crazy and noisy. After gaining medical history from family members, we also meet patients themselves and do some examinations. If I confirm he is mentally ill, I will tell his family members about his condition and propose inpatient treatment or taking medication at home. This is because family members as caregivers or guardians have to monitor that he does take his medication. Most of the family members think they are unable to do that, so they choose inpatient treatment.... In some cases, we have prescribed medication and family members take patients back home, but there is nothing they can do to ensure patients take the drugs on time. In fact, most patients with severe illness are like this, refusing medication. So, some family members say we can't deal with patients at home and

5 Interviews with H-psychiatrist, I-psychiatrist, J-psychiatrist, K-psychiatrist, L-psychiatrist, N-psychiatrist, O-psychiatrist.
6 Ibid.
7 Interview with H-psychiatrist.
8 Interviews with H-psychiatrist and L-psychiatrist.
9 *Training Textbook for Healthcare Professionals on the Mental Health Law of the People's Republic of China* (China Legal Publishing House 2013), 174. (*Training Textbook*)

request inpatient treatment. Of course, patients refuse. So, we will have a consent form for the family member to sign and we accept the patient.[10]

Participating psychiatrists also reported that they have dealt with service users who were taken by police or local Department of Civil Affairs only occasionally.[11]Chapter 4 explained that the MHL does not set a different procedure if a homeless person with a suspected mental disorder, who has no family member or his or her family member is out of reach, is taken by the government to a mental health facility. Instead, the Department of Civil Affairs simply assumes the role in decision-making that is typically assumed by a family member. Participating psychiatrists affirm that, in their practice at least, the decision-making framework of this type of service user is identical to those who are taken by their family members. The only exception is that psychiatrists have a larger say in deciding whether a person with a suspected mental disorder taken by the police should be detained for treatment.[12] Given the limitation in collecting data on service users taken by the police, this chapter will only focus on the situation in which service users are taken by family members.

To sum up, this section provides an overview of the daily practice of mental health admission and treatment in China. At a glance, the differentiation of being voluntary and involuntary relies on whether a service user complies with the diagnostic assessment and recommended treatment. The dangerousness standard, however, is merely a part of the consideration. Now, this chapter turns to explore the practice of decision-making at various phases in more detail.

5.3 Admission and Detention for Diagnostic Assessment

Chapter 4 has addressed that the MHL provides a voluntary principle of psychiatric diagnostic assessment. It provides that, except when laws specify otherwise, it is prohibited to force persons against their will to undergo a medical examination to determine whether or not they have a mental disorder.[13] Article 28, however, provides in the first paragraph that a person with a suspected mental disorder may be taken to a medical facility for a psychiatric assessment by a close family member,[14] without requiring any presence of harm or dangerousness to oneself or others. It is in contrast with its second paragraph, which explicitly authorises close family members, employers, or the local police to intervene and take the person against his or her will, when dangerousness is present.[15]

It is unclear under the MHL when there is no harm or evident dangerousness present, whether or not Article 28 authorises family members to decide detention for diagnostic assessment against one's will. In addition, the level of force

10 Interview with H-psychiatrist.
11 Interviews with J-psychiatrist, K-psychiatrist, L-psychiatrist, and N-psychiatrist.
12 Interviews with J-psychiatrist, K-psychiatrist, and L-psychiatrist.
13 MHL, Art 27.
14 Ibid., Art 28.
15 Ibid.

permitted under the provision that a person with a suspected mental disorder may be taken to a medical facility for a psychiatric assessment by a close family member[16] merits further examination.

5.3.1 Medical practice

All participating service users state that they have experience of admission against their will by their family members.[17] That said, some of the participants in the study chose to admit themselves when they realised their need for professional help.[18] Meanwhile, many participating psychiatrists acknowledged that, in their practice, more patients are 'uncooperative' and, therefore, are admitted against their will by family members.[19]

In these cases, the dangerousness standard is interpreted loosely. Some participating psychiatrists acknowledged that the trigger for admission for diagnostic assessment may be merely a 'verbal impulse' or abnormality in sleep.[20] The determination of dangerousness will be addressed fully later in this chapter. The point here is that none of the participating psychiatrists reported experience of refusing to undertake a diagnostic assessment because they believed that the family member had no authority to admit the service user against his or her will. Admittedly, Article 28 of the MHL provides that, when receiving a person with a suspected mental disorder, mental health facilities cannot refuse to run a diagnostic assessment.[21]

This book does not collect direct narrative accounts about the use of force during the admissions of this kind. The author chose not to ask participants in the study to further elaboration on the details of coercion during admission or detention for diagnostic assessment during the interviews. This was to prevent service users becoming distressed by further probing their experiences of a traumatising process. Similarly, this decision not to ask psychiatrists was to avoid psychiatrists becoming defensive, which might have affected their willingness to continue with the interviews. Nevertheless, the interviews reveal that some degree of coercion is acceptable in practice. A participating mental health social worker reported that one of her clients was admitted for diagnostic assessment by deception: the mother of the client told the client that the purpose of their visit to the city was sightseeing not assessment for admission to a mental facility.[22]

5.3.2 Judicial response

On the one hand, there are cases in which the courts understand that Article 28 of the MHL permits the family member to take a person with a suspected mental

16 Ibid.
17 Interviews with A-service user, B-service user, C-service user, D-service user, E-service user, F-service user, and G-service user.
18 Interviews with B-service user and C-service user.
19 Interviews with H-psychiatrist, K-psychiatrist, and L-psychiatrist.
20 Interview with J-psychiatrist.
21 MHL, Art 28.
22 Interview with Y-social worker.

disorder to a mental health facility for diagnostic assessment, without any presence of harm or dangerousness to oneself or others. In one case, Fu took his mother Qi against her will to a psychiatric hospital where Qi was detained for 30 days, primarily because of the disagreement about Fu's marriage choice and associated financial disputes.[23] After her discharge, Qi sued Fu and the hospital for violating her rights and dignity.[24] On whether Fu violated Qi's rights, after quoting Article 28 in full, the court ruled that

> When Fu found Qi had a suspected mental disorder, Fu had the right to take Qi into the hospital for diagnostic assessment. Since the assessment confirmed that Qi was mentally ill at that moment, the current evidence suggests that Fu's intention of taking Qi to the hospital was for Qi's health, not to violate her right to dignity or health. Therefore, Fu's action shall not be regarded as violating Qi's rights.[25]

This case indicates that the court was willing to tolerate coercion at this stage. In another case, where there was no evidence of the presence of harm or danger before admission, a woman in her 40s was taken by force to a mental health facility by police, her parents, and two of her colleagues from work.[26] The woman claimed that, in her neighbourhood, she was restrained and tied up before she was taken to a vehicle that transported her to the mental health facility.[27] The court found that the women had a history of repeatedly calling the police to report for other matters, but, due to the lack of evidence, the police had not built a case for her.[28] These statements in the judgment may imply the court's suspicion of her mental well-being, but the judgment did not identify any harm or dangerousness.[29] After 54 days of detention for involuntary treatment, the women sued the hospital and her two colleagues from work, who assisted the forced admission, for violating her right to liberty.[30] Citing Article 28 of the MHL, the court ruled 'no tort liability is found', because she had a history of mental illness and, therefore, 'it is reasonable and lawful that her father took her to the hospital for treatment'.[31]

In another case, a man's four children requested a mental health hospital to take the man from his home to the hospital for both diagnostic assessment and

23 *Zhenhua Qi v Peng Fu and Beijing Huilongguan Hospital* – Personality Right Dispute Appeal Case, First Intermediate People's Court of Beijing Municipality, Civil Appeal No 09354, 16 December 2015. (*Qi v Fu* 2015)

24 Ibid.

25 Ibid.

26 *Xu v The Hospital attached to Central South University* – Medical Damage Liability Dispute Case, Basic People's Court of Furong District, Changsha Municipality, Civil First Instance No 2938, 22 July 2015.

27 Ibid.

28 Ibid.

29 Ibid.

30 Ibid.

31 Ibid.

treatment against his will.[32] The man subsequently litigated claiming compensation after he was discharged. The court found that his four children had not violated his right to liberty.[33] There are a number of other judgments that adopted this low-threshold approach to admission against one's own will, possibly by force, without giving further reasoning.[34] This represents a loose interpretation by the courts of the relevant provisions of the MHL.

However, there is one case, also the only one collected by this study, where the court adopted a strict standard in scrutinising admission for diagnostic assessment against one's will. Wang was taken to a local mental health hospital by his daughter and son-in-law in 2015 for twelve days.[35] The medical record recorded that force used in his admission.[36] After his discharge, Wang sued his daughter, son-in-law and the hospital for violating his right to personal liberty.[37] The court ruled that there was no evidence of harm or dangerousness in respect of Wang's condition and as such did not warrant an involuntary admission by family members.[38] Regardless of whether Wang's daughter and son-in-law were motivated by benign intentions to cure the mental illness, the court ruled that Wang's liberty was violated.[39] Since no dangerousness was found, the admission against his will breached the voluntary principle of diagnostic assessment. Interestingly, the court also held that the hospital had no liability at the stage of admission because, as addressed earlier, Article 28 prohibits the hospital from refusing to run the diagnostic assessment.[40] The court awarded Wang a compensation of 10,000 RMB (approximately 1300 euros) from his daughter and son-in-law.[41] The defendants appealed, and the court of second instance upheld the judgment of the first instance.[42]

32 *Lianshui Du v Chinese Medical Psychiatric Hospital and others* – Personal Liberty Dispute, Basic People's Court of Lixia District, Jinan Municipality, Shandong Province, Civil First Instance No 1219, 08 September 2015. (*Du v the Hospital* 2015)

33 Ibid.

34 For example, see *Tongbo He v Third People's Hospital of Mianyang Municipality* – Personal Liberty Dispute Retrial Application Case, High People's Court of Sichuan Province, Retrial Application No 3761, 20 February 2017 (*He v Hospital* 2017); and *Hongmei Gou v Physical and Mental Health Hospital of Nanchong Municipality* – Right to Health Dispute, Basic People's Court of Yingshan County, Nanchong Municipality, Sichuan Province, Civil First Instance No 957, 18 August 2014. (*Gou v the Hospital* 2014)

35 *Zhengxi Wang v Min Wang and Yuanzheng Wu* – Tort Liability Dispute, Basic People's Court of Sanxiaba District, Yichang Municipality, Hubei Province, Civil First Instance No 13, 10 February 2017. (*Wang v Wang* 2017)

36 Ibid.

37 Ibid.

38 Ibid.

39 Ibid.

40 Ibid.

41 Ibid.

42 *Zhengxi Wang v Min Wang* – Tort Liability Dispute Appeal Case, Intermediate People's Court of Yichang Municipality, Civil Second Instance No 1311, 26 June 2017 (*Wang v Wang, Appeal,* 2017).

5.3.3 Section summary

To conclude, given the vagueness in the MHL, the practice of taking a person to a mental health facility for diagnostic assessment against his or her will, even without any evidence of harm or dangerousness, appears to be generally tolerated in both medical practice and legal proceedings. However, there also emerges a promising signal that some courts may begin to adopt stricter scrutiny in this regard.

5.4 Diagnostic Assessment

Diagnostic assessment in mental health facilities is a highly professional clinical activity, of which psychiatrists have considerable discretion. Accordingly, the MHL only provides in Article 29 that registered psychiatrists are the only professionals who can undertake a diagnostic assessment.[43] There is no further regulation concerning the content or procedure of the diagnostic assessment. This section will consider the psychiatric discretion in including family members' narrative in diagnostic assessment. Then, it will also address the common confusion or conflation between the detention for diagnostic assessment and the detention for treatment.

5.4.1 Diagnostic assessment interview: whose voice?

As discussed above, most patients are taken or 'accompanied' by their family members for diagnostic assessment in China. Since psychiatry highly relies on a clinical interview for diagnostic assessment, who answers the interview questions becomes very important. How the interviewing psychiatrists attaches credit to these answers is equally important to the diagnostic result. The practice in this regard significantly impacts service users' experiences within the mental health system.

5.4.1.1 Medical practice

Most participating psychiatrists in this study stated that they collect the description of medical history and behaviour problems at home from both the service user and his or her accompanying family member.[44] That is, unless a patient presents alone, which is rare but possible.[45] Sometimes psychiatrists may meet the service user and his or her accompanying family member together.[46] However, most participating service users complained that their diagnoses were decided solely based on the meetings between their psychiatrists and their family members.[47] The meetings between service users and psychiatrists were claimed to

43 MHL, art 29.
44 Interviews with H-psychiatrist, J-psychiatrist, K-psychiatrist, L-psychiatrist, M-psychiatrist, and N-psychiatrist.
45 Ibid.
46 Interviews with A-service user and C-service user.
47 Interviews with A-service user, F-service user, D-service user, and G-service user.

be too short and meaningless, and service users were not treated with patience or respect.[48] The dependence on family members' narratives is particularly common for new users who are regarded as being unreliable as that they have psychosis and are delusional. A participating psychiatrist reported that she values the description of family members over patients if she believes a patient has 'victim delusion'.[49]

Responding to one of the interview questions on how to determine if the narratives given by a service user and his or her family member differ in critical issues, a participating psychiatrist provided a vivid example:

> If descriptions vary, we will listen to different family members about their views and have a comprehensive idea. For example, if a female is taken by her husband or in-laws, we will normally ask her own parents and other close family members for more information. If her condition remains unclear, we will probably propose (to her family members) a longer period of observation.[50]

There is a clear sense of preventing abuse or conflict of interest in some cases. However, since the description given by family members is generally accepted, the motivation to strengthen the communication with service users directly may weaken, thereby marginalising the voices of users. A participating psychiatrist acknowledged 'we usually have difficulties in communicating with patients, so we have more communication with their family members'.[51]

A common ground of favouring family members' narratives is the issue of insight. Many participating psychiatrists used 'lacking insight' to explain why users' own words are at least questionable.[52] A participating psychiatrist said 'patients lacking insight do not acknowledge their (mental) illness', and, therefore, 'it is extremely difficult to talk with patients that have no insight'.[53] The next chapter will revisit the issue of insight, as it impacts on the communication and decision-making at all phases of the service users' journey.

5.4.1.2 Judicial response

As diagnostic assessment is a highly professional clinical activity, it is understandable that courts restrain themselves from making a judgment about how to do it. Nevertheless, the study of the judgments affirms the findings of the qualitative interviews that family members' narratives are recognised as a legitimate part of the assessment. In several of the collected judgments on the MHL the hospitals

48 Ibid.
49 Interview with H-psychiatrist.
50 Interview with K-psychiatrist.
51 Interview with K-psychiatrist.
52 Interviews with H-psychiatrist, I-psychiatrist, and L-psychiatrist.
53 Interview with I-psychiatrist.

defended the practice of obtaining medical histories and symptoms solely from family members, and the courts held that this did not breach of law.[54]

While the courts may be reluctant to second guess the diagnostic assessments, the courts may be willing to consider the procedural requirements around assessments. In one case the court found the mental hospital accountable because it did not fill in the 'mental status' part of the admission form when the hospital assessed a person, who was then detained for treatment, at the clinical department.[55] In this case, the plaintiff also claimed that her medical record was made up by the hospital based on her daughter's description, who had taken the plaintiff to the hospital against her will.[56] However, the plaintiff could not provide evidence on this point, and, therefore, the court did not accept this claim.[57] Without going into too much detail on this case, the point is that courts are prone to give respect to the psychiatric discretion during assessments but only likely to favour service users when the omission or fault is blatantly obvious. How to ensure the authenticity of medical history or narratives relevant in forming a psychiatric diagnosis given by family members is an important issue, meriting further research.

5.4.2 Detention for diagnostic assessment or detention for treatment?

As discussed earlier, family members have the power to take a person with a suspected mental disorder for diagnostic assessment against one's will; and the receiving psychiatric facility is obliged to accept the person to carry out an assessment.[58] Therefore, a time limit to the diagnostic assessment appears to be necessary as a safeguard. As discussed in Chapter 4, a draft of the MHL included a 72-hour limitation for assessment, which was deleted from the final MHL.[59] The MHL only requires that a diagnosis be made 'promptly', without any further guide or interpretation.[60] However, the deletion of an explicit time-limit does not appear to facilitate abuse in this regard. A municipal mental health regulation adopted the 72-hour rule as early as in

54 For example, see *He v Hospital* 2017, *Zhenyang Han v Psychiatric Hospital of Zhumadian Municipality* – Medical Damage Liability Dispute Appeal Case, Intermediate People's Court of Zhumadian Municipality, Henan Province, Civil Appeal No 179, 7 April 2017 (*Han v the Hospital* 2017), and *Qiao Jing v Third People's Hsopital of Mianyang Municipality* – Personal Liberty Dispute Retrial Application Case, High People's Court of Sichuan Province, Civil Retrial Application No 3745, 10 March 2017.

55 *Feng Liang v Zhongpei Wu Memorial Hospital of Shunde District, Foshan Municipality* – Right to Life, Right to Health and Right to Body Integrity Dispute Appeal Case, Intermediate People's Court of Foshan Municipality, Civil Appeal No 37, 7 March 2014.

56 Ibid.

57 Ibid.

58 MHL, Art 28.

59 Chapter 4, Section 4.4.2.1.

60 Ibid., Art 29.

2001 as this was seen to be good practice.[61] Participating service users also reported that their assessment interviews were too short and hasty, rather than too long.[62]

The study of courts' judgments suggests a potentially problematic issue concerning the procedure for detention for diagnostic assessment. As Chapter 4 suggests, the criteria for detention for treatment is significantly higher than the criteria for admission or detention for diagnostic assessment.[63] Detention for diagnostic assessment only requires a non-expert family member's suspicion that a service user has a mental disorder.[64] Under the MHL, it is possible that a person is legally detained for diagnostic assessment against his or her will but the condition does not warrant detention for treatment.[65] Thus, a distinction between detention for diagnostic assessment and detention for treatment becomes critical. Otherwise, the stricter standards of detention for treatment would be *de facto* replaced by the criteria for detention for assessment.

Based on the data collected in this research, this supposedly important distinction is not reflected sufficiently in practice. None of the participating psychiatrists placed an emphasis on such a distinction. More problematically, the courts also appear to ignore the distinction. In a number of cases in which service users challenged the lawfulness of their detention for treatment, the courts invoked Article 28, which is only about admission and detention for diagnostic assessment, to justify the detention for treatment. The courts did so without examining whether the legal criteria for detention for treatment was met. For example, in a case where the plaintiff was taken to a mental health facility by his sister, brother-in-law and ex-wife and treated for thirty-one days, the court ruled:

> The second paragraph of Article 28 MHL provides that "[w]hen persons with a suspected mental disorder harm themselves, harm others, or endanger the safety of others, or when they are at risk of harming themselves or others, close family members, employers, or local police shall immediately intervene and subsequently take these individuals to a medical facility for a psychiatric assessment. Medical facilities cannot refuse to conduct diagnostic evaluations on persons sent to the facility with a suspected mental disorder." On 11 February 2015, [the defendants] took [the plaintiff] into the Fifth People's Hospital of Zibo Municipality because of [the plaintiff]'s symptoms of mental disorders. Both [the defendants]' action of sending and the hospital's action of treatment are, therefore, in accordance with the law above.[66]

61 The Mental Health Regulation of Shanghai (the version before amendment according to the MHL was passed on 28 December 2001 by the Standing Committee of Shanghai Municipal People's Congress, entered into force on 7 April 2002), art 31.
62 Interviews with A-service user, F-service user, D-service user, and G-service user.
63 Chapter 4, Section 4.4.2.
64 MHL, Art 28.
65 Ibid., Art 28, 30–32.
66 *Yonghao Yu v Yongbo Yu, Feng Zhang and others* – Tort Liability Dispute Appeal Case, Intermediate People's Court of Zibo Municipality, Shandong Province, Civil Appeal No. 551, 18 April 2016.

The next section will address the decision-making in detention for treatment. The issue here is that, whatever criteria the MHL sets, it would be bypassed as long as the courts confuse detention for assessment with detention for treatment. The confusion has been put forth in another case, in which the court adopted the term 'diagnostic inpatient treatment'.[67] After a quote of Article 28, the court ruled that 'diagnostic inpatient treatment is one of the common measures used in clinical hospitals, especially in psychiatric diagnoses'.[68] The court did not offer a precise determination whether the detention was for diagnostic assessment or treatment.

This study collected over 200 MHL-related cases within five years since its entry into force. There is only one case in which the court made such a distinction. In this case, a man, Wang, was taken by his daughter and son-in-law to a mental health facility for diagnostic assessment and, then, treatment for eleven days. Because Wang did not meet the criteria for involuntary treatment, the court ruled the hospital did not violate Wang's right for undertaking the diagnostic assessment but was liable for detaining him for further treatment.[69]

5.4.3 Section summary

This section considers two issues in the phase of diagnostic assessment, and both of them concern the professional discretion of psychiatrists. This study acknowledges that medical discretion is necessary for diagnostic assessment and clinical decision-making. This section only aims to explore its potential impact on service users' decision-making and to observe how judicial practice responds to psychiatric discretion in the procedure for detention for assessment.

Accordingly, this study finds that psychiatrists usually put more weight on the narrative provided by family members over service users themselves in diagnostic assessment. The courts are also unlikely to intervene, unless a significant fault presents. Neither do the courts adopt a clear distinction between criteria for detention for diagnostic assessment and detention for treatment.

5.5 Detention for Involuntary Treatment

This section considers how a decision of inpatient treatment is made following a diagnosis. The MHL provides a relatively clear guide that, unless a diagnostic threshold of a severe mental disorder is met and harm or dangerousness to oneself or others is established, inpatient treatment should be voluntary.[70] However, based on the data collected in this research, some issues concerning the diagnostic threshold and risk determination have emerged, which will be addressed in turn.

67 *Gou v the Hospital* 2014.
68 Ibid.
69 *Wang v Wang, Appeal,* 2017.
70 MHL, Art 30.

5.5.1 Diagnostic threshold

Chapter 4 notes that there exist different interpretations and understandings of the definition of a severe mental disorder under the MHL. On the one hand, Article 83 of the MHL provides a comprehensive but vague definition. It defines severe mental disorders as 'characterised by severe symptoms that result in serious impairments in social adaptation or in other types of functioning, in impaired awareness of objective reality or of one's medical condition, or in an inability to deal with one's own affairs'.[71] This definition is described as potentially allowing psychiatrists to take decision-making functionality or mental capacity into consideration.[72]

On the other hand, without available reference to any other piece of legislation, an authoritative guidebook to the MHL, published by the *de facto* law-making office of the Standing Committee of the National People's Congress, interprets severe mental disorders as 'including six types of mental illness mainly: schizophrenia, bipolar disorder, paranoid psychosis, schizoaffective disorder and others'.[73] In its interpretation of Article 30 on detention for involuntary treatment, the guidebook first repeats the wording of Article 83 as involving considerations of both symptoms and social adaptation or functioning.[74] It then provides a list of examples of severe mental disorders defined as: 'schizophrenia, bipolar disorder, paranoid psychosis, schizoaffective disorder, mental disorder due to epilepsy, and mental retardation'.[75] The guidebook interpretation strongly implies that the severe mental disorders defined by the MHL are a fixed category, not depending on the individual severity of symptoms or the impairment of functionality. As a commentator rightly points out, service users labelled with one of these six conditions may not have such severe symptoms; whilst people with other conditions of a severe degree may pose a threat to oneself or others, depression with suicidal ideation for example.[76]

This section will examine the determinations of the diagnostic threshold in practice and the courts' response to the psychiatric discretion.

5.5.1.1 Medical practice

Based on the qualitative interviews of this study, there is no universal pattern of deciding what is a severe mental disorder, as defined in the MHL, and what is not. A participating psychiatrist said

71 Ibid., Art 83.
72 John Dawson, 'A Realistic Approach to Assessing Mental Health Laws Compliance with the UNCRPD' (2015) *International Journal of Law and Psychiatry* 70, 75.
73 Chunying Xin (eds) *The interpretations of the Mental Health Law of the People's Republic of China* (Law Press China 2013), 242.
74 Ibid., 91.
75 Ibid.
76 Xiangfei Qu, 'UN CRPD and rights protection of persons with disabilities' (2013) *Legal Studies* 105, 107.

> Patients with these six kinds of illness are all posing a danger to society, so involuntary treatment must be imposed. If one's condition is not on the list, it is up to you (family members) to take the treatment or not. So many people end up in poverty because of the cost of mental health treatment, so a lot of them just give up and do not have any treatment.[77]

However, more participating psychiatrists pointed out that it is a 'comprehensive judgement'.[78] Some said their daily practice takes both the category of illness and the severity of symptoms into account.[79] Some relied on the concept of insight as the most important working standard.[80] There are also some psychiatrists who disregarded the importance of the diagnostic threshold but relied on the decision of family members, which will be discussed later.[81] A participating psychiatrist said, off the record, when the audio recorder was switched off, that it is not uncommon that psychiatrists may change a diagnosis at the request of family members. It is because the patients of the six listed severe mental disorders could receive some subsidies for medication. The economic drive behind this will be discussed in the next chapter, but it is safe to note here that, based on the evidence collected in the study, the concept of severe mental disorder appears not to be given much weight in medical practice.

However, this is not to suggest that psychiatrists never say no to detention for involuntary treatment. Some participating psychiatrists reported that they have experience of proposing clinical treatment under the request of involuntary detention for treatment by family members.[82] Whether or not proposing detention for treatment requires a comprehensive judgement that take a broad range of factors into account. By contrast, the definition of a severe mental disorder, as a legal term, seems not carry much weight.

5.5.1.2 Judicial response

Based on the analysis of the collected judgments, the courts rarely, if ever, challenge the determination of a severe mental disorder. Similar to the approach to diagnostic assessment, the court only intervene when a formal and substantive breach of law is found. In one case a man in his 60s was taken to a mental health facility by his son, the court held the involuntary detention for treatment was unlawful partly because the hospital detained him for involuntary treatment without recording any diagnosis of mental disorder in his medical record.[83]

77 Interview with I-psychiatrist.
78 Interviews with H-psychiatrist, J-psychiatrist, L-psychiatrist, and O-psychiatrist.
79 Interview with H-psychiatrist.
80 Interview with O-psychiatrist.
81 Interviews with L-psychiatrist, M-psychiatrist, and N-psychiatrist.
82 Interviews with H-psychiatrist and J-psychiatrist.
83 *Delin Wang v Anding Hosptial of Tianjin Municipality* – Medical Damage Liability Dispute First Instance Case, Basic People Court of Hexi District, Tianjin Municipality, Civil First Instance No 4915, 21 July 2017 (*Wang v the Hospital* 2017).

The study identified only one case where the court of the first instance found involuntary detention for treatment unlawful on the ground of not meeting the diagnostic threshold. The court reasoned that the initial diagnosis of 'dubious or hard-to-treat cases', as written in the medical record, does not meet the criteria of severe mental disorder.[84] However, the hospital argued in its appeal that the court of the first instance 'misunderstood that bipolar disorder is not a severe mental disorder'.[85] The court of second instance held that the detention was still unlawful. However, the judgment of the second instance did not address the determination of severe mental disorder.[86] Without more information, it appears to reflect the court's reluctance to enter into a dispute on a medical determination with psychiatrists.

5.5.2 Risk evaluation

The MHL provides even less clear guidance on how to evaluate the harm or dangerousness to oneself or others. It does not require any standard of evidence or include any term such as 'immediate', 'material', or 'significant' before the risk, thereby leaving considerable room to psychiatric discretion.

5.5.2.1 Medical practice

The participating psychiatrists in this research suggested that their risk evaluation in practice is based on two risk evaluation forms: one for provoking a disturbance to others and one for suicide.[87] Without going into the technical issues about the two forms, it is evident from the qualitative interviews that psychiatrists have enormous discretion in determining the harm or dangerousness to oneself or others. The only exception is when a person is taken by the police who would provide a description of the risk.[88]

For example, a participating psychiatrist considered being naked on the street a dangerous behaviour:

> A naked man walking on the street, is this dangerous? What do you think? Maybe it is not in another country, but in China he is dangerous. An adult man wears nothing, walking from east to west and from west to east. Is this normal?[89]

The psychiatrist continued to generalise harm or dangerousness by saying 'all thoughts or actions that are not normal to general standards are dangerous'.[90]

84 *Wang v Wang* 2017.
85 *Wang v Wang, Appeal,* 2017.
86 Ibid.
87 Interviews with H-psychiatrist, K-psychiatrist, and M-psychiatrist.
88 Interviews with N-psychiatrist.
89 Interviews with I-psychiatrist.
90 Ibid.

However, some participating psychiatrists believed it is a positive result of awareness raising among family members. By some community education, family members have become able to identify some conditions or early symptoms, like sleeping difficulty or expression problems but without behaviour problems, and take service users for treatment, possibly against their will, to 'prevent the crisis'.[91]

The participating psychiatrists also suggested a link between dangerous behaviours and delusion. A psychiatrist said:

> For some patients, their risk is shown. But more people have dangerous factors that are not easy to see. If a person has delusions, the delusions may lead him or stimulate him to have extreme behaviours. So, this patient must be detained and treated. You have to consider the unseen factors. You cannot wait for the bad things to happen and do something then.[92]

Differential attitudes towards the same behaviour of persons with and without a mental disorder were also expressively suggested in the interviews. One of the interview questions to participating psychiatrists asked how they determine who is telling the truth, since both service users and family members may give different narratives about the same thing.[93] For the purpose of this research, the author used following scenario in the interviews with participants. A girl is complaining about her father being too paternalistic: when she is upset by something and throws a pillow at her father, which is common to every teenage girl, her father tells their doctor that she is hitting him. The question posed to the participating psychiatrists was how would they determine whether there is harm or dangerousness to oneself or others, warranting detention for treatment. One of the participating psychiatrists said:

> Indeed, what you ask is a difficult one. Why? If the impulse comes from mental illness, it may be unpredictable. So, if the behaviour of throwing a pillow is presented to me, we will agree with the father, because we have to prevent any possibility of harm.... To a normal person, throwing a pillow may be merely playful. But to a mental patient, she can throw a pillow this time, and she may throw a brick next time. If that happens, we will be responsible for what happens to her father. If we disregard it, and next time she throws a knife, we, as psychiatrists, are accountable.[94]

These findings suggest how the psychiatrists' discretion operates in practice, which is facilitated by the vague provisions adopted in the MHL. As this sub-section focuses on the findings from qualitative interviews, Chapter 6 will revisit the issue

91 Interviews with J-psychiatrist and O-psychiatrist.
92 Interview with O-psychiatrist.
93 Chapter 5, Section 5.4.1.
94 Interview with N-psychiatrist.

of risk evaluation, illustrating the enormous power imbalance weighted in favour of psychiatrists in deciding on mental health detention and treatment.

5.5.2.2 Judicial response

In contrast to the approach of the court in determining whether the diagnostic threshold of a severe mental disorder is met, the court appears to be playing a much more active role in determining whether the dangerousness requirement is fulfilled. Before proceeding to a closer examination of this active role, it has to be noted that the judicial position on this matter is mixed. There are many cases in which family members decided detention for treatment without any evidence of harm or dangerousness and the courts did not find a breach of the law.

For example, in one case a woman was taken to a mental health facility by her husband and treated against her will.[95] After discharge, she sued the hospital for violating her right to liberty, arguing that her condition did not fulfil the dangerousness standard.[96] The hospital argued that the treatment was voluntary because the plaintiff was 'accompanied' by her husband who completed the procedure of hospitalisation.[97] The court rejected the plaintiff's claim for not providing sufficient evidence to suggest the hospital's fault in the delivery of treatment, without any elaboration on whether the dangerousness standard was met.[98] A particularly problematic point here is that the court assigned the duty of proof to the service user, which is by nature extremely difficult for her to prove she was not posing any risk. Many cases were decided following similar reasoning.[99] It is therefore evident that the practice that family members decide detention for treatment without any presence of harm or dangerousness, so-called 'medical protective admission', is still widely accepted by the courts.

However, there are also several cases in which the courts find involuntary detention for treatment unlawful from a formal perspective. The hospitals in these cases failed to provide evidence of dangerousness. In one case, after quoting the dangerousness standard provided by Article 30 MHL, the court ruled that

> In this case, the defendant did not provide evidence to suggest the plaintiff had behaviour that harms or endangers the safety of others. Only under the request of the plaintiff's mother by phone, the defendant sent its staff

95 *Shuhua Sun v Fourth People's Hospital of Linyi Municipality* – Medical Damage Liability Dispute First Instance Case, Basic People's Court of Lanshan District, Linyi Municipality, Shandong Province, Civil First Instance Case No 2487, 16 November 2015.

96 Ibid.

97 Ibid.

98 Ibid.

99 See *Qi v Fu* 2015, *Han v the Hospital* 2017, and *Wenjie Mai v Third People's Hospital of Foshan Municipality* – Medical Damage Liability Dispute Appeal Case, Intermediate People's Court of Foshan Municipality, Guangdong Province, Civil Appeal No 1887, 18 September 2015.

> members to take the plaintiff to the hospital and impose involuntary inpatient treatment. This arrangement violated the right to bodily integrity and the right to personal liberty of the plaintiff, and therefore the defendant is liable for the plaintiff's damage.[100]

A number of other cases follow this reasoning.[101] Additionally, there is another case in which the court adopted a more substantial approach. The court examined the full record of diagnostic assessment and the medical history, and, then, found the dangerousness standard was not met.[102]

There is also a case in which the court found the dangerousness standard was not met, based on their review of the service user's medical records, which suggested the presence of dangerous thoughts at very least. In this case, the wife of a gay man took him to a mental health facility, where the man was diagnosed as having an anxiety disorder.[103] The facility wrote in his medical record 'no dangerous or impulsive is observed. [The plaintiff] has thoughts of suicide but has not acted on those thoughts'.[104] In the medical record, his wife suggested that the plaintiff had emotional issues; but he did not pose a risk at his family members but himself.[105] However, the medical record did not assess the level of 'risk' he posed or elaborate on his specific behaviours. Despite the medical record, the court found 'it cannot be established that the plaintiff has suicidal behaviour, harming others, or damaging things'.[106] On this basis, the court found a violation of the plaintiff's right to liberty.[107]

Although it adopted a substantive approach to determining the presence of dangerousness, the courts did not identify to whom the harm or dangerousness is directed. It is a critical factor under the MHL, as explored in the next subsection.

5.5.3 Harm or dangerousness to whom?

The psychiatric discretion also reflects on the determination of the object of harm or dangerousness. According to the MHL, when the diagnostic threshold of a severe mental disorder is met, if a person poses a danger to themself, the guardian

100 *Mengyan Jing v Mental Hospital of Luohe Municipality* – Tort Liability Dispute First Instance Case, Basic People's Court of Yancheng District, Luohe Municipality, Civil First Instance No 219, 24 May 2016.
101 See *Du v the Hospital* 2015 and *Wang v the Hospital* 2017.
102 *Lianqiong Zhang v Stomatological Hospital of Jinmen Municipality* – Right to Health Dispute First Instance Case, Basic People's Court of Dongbao District, Jinmen Municipality, Hubei Province, Civil First Instance No 238, 11 March 2016 (*Zhang v the Hospital* 2016).
103 *Yu v Mental Hospital of Zhumadian Municipality* – Right to Personal Liberty Dispute First Instance Case, Basic People's Court of Yicheng District, Zhumadian Muncipality, Henan Province, Civil First Instance No 4122, 26 June 2017.
104 Ibid.
105 Ibid.
106 Ibid.
107 Ibid.

decides on detention for treatment; by contrast, if the harm or dangerousness is to others, however, the psychiatrist should assume the role of decision-maker.[108] Thus, this subsection explores the practice of this particular arrangement of decision-makers for detention for treatment.

5.5.3.1 Medical practice

As discussed above, if the dangerousness is to oneself, family members decide detention for treatment; where the dangerousness is to others, psychiatrists are the ultimate decision-makers. Therefore, the determination of who is at risk is critical and a potentially contentious issue. The study of medical practice, however, suggests otherwise. Based on the qualitative interviews, all participating psychiatrists understood their role as only proposing medical recommendations; it is the family members who decide the detention for treatment.[109] This is so regardless of the focus of the dangerousness, as long as the family member takes responsibility for the service user. The basis of this common practice is that dangerousness to oneself or others is not determined clearly.

In order to better understand the practice, the participating psychiatrists were asked to answer a hypothetical question: if a person with a severe mental disorder is taken by his family on the grounds of physically hurting his or her family members, is the harm to oneself or others? In this question, the harm, however serious it may be, is to 'others' not 'oneself'. Therefore, the MHL grants psychiatrists the authority to impose detention for involuntary treatment, even against the will of the service user and the dissenting family members.[110]

However, the common answer from the interviewees is that they may propose inpatient treatment, but the final decision shall be made by the family member.[111] A participating psychiatrist responded:

> We do not distinguish these two conditions very clearly. If a person beats his parents, for example, it is up to the parents whether to take him or not.... As doctors, we can only say what is suitable and what is not, which is informed by our professional background, and you (the family member) make the choice.... The decision maker has to be a family member, not the patient himself or us doctors.[112]

This practice of 'psychiatrists proposing and family members deciding', conceptualised as 'Shared Power', is also applicable to service users where they pose no harm or dangerousness. Another question asked in the interviews was how psychiatrists deal with a service user if he or she is not complying with the

108 MHL, Art 30–32.
109 Interviews with H-psychiatrist, I-psychiatrist, J-psychiatrist, K-psychiatrist, L-psychiatrist, M-psychiatrist, N-psychiatrist, O-psychiatrist, and P-psychiatrist.
110 MHL, Art 32.
111 Interviews with K-psychiatrist, N-psychiatrist, and O-psychiatrist.
112 Interview with N-psychiatrist.

treatment proposal but posing no harm or dangerousness. A participating psychiatrist answered:

> We will explain to the family member about two options, inpatient treatment or clinical outpatient treatment. Many family members do not have much experience in dealing with these matters, so our recommendation is usually taken seriously.[113]

Family members' decision-making authority in medical practice is evident. By contrast, the voices of service users are much weaker. Most participating psychiatrists use the term 'patient's side' to refer to patients and their family members as one unified side. However, when the conversations went deeper in the interviews, it appeared to be the case that the voice of the service user is usually absent in the so-called 'patient's side'. Referring to the decision of the patient's side, what psychiatrists mostly expect is a unitary position among different family members.[114]

> We must ensure that all family members have the same position in the matter of hospitalisation or not. For a female patient, if her husband is potentially in the conflict of interest with her, we must notify her parents. If they disagree with each other, we only follow the unified decision given by them.[115]

This study conceptualises this practice as 'Silenced Service Users'. Nevertheless, it is not to suggest the voice of service users is definitely silenced in all cases. There are service users who shared their experience of a positive experience of communicating with their psychiatrists.[116] Some participating service users have also gradually earned trust from their family members, after years of communication, so that they can participate in the decision-making.[117] This suggests that under this framework, having your family members on your side is essential in retaining one's autonomy.

To sum up, psychiatrists are prone not to exercise their decision-making authority in detention for treatment. It is so even when the harm is to a family member so that the MHL explicitly grants psychiatrists the authority to impose detention for treatment. As addressed earlier in this chapter, when the police take a person with a mental disorder, who is most likely in crisis, psychiatrists may have stronger decision-making authority. Even in this scenario, based on the data collected from the interviews, every effort is given to find his or her family members and persuade them to decide detention for treatment.[118]

113 Interview with L-psychiatrist.
114 Interviews with H-psychiatrist, K-psychiatrist, and N-psychiatrist.
115 Interview with N-psychiatrist.
116 Interview with F-service user.
117 Interviews with A-service user and G-service user.
118 Interviews with D-service user, L-psychiatrist, N-psychiatrist, and O-psychiatrist.

5.5.3.2 *Judicial response*

There are a few cases where the courts have drawn a clear line between the decision for detention for treatment decided by psychiatrists or family members. In one case, a woman was taken to a mental hospital and treated for more than a month for engaging in a physical conflict with her ex-father-in-law, who called the police.[119] The women sued the hospital and her ex-father-in-law after being discharged by another family member.[120] The court found that the hospital was accountable because the hospital detained the woman without seeking the consent of the service user's guardian. The court ruled:

> Even if under circumstances where the patient with a mental disorder is posing harm or dangerousness to others and involuntary detention for treatment should be imposed, it still needs the consent of the patient or the guardian. If the guardian obstructs hospitalisation, the procedure for inpatient treatment shall be completed by the police. If the guardian refuses hospitalisation, the plaintiff's work unit, village committee or neighbourhood committee shall complete the procedure.[121]

The court's reasoning is problematic. When the harm or danger is towards others the MHL only grants the guardian the right to apply for a reassessment and medical certification, not a right to veto the detention.[122] Since the dangerousness to others was confirmed by the police, the psychiatrist and the mental health facility have the authority to impose detention for treatment.

Why had the court believed the hospital should seek consent from the guardian? It seems possible that the court read the second paragraph of Article 35 of the MHL without having a consistent understanding of other relevant provisions. Article 35 provides that if the reassessment or the certification affirms the proposal of inpatient treatment, 'the guardians shall agree to the imposition of inpatient treatment for the patient'.[123] This provision reaffirms that the guardian should be informed about the detention for treatment and the guardian's right to apply for reassessment and certification.[124] However, if the guardian still refuses to complete the procedure after reassessment and certification, Article 36 provides that his or her work-unit or relevant village/neighbourhood committee should complete the procedure, as quoted in the judgment.[125] Therefore, it has become clear in law that when the identified

119 *Ding v Mental Hosptial of Xuzhou Municipality and Ding* – Medical Damage Liability Dispute First Instance Case, Basic People's Court of Gulou District, Xuzhou Municipality, Jiangsu Province, Civil First Instance No 3401, 29 June 2017 (*Ding v Hospital and Ding* 2017).
120 Ibid.
121 Ibid.
122 Chapter 4, Section 4.4.2.2.
123 MHL, Art 35.
124 Ibid., Art 37.
125 Ibid., Art 36.

dangerousness is to others and the psychiatric opinions favour detention for treatment, it will happen after all. The only method for a guardian to object is to apply for reassessment and medical certification.

Putting the legal details aside, it has become apparent that, when the dangerousness is to others, the courts, as well as the MHL itself, still place emphasis on the guardian's role. The court's approach in the above case indicates that family members are still the dominant decision-makers for detention for treatment even when the MHL authorises psychiatrists to decide. It echoes the findings from the interviews with service users and psychiatrists.

5.5.4 Section summary

This section considers the psychiatrists' broad discretion in the phase of deciding detention for treatment, as well as the responses from the courts. The main finding is that the courts appear to adopt an active approach in examining the psychiatrists' discretion in risk evaluations. By contrast, psychiatrists' authority in determining the diagnostic threshold is rarely, if ever, challenged by the courts.

The section also suggests that psychiatrists and family members share the authority of deciding detention for treatment. 'Psychiatrists propose, and family members decide'. Moreover, psychiatrists are avoiding deciding on detention for treatment even when the MHL grants them such authority. The MHL-related judgments also illustrate the emphasis on family members' decision-making role. By contrast, the voices of service users become easy to ignore. The book conceptualises this phenomenon as 'Shared Power and Silenced Service Users'. Chapter 6 will address the driving forces of financial and liability concerns behind this phenomenon.

5.6 Administration of Treatment

The MHL does not set different standards or procedures for detention and treatment. Therefore, when a person with a severe mental disorder is detained for treatment, involuntary treatment is expected. This section suggests how the treatment is administered and analyses the judicial response.

5.6.1 Medical practice

Both participating service users and psychiatrists reported that a voluntary service user has full control of their treatment plan.[126] A participating psychiatrist even considered voluntary users have 'too much freedom' because 'patients' free choices make the management of wards more difficult and chaotic'.[127]

Regarding involuntary treatments, however, both participating service users and psychiatrists acknowledged that the communication about the treatment plan

126 Interviews with B-service user, C-service user, H-psychiatrist, and J-psychiatrist.
127 Interview with J-psychiatrist.

always involves family members.[128] In some cases, the communication is primarily between psychiatrists and family members,[129] and service users' opinion is always ignored.[130] In most cases the paperwork is signed by family members.[131]

However, the quality of communication depends on the interactive relationship among service users, family members and psychiatrists. Some participating service users reported that they never had a chance to talk with their psychiatrists properly, and some complained that they were not even allowed to know their diagnosis or what drug they were taking.[132] On the other hand, a participating service user reported that they managed to establish an excellent working relationship with their psychiatrist, who has a good reputation for being patient and respectful to patients.[133]

That said, the decision-making for the treatment plan in practice is subject to psychiatrists' influence and the reality is that the choices are limited. A participating psychiatrist said:

> In theory, the doctor's job is to propose a treatment plan, and family members decide to accept or not. However, the options for treatment are limited. The real choice is normally between different drugs. In this way, family members of involuntary patients and patients themselves in voluntary services are following what doctors recommend.[134]

To sum up, the proposal and delivery of treatment largely depends on the interaction among different stakeholders in individual cases. Meanwhile, considering the limited choices available, psychiatrists usually take a leading role because of their professional background and authority.[135]

5.6.2 Judicial response

This study does not find any judgment that addresses the lawfulness of the administration of treatment. There are a large number of cases in which users claimed in their indictments that they were unlawfully treated with physical or chemical restraint, but in most of these cases the courts did not address this issue.

128 Interviews with A-service user, B-service user, C-service user, F-service user, G-service user, H-psychiatrist, I-psychiatrist, J-psychiatrist, K-psychiatrist, L-psychiatrist, M-psychiatrist, N-psychiatrist, and O-psychiatrist.
129 Interviews with A-service user and K-psychiatrist.
130 Interviews with B-service user, F-service user and G-service user.
131 Interviews with H-psychiatrist, J-psychiatrist, and K-psychiatrist.
132 Interviews with F-service user and G-service user.
133 Interview with C-service user.
134 Interview with K-psychiatrist.
135 During the interviews and my presence at the mental health facilities, an observation could be made that the use of physical restraint is common and electric-shock therapy is possibly administered with the consent of family member only. However, it is a sensitive topic, so I did not chase this issue in most interviews.

Another factor relevant here is that most of the courts highly rely (perhaps overly rely) on the experts' opinions in medical certifications to determine whether the mental health facility is accountable. There is only one case on the MHL in which the court expressly chose not to accept the opinion of medical certification and found the mental health facility accountable.[136] Medical certifications have been long criticised as lacking independence, as the experts conducting the certification are very likely to be the colleagues of the doctors.[137] This criticism applies to all medical dispute cases in China and is beyond the scope of this book.

5.6.3 Section summary

This section suggests that the planning and delivery of mental health treatment is co-decided by psychiatrists, service users and family members, with psychiatrists taking a leading role. However, the amount of control a service user retains depends upon the subtle interactions among these parties, which may vary from case to case.

Based on the study of the MHL-related judgments, the courts also restrain themselves from intervening in this highly professional clinical activity.

5.7 Discharge

As addressed earlier, the MHL grants family members a critical decision-making role for detention for involuntary treatment. This critical role is even more evident in the decision-making relating to discharge.

The MHL provides different procedures for discharge for different types of inpatient treatment. First, a voluntary service user may request discharge at any time, and 'medical facilities shall comply with such requests'.[138] Second, an involuntary service user who is detained on the ground of posing harm or dangerousness to oneself, the guardian requests discharge.[139] Third, in the cases that an involuntary service user is detained for being harmful or dangerous to others, the medical facility 'shall immediately inform the patient and the guardian' when the medical facility sees appropriate.[140]

However, Article 45 only provides 'when persons with mental disorders are unable to complete the hospital discharge themselves, these procedures shall be completed by their guardians'.[141] The MHL does not provide any rule on the legal consequence if a guardian refuses to complete the procedure. This section will examine the family members' status in the stage of discharge in medical practice and the courts' responses.

136 *Wang v Wang* 2017.
137 Interview with K-psychiatrist.
138 MHL, Art 44.
139 Ibid.
140 Ibid.
141 Ibid., Art 45.

5.7.1 Medical practice

Based on the qualitative interviews, the discharge must be completed by the family member who decided on the detention for involuntary treatment in the first place.[142] Under the MHL, the premise of this practice is that the service user is unable to complete the discharge procedure, which may imply a consideration of his or her ability in some aspect. However, the findings from the interviews suggest there is no formal assessment or guide in determining such ability. Instead, the driving force behind this approach is mostly pragmatic.

Many participating psychiatrists reported that they have experience of dealing with service users who were appropriate for discharge, from a professional perspective, but their family members refused to complete the discharge procedure or were extremely negative about doing so.[143] A participating psychiatrist described the situation at his hospital:

> Unlike operations in other medical departments, mental illness is a long term and relapsing illness. So, it is very important to clearly divide the responsibility. This is why we have to stick to the principle of 'the discharge must be completed by the family member who decided on the detention for involuntary treatment in the first place'. Family members have the duty to monitor the patient to ensure they take their medication. We can say a patient is okay in our ward, but we cannot guarantee that the patient will be okay at home, as he can refuse to take medication at home. If we do so according to the MHL, family members may make trouble with us, saying it is not us but you doctors allowing him to leave.... If the patient relapses and makes trouble with others, their family members may be accountable according to our law. Then family members may go after us.... Another reason why we have to rely on family members is about fees. We cannot sustain if family members are not paying.[144]

Under these considerations, psychiatrists are counting on family members' cooperation in proceeding with their work. Where family members are not willing to support discharge, psychiatrists have to spend much time in communication,[145] send some service users back home with the hospital staff,[146] or attempt to make family members accountable for the crime of abandonment.[147]

142 Interviews with A-service user, B-service user, C-service user, D-service user, F-service user, G-service user, H-psychiatrist, J-psychiatrist, K-psychiatrist, L-psychiatrist, M-psychiatrist, N-psychiatrist, and O-psychiatrist.

143 Interviews with H-psychiatrist, J-psychiatrist, K-psychiatrist, L-psychiatrist, M-psychiatrist, and N-psychiatrist.

144 Interview with N-psychiatrist.

145 Interview with H-psychiatrist.

146 Interviews with J-psychiatrist, K-psychiatrist, and O-psychiatrist.

147 Interviews with K-psychiatrist and M-psychiatrist.

The lack of community-based services, addressed in Chapter 3, is reaffirmed by participants of this study.[148] It partly explains why family members have difficulties in taking detained service users back to their own home. Two other issues, responsibility and financial concerns, have also emerged from the interviews. Chapter 6 will address these factors in more depth.

5.7.2 *Judicial response*

As service users under involuntary detention have limited access to justice, very few cases have come before the courts relating to the unlawfulness of refusing discharge. This study only identified one case in which a detained service user sued for discharge, with legal support from a public interest law institute in China.[149] In this case, a man was detained for thirteen years after having conflict with his father.[150] When his father passed away, his older brother became his guardian, and he refused to take the man out of the hospital.[151] The court did not consider whether the plaintiff had the capacity to complete the discharge procedure by himself but found the guardian 'has the right to decide what is the right way to fulfil his duty as a guardian'.[152] As discussed in Chapter 4 under the guardianship law, the plaintiff was found to have limited capacity for civil conduct.[153] It means he can independently undertake civil conduct that is appropriate to his capacity for civil conduct.[154] The court's decision mentioned this but did not give any clear finding on whether the discharge fell in or beyond the scope of capacity.[155] Neither the judgment that rejected the plaintiff's claim of discharge reflects any effort made by the court to identify whether a guardian was necessary for discharge.[156]

In another case in which the court quoted Article 45 in the judgment, the hospital sued the service user under detention and family members, asking for discharge and payment of the outstanding fees.[157] In this case, a middle-aged woman with a mental health condition was detained for treatment.[158] The woman

148 Interviews with A-service user, B-service user, I-psychiatrist, L-psychiatrist, and N-psychiatrist.

149 *Lixin Xu v Shanghai Qingchun Mental Rehabilitation Hospital and Canxing Xu* – Right to Personal Liberty Dispute Appeal Case, First Intermediate People's Court of Shanghai Municipality, Civil Appeal No 2108, 15 September 2015. (*Xu v the Hospital and Xu* 2015).

150 Ibid.

151 Ibid.

152 Ibid.

153 Ibid.

154 The General Provisions of Civil Law of the People's Republic of China (passed on 15 March 2017 by the National People's Congress, entered on 1 October 2017), Art 21.

155 *Xu v the Hospital and Xu* 2015.

156 Ibid.

157 *Beijing Anding Hosptial v Yang* – Medical Service Contract Dispute First Instance Case, Basic People's Court of Xicheng District, Beijing Municipality, Civil First Instance No 24789, 19 December 2014.

158 Ibid.

was living with her father until the father passed away in 2011.[159] The father made a will before his death that the defendant's cousin would inherit his apartment on the condition that the cousin must ensure the woman could continue to live in the apartment.[160] Two days after the father's death, however, the cousin took the woman into a mental hospital on a ground which was unspecified in the judgment. The will was the only supporting evidence for the cousin to act the role of guardian, and no legal procedure of guardianship was initiated.[161] When the woman had lived in the hospital for three years, the hospital sued the woman, the cousin and the woman's sister, because: (a) the hospital believed the woman was recovered enough to be discharged, and (b) none of the three defendants paid the hospital fee, approximately 7,000 euros.[162] The hospital asked the court to rule: (a) the women should be discharged, and (b) the fee must be paid by any one of the three defendants.[163] The court attempted to rely on medical certification to rule on whether the women should be discharged, but two certification agencies refused to give their opinion.[164] Eventually, the hospital withdrew this claim, possibly under pressure from the court.[165]

This case illustrates that the court may also be unwilling to challenge the family member's authority in deciding discharge. As discussed above, it also reaffirms the financial reasons why family members have a critical role in decision-making.

5.7.3 Section summary

To conclude, this section reveals, in both medical and judicial practice, the family members are still the most important stakeholders in deciding discharge. Moreover, although the MHL provides the family member is only necessary when a service user cannot complete the discharge procedure, no assessment is observed in medical practice or required by the courts. The *de facto* denial of legal capacity in the decision-making process of discharge is at the complete discretion of the psychiatric professionals. The determinations are essentially based on the diagnosis, rather than tailored to a specific task for specific timing. It is, therefore, a form of 'status approach' in restricting legal capacity.[166] The lack of legal clarity on this point also appears to prevent treating psychiatrists from giving better respect to service users' wishes for discharge. The courts are not active in clarifying the vagueness in the law either. Chapter 6 will explore these broader socio-legal factors behind the conservative practice in both medical and judicial practice.

159 Ibid.
160 Ibid.
161 Ibid.
162 Ibid. The full cost was about 45,000 euros and the insurance only covered part of the cost.
163 Ibid.
164 Ibid.
165 Ibid.
166 Mary Keys, 'Legal Capacity Law Reform in Europe: An Urgent Challenge' in Gerard Quinn and Lisa Waddington (eds), *European Yearbook of Disability Law*, vol 1 (Intersentia 2009).

5.8 Complaint Mechanism

Chapter 4 has addressed the internal complaint mechanism provided by the MHL. The guardian of a service user who is detained for treatment on the ground of posing harm or danger to others can apply for a reassessment to the detaining facility and medical certification from an external agency.[167] By contrast, for those service users where detention is decided by their family members, there is no complaint mechanism to challenge the family member's decision, unless going to a court, like the above case *Xu v the Hospital and Xu* 2015. Since most involuntary service users are taken by their family members, the internal complaint mechanism is rare in practice.

5.8.1 Medical practice

None of the participating psychiatrists of this study reported any experience of dealing with family members who applied for reassessment and certification. However, a participating psychiatrist, whose employer is the most authoritative psychiatric facility of the province, reported that her employer also assumes the role of doing psychiatric certification in that province.[168] Although there is no evidence suggests the certification is widely used in practice, this reality raises a doubt about its independence.

5.8.2 Judicial response

Of the MHL-related cases collected in this study, only two judgments involve a ruling based on Article 32 on the complaint mechanism. In a case, a man had a conflict with his father, and his father called the police who then took him to the mental hospital.[169] However, his father signed the paperwork for detention for treatment.[170] The man was treated for 20 days, despite his protest and that of his wife.[171] After discharge, the man sued his father and the hospital for unlawful detention. His risk evaluation suggested that he was carrying a knife, damaging goods and having persecutory delusions.[172] The court found the hospital did not violate the man's right to liberty, partly because the man or his father had not applied for a reassessment or certification under Article 32.[173] The court did not further elaborate on the internal complaint mechanism, highlighting the importance of accessing information on the complaints mechanism to service users.

167 MHL, Art 32.
168 Interview with K-psychiatrist.
169 *Guo Zhu v Shu Zhu and Wanchun Mental Hosptial of Wenjiang District*, Chengdu Municipality – Medical Damage Liability Dispute First Instance Case, Basic People's Court of Wenjiang District, Chengdu Municipality, Sichuan Province, Civil First Instance No 2035, 29 September 2014 (*Zhu v Zhu and the Hospital* 2014).
170 Ibid.
171 Ibid.
172 Ibid.
173 Ibid.

The court in another case gave explicit emphasis on the obligation of information and rights disclosure. Article 37 provides that medical facilities and the health care providers in these facilities shall inform patients or their guardians of the rights that patients with mental disorders have during the process of diagnosis and treatment.[174] The court found the hospital liable partly because the hospital failed to fulfil this procedural requirement.[175] Although the key to this case is that there was no evidence to prove the service user's dangerousness, the court's approach is still worth applauding. By contrast, the court in the above *Zhu v Zhu and the Hospital* 2014 appears to 'blame' the service user for not utilising the internal complaint mechanism.

5.8.3 Section summary

This section suggests that, based on the data collected by this study, the internal complaint mechanism provided by Article 32 of the MHL is not widely used in medical practice. Its application in the courts' judgments is also at an early stage. It is unsurprising, since most service users are taken by their family members and, therefore, no internal complaint mechanism is available to them. To explore why service users are silenced in the decision-making, Chapter 6 will address the barriers in accessing the external mechanism through the courts.

5.9 Who is the Guardian?

Throughout the book, the term 'family member(s)' is used wherever possible, unless 'guardian(s)' is directly used in quotes. It is based on the reality that very few guardians of service users are appointed by court proceedings.[176] When the MHL was under the consideration and review of the Standing Committee of the National People's Congress, a member of the Standing Committee acknowledged that in practice the guardian is mostly 'identified' by psychiatrists but not appointed in accordance with the procedures provided in the Civil Procedure Law.[177] The study reaffirms this reality that the procedural requirement of appointing a guardian, as explained in Chapter 4, is generally absent in medical practice and in the MHL-related cases.

5.9.1 Medical practice

The participating psychiatrists reported that they do not distinguish between guardians and family members in their daily practice.[178] Some of them also expressed their confusion about who should be the decision-maker among various

174 MHL, Art 37.
175 *Zhang v the Hospital* 2016.
176 *Training Textbook* (n 9) 19.
177 Xin (n 73) 273.
178 Interviews with K-psychiatrist and L-psychiatrist.

family members 'who may assume the role of the guardian', as provided by the MHL.[179] In such scenarios, the only guidance for psychiatrists is the hierarchy of different family members, as set out in the Civil Law.[180]

As addressed earlier, participating psychiatrists seek to prevent conflicts of interest, by seeking a unified decision from all concerned family members as the guardian's decision.[181] In circumstances where the psychiatrist determines that there is no apparent conflict of interest, it is possible that any close family member that takes the user to a hospital may be automatically regarded as the legitimate substituted decision-maker.[182]

Sometimes the 'appointment' of a guardian could be very flexible in practice. A participating service user reported, when he was under detention for treatment, it was his girlfriend, which has no legal status under Chinese law, who signed his documents and completed all procedures of his detention for treatment and discharge.[183] This flexibility allows the most respecting person to play a role, thereby significantly benefiting the service user. However, the flexibility also enables psychiatrists to choose the most compliant family member as the guardian. Unfortunately, the study was unable to collect more information on this point from the interviews.

5.9.2 Judicial response

The judgments in the MHL-related cases do not address whether a guardian is appointed by a court. Therefore, an accurate examination of how the courts use the term 'guardian' is impossible to ascertain. Nevertheless, the study of the judgments suggests that, at least in some cases with no indication of a prior declaration of one's capacity for civil conduct, the courts still used 'guardian' and 'family member' interchangeably.[184] It reflects a worrying reality that the courts routinely ignore the procedural requirements around the appointment of guardians.

5.9.3 Section summary

The limited findings of this section echo the widely criticised practice that the procedural requirements of appointing a guardian are generally ignored in mental health practice. Moreover, it appears that the courts do not challenge the practice.

As addressed, the broad discretionary use of the law has mixed effects on service users, depending on their relationship with their family members. On the one

179 Interview with L-psychiatrist.
180 Ibid. Also, see Chapter 4, Section 4.5.3.
181 Interviews with H-psychiatrist and K-psychiatrist.
182 Interviews with H-psychiatrist, I-psychiatrist, J-psychiatrist, K-psychiatrist, L-psychiatrist, M-psychiatrist, N-psychiatrist, and O-psychiatrist.
183 Interview with F-service user.
184 For example, *Zhu v Zhu and Hospital* 2014, *Ding v Hospital and Ding* 2017, and *Xiangyu Wang v Kangning Veteran Hospital of Liaoning Province and Qiuyue Wang* – Medical Contract Dispute Appeal Case, Intermediate People's Court of Huludao Municipality, Liaoning Province, Civil Appeal No 01257, 11 February 2015.

hand, the flexibility of 'appointing' a guardian provides the possibility that the most suitable family members who respect the service user's will and preference. Under the MHL, it could free the service user from the state coercion that is exercised by psychiatrists. However, this flexibility could also facilitate abuse. Psychiatrists will not contravene the law as long as they follow the decisions by anyone 'who may assume the role of the guardian'. This is the case even where the so-called 'guardian' has not met the service user for years or the service user strongly resists the appointment of a particular person.

5.10 Chapter Conclusion: A Need for Further Explanation

Using the data collected from the qualitative interviews, this chapter provides a detailed examination of the practice in different stages of mental health treatment. The analysis of the MHL-related cases also suggests how the judicial system responds to medical practice across the spectrum of legal issues relating to assessment, involuntary treatment, discharge, the complaints mechanism and guardianship. A common theme emerging from the findings is that psychiatrists and family members share the decision-making power and authority in China. Where a person with a diagnosis of a severe mental disorder poses harm or dangerousness to others, psychiatrists are the ultimate decision-makers in respect to detention for treatment. However, even in this scenario, family members are still the most important stakeholders. Psychiatrists understand their role as proposing the treatment plans and rely on family members for final decisions. By contrast, detention for treatment is often exercised by psychiatric professionals in other jurisdictions.

Simultaneously, the courts in general are not actively responding to legal issues arising in medical practice. The courts adopt a more substantive approach in some issues and are more deferential to psychiatrists' professional discretion and the family members' decision-making role in others. In general, the courts are prone not to intervene, unless an apparent breach of the MHL is found.

As revealed in Chapter 4, the MHL has made a progressive step in the direction of maximising the autonomy of persons with mental health issues. This chapter, however, finds that this step forward in the law has not been translated into practice. The so-called 'medical protective admissions', in which family members decide detention for treatment without any requirement of providing evidence of dangerousness, still operates widely in medical practice. The MHL-related cases indicate that the courts have not offered a clear signal on this matter either.

The exploration of different stages of decision-making in this chapter partly explains why the change from the 'law in the book' to the 'law in action' is so difficult. Nevertheless, there are some other factors that may have an impact on the overall system. These factors include the power imbalance among stakeholders, the lack of an independent oversight mechanism, the economically driven nature of mental health facilities, and barriers faced by service users in accessing justice. These factors have shaped and continue to shape every single part of the system of mental health treatment decision-making. Chapter 6 will attempt to deliver further analysis of these important factors.

6 Shared Power and Silenced Service Users

6.1 Chapter Introduction

Based on the qualitative interviews with stakeholders, Chapter 5 provides a descriptive account of the decision-making for detention and treatment in the Chinese mental health system. Chapter 5 also explores the judicial responses to the medical practice by analysing the relevant court judgments. The most important finding is that family members in China share the power in deciding treatment, which is exercised exclusively by psychiatric professionals in many other jurisdictions; whilst the respect for the voices and decisions of service users largely depends on the individual interactive relationship between a service user and his or her family member. This book conceptualises this phenomenon, which does not comply with the voluntary principle adopted in the Mental Health Law,[1] as 'shared power and silenced service users'. This chapter turns to examine the critical factors that have shaped this phenomenon.

It has to be noted that most social phenomenon result from multiple factors. The explanations offered below do not claim to be a definitive or exhaustive account, and other factors may also apply. Instead, this chapter aims to present a set of factors that are most pertinent in understanding the 'shared power and silenced service users'. As will be discussed below, this chapter attempts to reveal that the gap between practice and the law reform brought by the MHL in promoting the voluntary principle cannot be filled unless the power structure behind it is altered.

This chapter starts with an examination of how and why psychiatrists and family members in China share the decision-making authority in mental health treatment. As will be revealed, psychiatrists still retain a power imbalance over service users. Family members, however, earn their status of decision-maker by bearing most responsibility towards service users, in particular paying the hospital fee and being liable for compensating third parties in any (potential) tort action resulting from the conduct of a service user. Section 6.3 will discuss the reasons for the marginalisation of service users' voices in the decision-making process, using the

1 Mental Health Law of the People's Republic of China (passed by the Standing Committee of the National People's Congress on 26 October 2012, entered into force on 1 May 2013) (MHL).

DOI: 10.4324/9781003212034-6

lens of access to justice. Before the conclusion of the chapter, Section 6.4 discusses how the factors examined in Section 6.2 and 6.3 respectively are connected to one another in practice.

6.2 Unpacking 'Shared Power'

The term 'shared power' describes the practice where family members exercise considerable power in making most treatment decisions. These decisions include detention for diagnostic assessment, detention for treatment, making and delivery of the treatment plan, and discharge. By contrast, in common law jurisdictions psychiatrists are usually the ultimate decision-makers over these matters, whilst family members do not have a formal decision-making status in the mental health treatment. For example, family members in Ireland do not have any formal role under the Irish Mental Health Act 2001 but can only initiate the process of assessment for detention and involuntary treatment by reporting to approved professionals.[2]

However, it does not mean that the power imbalance in psychiatry, which is well documented in academic works and by international and regional human rights bodies,[3] does not exist in China. On the contrary, the power imbalance is severe and obvious. The difference is that in China some decision-making roles are undertaken by family members who are also heavy influenced by psychiatrists. A participating lawyer in this research, who has extensive experience of dealing with MHL-related cases, makes a thought-provoking analogy of the relationship between family members and psychiatrists. The lawyer found that the relationship in Chinese mental health system is 'like two parties to a contract for services: family members give some basic requirements, and psychiatrists work out the details'.[4]

This section explores the power imbalance that is weighted in favour of psychiatrists over service users first. Then it discusses why family members have the significant role in the decision-making.

6.2.1 Psychiatrists' power in decision-making

As suggested above, Chinese psychiatrists still exercise enormous authority over service users. In order to better illustrate the power imbalance, this subsection partly borrows the analysis model of the power imbalance in the context of service user involvement in the Irish mental health system.[5] Under this framework, power

2 Mental Health Act 2001 (Ireland), s 9. Also, see Mary Donnelley and Claire Murray, 'The Role of Family in Mental Health Law: A Framework for Transformation' (2013) 25 *Child and Family Law Quarterly* 380.

3 For example, see Human Rights Council, 'Report of the Special Rapporteur on the right of everyone to the enjoyment of the highest attainable standard of physical and mental health' (28 March 2017) A/HRC/35/21.

4 Interview with U-lawyer/NGO.

5 Liz Brosnan, 'Power and Participation: An Examination of the Dynamics of Mental Health Service-User Involvement in Ireland' (2012) 6 *Studies in Social Justice* 45.

operates in different forms.[6] Some performance of power is visible and explicit: the professionals have apparent authority and discretion in the decisions that have significant effects on service users. This form of power reflects the determination of who makes a decision, the content of a decision, and the procedure for decision-making and relevant consultation.[7] On the other hand, power also operates in a hidden and invisible way, which requires a closer examination to identify.[8] For example, 'what is or is not allowed onto the agenda', 'what knowledge is valid for consideration', and even 'the psychological and ideological boundaries of participation' are also exercises of power in the context of service user involvement in Ireland.[9]

Learning from the analysis of the Irish service users' involvement, this subsection examines the psychiatrists' remaining power over service users in China. The subsection applies the different forms of power to the evidence collected by this research. It not only explores the legal and formal reflections of the power imbalance but also briefly discusses the cultural or attitudinal underpinnings. The subsection, however, does not attempt to suggest the psychiatrists' professional authority, based on its biomedical basis, is by nature unjustifiable in understanding mental health conditions. Due to the legal nature, this book focuses on the institutional perspective of psychiatric power rather than a sociological or cultural one, which merits further interdisciplinary research.

6.2.1.1 Visible and explicit power

The discretion in determining a number of critical issues, particularly the imposition of restraints on service users, reflect the visible and explicit power retained by Chinese psychiatrists.

A. CLINICAL DISCRETION IN RISK DETERMINATION

As explored in Chapter 4, detention for involuntary treatment is permitted by the MHL when a service user meets the diagnostic threshold of a severe mental disorder and poses harm or dangerousness to him/herself or others.[10] If the harm or danger is to him/herself, their family member decides on whether or not to impose detention for treatment; if the harm or danger points to others, psychiatrists make the ultimate decision.[11] The empirical findings in Chapter 5, however, reveal that psychiatrists tend not to exercise their decision-making authority in the latter situation but rely on family members' decisions.[12] That said, psychiatrists' power in this process is still visible and explicit.

6 Ibid., 56.
7 Ibid.
8 Ibid.
9 Ibid.
10 MHL, art 30.
11 Ibid, Art 31–36. Also, see Chapter 4, Section 4.4.2.
12 Chapter 5, Section 5.3

Psychiatrists exercise great authority in clinical decision-making. The issues to determine include: whether a person has a mental disorder, whether the mental disorder is 'severe' as defined in the MHL, and whether there exists harm or danger. The determination of risk is particularly critical here. If the psychiatrist finds no harm or dangerousness, involuntary detention for treatment is not permissible for a service user, even if he or she has a severe mental disorder. The different objects of the harm or danger, oneself or others, also denote different decision-makers.

As discussed in Chapter 4, the MHL provides both an internal and an external complaint mechanism for a service user and his or her family member to challenge a psychiatrist's determination.[13] The internal one refers to reassessment and medical certification upon application[14]; whilst the external one refers to litigation in courts, which will be discussed later in this chapter.[15] The MHL does not set up any specialised or interdisciplinary body that provides independent and periodic oversight, unlike the tribunals set up under the Irish Mental Health Act 2001.[16] The collected empirical data is insufficient to suggest whether the internal mechanism to check a psychiatrist's diagnosis or the determination of risk is meaningful. This is mainly due to the lack of either national or local data. The number of applications for reassessment and medical certification every month or year and their results are unknown to the public. Nevertheless, none of the seven participating psychiatrists in this study reported any experience of having their diagnosis or determination reassessed upon application.

Setting up mental health tribunals does not necessarily entail the meaningfulness and effectiveness of the oversight. For example, there has long been fierce criticism towards the tokenism of the tribunals in the US[17] and the paternalism of their Irish counterparts.[18] The meaningfulness of the judicial oversight over the decisions made by Irish mental health tribunals is also a mixed package. The case law indicates the courts' reluctance in undertaking substantive reviews or finding detention unlawful.[19] Nevertheless, the point here is that such an independent complaint mechanism at least provides a platform for hearing the voices of detained service users.[20] It also provides a formal basis for future law reform.[21]

13 Chapter 4, Section 4.4.2.
14 MHL, Art 32.
15 Ibid., Art 82.
16 Mental Health Act 2001 (Ireland), s 48.
17 See, generally, Michael L Perlin, *International Human Rights and Mental Disability Law* (Oxford University Press 2011).
18 Darius Whelan, 'Protecting Rights in Mental Health Law: The Relationship between the Courts and Mental Health Tribunals' in Mary Donnelly and Murray Claire (eds), *Ethical and Legal Debates in Irish Healthcare: Confronting Complexities* (Manchester University Press 2016).
19 Ibid.
20 Darius Whelan, 'Mental Health Tribunals: A Significant Medico-Legal Change' (2004) 10 Medico-legal Journal of Ireland 84.
21 Ibid.

Without such a mechanism in place, the clinical discretion of Chinese psychiatrists receives no formal oversight.

Meanwhile, a substantive enquiry into the clinical determination is also worth raising here. The analysis of the interviews in Chapter 5 suggested that determinations are made with an arguably excessive scope of medical discretion.[22] A diagnosis of certain mental disorders or symptoms, like schizophrenia or delusion, is believed to automatically entail harm or danger, thereby justifying the detention and involuntary treatment.[23] The legal basis of this common practice is the fact that the MHL does not adopt any limitation, like 'substantive' or 'immediate', to the harm or danger requirement.[24] The MHL does not provide any specific guide or tool for risk assessment either. An authoritative textbook on the MHL for medical and psychiatric professionals[25] even widens the broad medical discretion in risk assessment, whose accuracy is in doubt.[26]

For example, in answering the question 'Should involuntary detention for treatment be imposed on patients with schizophrenia who have no behaviour of harm but refuse treatment?', the *Training Textbook* explains:

> Obviously, 'harm to oneself' has a broader scope than suicide. 'Harm to self' must include all behaviours that may harm the patients, intentionally or unintentionally. These behaviours include, for example, *stiffness, excitement*, food or water refusal, and long periods of sleepless. So, patients with a diagnosis of schizophrenia may have no behaviour or risk of suicide or harming others. However, if a patient who refuses treatment has these above conditions (referring to stiffness, excitement, food or water refusal, and long periods of sleepless) that may potentially harm the patient, the criteria for detention for involuntary treatment based on imposing harm or dangerousness to him/herself is fulfilled.[27]

The *Training Textbook* also reminds psychiatrists to uphold the 'principle of accurate diagnosis' and avoid an approach that is 'too loose'.[28] Its effectiveness in

22 Chapter 5, Section 4, 5, and 9.
23 Chapter 5, Section 5.
24 MHL, Art 30.
25 *Training Textbook for Healthcare Professionals on the Mental Health Law of the People's Republic of China* (China Legal Publishing House 2013). (*Training Textbook*)
26 This book does not find any meta-analysis about the accuracy of risk assessment in China. An international study shows the extremely low accuracy of risk assessment: if one hundred persons are regarded as having the risk of committing suicide only less than two persons would eventually have suicidal behaviours. See Matthew Large et al., 'Systematic Review and Meta-Analysis of the Clinical Factors Associated with the Suicide of Psychiatric In-Patients' (2011) 124 *Acta Psychiatrica Scandinavica* 18. More discussion on this point, see Anna Nilsson, 'Objective and Reasonable? Scrutinising Compulsory Mental Health Interventions from a Non-Discrimination Perspective' (2014) 14 *Human Rights Law Review* 459.
27 *Training Textbook* (n 25), 109. Emphasis added.
28 Ibid.

practice, however, is questionable, especially when other psychiatrists undertaking reassessments and medical certifications are most likely to be trained with the same standards and interpretations and are not sufficiently independent from the mental health facility where the person is detained. As Chapter 5 reveals, Chinese courts are also prone to limit their review into a procedural check.[29] Rather than carrying out substantive scrutiny, the courts are more likely to merely examine whether one's medical records include the risk determination.[30] This reluctance of intervention may deter a more precise standard of risk assessment being developed by the courts through its case law.

B. POWER OF IMPOSING 'PROTECTIVE MEDICAL MEASURES'

Another example of visible and explicit power is the imposition of restraint, isolation, or other protective medical measures in Chinese psychiatric wards. The MHL provides that, when persons with mental disorders who are in a medical facility engage in or are about to engage in self-harm, in behaviour that endangers the safety of others, or in behaviour that disrupts the facility's functioning, the medical facilities and health care providers in these facilities may use restraints, isolation, or other protective medical measures if no alternative measures are available, but any punitive use is prohibited.[31] After the imposition of the measures, only family members shall be informed.[32] The medical facility has no specific duty to report to any oversight body.

Psychiatrists in China are usually sensitive to questions about the use of restraints, isolation and other protective measures in psychiatric wards. During the qualitative interviews, therefore, the author chose not to ask questions related to this issue. However, abuse of restraints, sometimes as punishment, is well documented by several civil society reports and justifies this practical choice by the author not to ask the question.[33] A report observes that physical restraints and forced electroconvulsive therapy or medication were 'routinely used' on the persons who refused treatment or were considered to be disobedient.[34]

The civil society reports may attract criticism for lacking representation or only highlighting extreme cases. Thus, it should be helpful to draw insights from the official publication which supposedly adopts a less critical perspective. In the *Training Textbook*, a section on 'questions and answers' relates to protective

29 Chapter 5, Section 5.2.2.
30 Ibid.
31 MHL, Art 40.
32 Ibid.
33 Chinese Human Rights Defenders, 'The Darkest Corners': Abuses of Involuntary Psychiatric Commitment in China <www.nchrd.org/2012/08/the-darkest-corners-abuses-of-involuntary-psychiatric-commitment-in-china> accessed 1 July 2021; Jonathan Tcheng and Human Rights Watch, '"Have You Considered Your Parents' Happiness?": Conversion Therapy against LGBT People in China' (2017) < www.hrw.org/report/2017/11/15/have-you-considered-your-parents-happiness/conversion-therapy-against-lgbt-people> accessed 1 July 2021.
34 Ibid., 22–24.

medical measures. One question is as follows, 'When involuntary patients refuse treatment, is it permissible to impose restraint?' After explaining the purpose of restraint and a summary of the World Health Organisation recommendations, the *Training Textbook* concludes:

> A patient refuses treatment means nurses cannot perform the treatment plan. The goal of involuntary detention for treatment, which is lowering or eliminating the risk of any dangerous behaviour of the patient, becomes difficult to achieve. Therefore, this could be considered to be '*behaviours that disrupt the facility's functioning*' and, according to the MHL, restraint could be imposed. However, in order to prove the necessity and irreplaceability of restraint, a warning or less restrictive measures, for example limiting activity space, should be adopted before the imposition of restraint.[35]

It is clear that psychiatrists in China are trained to exercise the power of imposing restraint over any service user who refuses treatment, without adequate oversight. It reflects the significant power imbalance that operates both visibly and explicitly. A common criticism of the mental health laws in the West is that the law creates a coercive environment.[36] Under the threat of detention and involuntary treatment, any attempt to negotiate the treatment plan is refused as it is 'not accepted as a legitimate part of the clinical interaction'.[37] Even a service user's 'efforts to establish a dialogue' may not be encouraged but 'tends to be interpreted as "non-compliance"'.[38] In the Chinese context, however, although sharing the power of deciding detention and discharge with family members, psychiatrists' power of imposing restraint remains a vivid reflection of the power imbalance of the doctor-patient relationship.

6.2.1.2 Hidden and invisible power

As mentioned earlier, power may also operate less visibly but still impose a heavy influence on the decision-making process of mental health treatment. Chapter 5 reveals that family members are often the primary narrative providers in the diagnostic assessment; nevertheless, it is at the psychiatrists' discretion to decide what to take seriously into account.[39] Participating psychiatrists refer to this discretion as a 'comprehensive consideration', especially when a potential conflict of interest or disagreement among different family members comes to their attention.[40]

35 *Training Textbook* (n 25) 112–113. Emphasis added.
36 Penelope Weller, *New Law and Ethics in Mental Health Advance Directives: The Convention on the Rights of Persons with Disabilities and the Right to Choose* (Routledge 2012), 9.
37 Ibid.
38 Ibid.
39 Chapter 5, Section 5.4.
40 Ibid.

Admittedly, this discretion is a part of the clinical autonomy of psychiatrists. Nevertheless, it also reflects the hidden power to decide what is a piece of valid narrative and what to consider seriously. Similarly, as addressed in Chapter 5, the psychiatrists also have the authority of setting the agenda within the wards, including when psychiatrist-service user communication can occur and how long it will take.[41] A participating NGO worker who had work experience in psychiatric hospitals observed:

> In the psychiatrist' morning rounds they only ask whether patients are still having certain symptoms. If you answer yes, I (psychiatrists) may consider reducing your medication. If you say no, I will not let you out. Doctors are pleased when compliant patients acknowledge they have symptoms like delusions.[42]

These exercises of power are hidden and informal but still noticeable. This subsection also considers another reflection of the power imbalance that may be more difficult to identify. That is psychiatrists' power in shaping the invisible epistemological foundation for all decision-making in mental health treatment. It will look at what beliefs people are holding and what terminology is in use concerning service users and their treatments.

For example, it is a general belief among Chinese psychiatrists that voluntary treatment for some kinds of mental illness, like schizophrenia, is inherently impossible. This belief is so dominant that such a position, without necessary supporting evidence or justification, has become widespread. In the brief of a draft of the MHL, the Legal Affairs Committee of the National People's Congress states 'patients with severe mental disorders have no insight and are usually unwilling to accept inpatient treatment'.[43] Without any further supporting evidence, this proposition served as the rationale for deleting service users' rights to apply for reassessment and medical certification, against psychiatrists and family members, from that draft.[44]

The belief is so prominent that even service users have learnt to accept the proposition when their personal experience suggests otherwise. A participating service user, who had experience of both voluntary and involuntary treatment, acknowledged that involuntary treatment is always inevitable for people with a diagnosis of a severe mental disorders.[45] In the same interview, however, the participating service user explained in depth how their peer support worked out in their community, including preventing new service users from involuntary interventions.[46]

41 Ibid., Section 6.
42 Interview with T-lawyer/NGO.
43 Xin Chunying (ed.) *The Interpretations of the Mental Health Law of the People's Republic of China* (Law Press China 2013), 297.
44 Ibid.
45 Interview with C-service user.
46 Ibid.

Another reflection of this epistemological or ideological dominance is the widespread use of the medical term 'insight'. Previous chapters note that the Mental Health Regulation of Shanghai[47] (before amendment according to the MHL in 2014) used insight as a threshold for exercising the right to informed consent in mental health treatment.[48] Although no longer a part of legal standards in the MHL, its influence in practice is still apparent. 'Lacking insight' is still a common term used in the various authoritative interpretations of the MHL.[49] Participating psychiatrists stressed that the lack of insight makes mental illness unique and the coercive nature of psychiatry necessary.[50] Participating social workers reported that psychiatrists dominate the assessment of insight in which social workers have no place.[51]

Moreover, not only do psychiatrists always refer to the concept of insight, but participating service users have also learnt to use 'lacking insight' to describe their condition in crisis.[52] As a researcher in law, the interviewing experience leaves an impression that service users had to use the medical term 'insight' to show they understood their condition. Otherwise, they have no other language to talk about their experience of distress and crisis. Chapter 3 notes that for historical and political reasons, a social perspective of understanding mental health conditions had been long absent; while the biomedical model was the only legitimate source of knowledge in understanding and 'curing' mental health issues.[53] The finding from qualitative interviews echoes these statements.

More importantly, the dominance of medical terminology in understanding mental health and the widespread belief that the 'voluntary treatment for people with a severe mental disorder is impossible', oversimplify the complicated issue of refusing treatment. The common belief restates as below:

> Because, (a) patients with severe mental disorders have no insight, and (b) these patients refuse treatment due to the lack of insight.
>
> Then, (a) and (b) imply (c) if they have insight, they will not refuse treatment.
>
> Thus, (d) involuntary treatment for people without insight is justified and desirable, in order to restore their autonomy.

47 The Mental Health Regulation of Shanghai (the version before amendment according to the MHL was passed on 28 December 2001 by the Standing Committee of Shanghai Municipal People's Congress, entered into force on 7 April 2002). (Shanghai Regulation (2002))

48 Chapter 4, Section 4.3.2; Shanghai Regulation (2002), art 36.

49 For example, the *Training Textbook* interprets the ability to complete the discharge procedure as lacking insight or capacity for civil conduct. See *Training Textbook* (n 25) 129.

50 Interviews with H-psychiatrist, L-psychiatrist, N-psychiatrist, and O-psychiatrist.

51 Interview with Y-social worker.

52 Interviews with A-service user and C-service user.

53 Chapter 3, Section 3.2.1.

However, whether or not to accept treatment for a specific time being involves various considerations for any individual. In the interviews, with participating psychiatrists they always emphasised the medical proposition (a) patients with severe mental disorders have no insight, regardless of whether the proposition is factually true or false. By contrast, very little attention directs to whether proposition (b) or (c) is true, or to explore what personalised reasons are deterring a service user from seeking treatment willingly. Peer support among service users, a model that has received increasing attention as a tool to promote access to treatment and prevent involuntary intervention,[54] is only emerging. Initiated and led by a group of self-advocates, peer support programmes in China have no public funding and rely solely on individual entrepreneurship.

Within this highly medicalised discourse, psychiatrists simplify a complicated matter into a quick judgement: if you refuse treatment, you have no insight; and because you have no insight, involuntary treatment is necessary. This judgement may have significant practical implications. Since consent from family members is sufficient, psychiatrists are less motivated to make efforts to foster a mutual-trust relationship or listen to those who are presumed as having no insight.

To conclude, the dominance of the overly simplistic belief that 'voluntary treatment for people with a severe mental disorder is impossible' and the biomedical model reflects a hidden and invisible layer of power imbalance. Beyond agenda setting, like when a service user can talk to a psychiatrist and what narrative is valid, psychiatrists' professional authority has also shaped the epistemological foundation of understanding mental health conditions.

6.2.1.3 Subsection summary

Mental health laws worldwide have created coercive environments and power imbalances within mental health services. This subsection has addressed its reflection in the Chinese context. The legal framework and the empirical findings reveal that family members are the primary decision-makers for mental health treatment in China. That said, this subsection serves as a reminder that psychiatrists are still exercising enormous power imbalance over service users. Psychiatrists have almost unlimited and explicit authority to impose restraint and determine harm or dangerousness. They decide when and how a conversation occurs with service users and what to consider from various and perhaps conflicting narratives. Psychiatrists also profoundly influence how service users and their family members think of mental health conditions and treatment.

The following subsection will turn to explain why family members have gained their formal role in the decision-making structure, which makes the MHL special to its counterparts in many other jurisdictions.

54 See, generally, Piers Gooding, *A New Era for Mental Health Law and Policy: Supported Decision-Making and the UN Convention on the Rights of Persons with Disabilities* (Cambridge University Press 2017).

6.2.2 Family members' power in decision-making

Chapter 4 reports that family members have a formal decision-making role under the involuntary procedure.[55]Chapter 5 further reveals that family members' decision-making power extends beyond what the MHL provides. When taking a service user who poses harm or dangerousness to others to a mental health facility, family members usually decide on the detention for treatment in practice. Although it is a fact that the MHL authorises psychiatrists to decide in this scenario.[56] The structure of shared power is most evident in the decision-making for detention for treatment and discharge. This subsection will address why family members earn their decision-making status at these two stages respectively.

6.2.2.1 Deciding detention for treatment

Chapter 5 has revealed that most service users are taken to mental health facilities by their family members, who make decisions for detention for treatment under the psychiatrists' recommendation.[57] It does not comply with the MHL, which authorises psychiatrists to decide when harm or dangerousness is posed to others.[58] This subsection attempts to answer the unexplained question in Chapter 5: why psychiatrists avoid exercising their authority in deciding on detention for treatment but rely on family members? The findings from interviews discussed in Chapter 5 indicate that the psychiatrists' understanding of the decision-making structure in most cases is as follows: psychiatrists propose, and family members decide. However, due to the limitation of the field work in this study, no family member was included in this study formally. In order to avoid a biased account of who makes decisions, the narratives provided by participating psychiatrists, service users and social workers help develop a balanced understanding.

A participating NGO worker who has experience of working as a social worker in mental health facilities stated the following in relation to the decision-making process:

> Experienced psychiatrists are more likely to discuss treatment plans with family members or sometimes even with service users. The discussion may include the considerations of the specific family situation, like the financial ability of the family or other social factors. For example, whether you have someone who can care for the patient at home, or whether the parents of a patient are both employed, may have an impact on the treatment proposal.[59]

The family and financial conditions are important here because different treatment plans may differ significantly in terms of financial cost. For example, there are

55 Chapter 4, Section 4.4.2.
56 Chapter 5, Section 5.3.
57 Chapter 5, Section 5.5.
58 Chapter 5, Section 5.3.
59 Interview with T-lawyer /NGO.

usually two options for inpatient wards in Chinese mental hospitals: open or locked. In open wards, service users enjoy more freedom of movement, due to flexibility in ward management.[60] In the Chinese context, open wards charge higher rates, and it is a general requirement that service users must have an accompanying person, which also increases the cost.[61] Therefore, the choice between open or locked wards is not only up to psychiatrists' assessment, but is also based on symptoms and other medical considerations. It also depends on whether family members acknowledge the benefit of open wards and whether they can afford and are willing to pay the higher cost. In relation to the financial consideration, as briefly introduced in Chapter 3, not all service users have healthcare insurance; and, even for those service users who have, their insurance will not cover all the cost.[62]

Healthcare insurance in China, public or private, is a very complicated issue.[63] Even narrowing it down to the health insurance of mental health service users, a precise account of how many service users have health insurance and what the insurance policies cover is beyond the scope of this book. Instead, the available data from a middle-income province provides a reasonable snapshot of the situation.

Sichuan Province is a southwestern inland province has a population of more than 80 million.[64] For employed urban residents, public insurance schemes cover 65% to 85% of the hospital fees for psychiatric facilities.[65] For unemployed urban residents, the percentage of reimbursement is from 42% to 65%.[66] By contrast, for village residents, the coverage ranges from only 32% to 85%.[67] In more prosperous regions, access to more benefits may be available. Some participating service users reported that their hospital fees are fully covered, and their family members only need to pay for food and other daily necessities during the period of inpatient treatment.[68] However, for most people and their family members, the part of financial cost that is not covered by health insurance and constitutes a considerable burden.[69]

According to a study of the hospital fees charged to 5,439 service users, the median costs for 30 days was 7,885.73 RMB (approximately 1,000 euros) and 60

60 Binglong Wen et al., 'Inventory survey on clinical features of patients in open wards and locked wards of psychiatric department' (2018) 49 (11) *Journal of Shanxi Medical University* 1378, 1381.
61 Interview with B-service user.
62 Chapter 3, Section 3.2.5.
63 See, generally, Keyong Dong, 'Medical Insurance System Evolution in China' (2009) 20 *China Economic Review* 591.
64 China National Bureau of Statistics, <www.citypopulation.de/China-Sichuan.html> assessed on 29 January 2019.
65 Xin (n 43) 395.
66 Ibid.
67 Ibid.
68 Interview with B-service user.
69 Junfang Xu et al., 'The Economic Burden of Mental Disorders in China, 2005–2013: Implications for Health Policy' (2016) 16 *BMC Psychiatry* 6.

days for 14,801.15 RMB (approximately 2,000 euros),[70] which is also confirmed by the data collected by the empirical study.[71] However, the GDP per capita of China is only approximately 14,000 euros in 2017, approximately 1,200 euros per month.[72] Even taking the insurance reimbursement into account, the hospital fee is still a heavy burden on most families in China. It is worth noting here that the healthcare insurance policies in China usually mainly cover the inpatient cost.[73] The *Training Textbook* also acknowledges that community services, including home care and personal illness management education, is generally absent.[74] Therefore, the actual cost of caring for a service user in daily life is even higher.

In the context that family members are fee payers for most service users, psychiatrists have to ensure family members agree with the proposed treatment plan and, accordingly, are willing to pay. This motivation is evident, as it is a general rule that any hospitalisation in China, not just in psychiatry, that a precondition of treatment is prepayment of the hospital fee.[75]Chapter 5 considers a case that a mental hospital sued a detained service user and her family members because none of the defendants paid the hospital fee.[76] The institutional basis of the financial motivation is the fact that the government has moved away from fully funding public hospitals in China.[77] Official data suggests that 'in the past two decades, government financial support has only accounted for around 7 per cent of the total income of public hospitals' and that '[a]pproximately 90 per cent of their revenue comes from healthcare services and drug sales'.[78] The profits-seeking nature of public hospitals in China has received much criticism for its impact on patients' rights.[79] It is suggested in this book that this is particularly problematic in psychiatry, in circumstances where profits-seeking motivation and coercive power combine.

However, the participating psychiatrists consider the above consideration of financial cost to be a mechanism that prevents abuse from family members. Some participating psychiatrists believe most family members who take service users to mental hospitals for treatment do so out of kindness, because it shows they are

70 Bingjie Wang and Xiping Li, 'Analysis of factors influencing hospitalization expenses of 5439 psychiatric inpatients' (2013) 20 (1) *Chinese Journal of Hospital Statistics* 30, 32.

71 Interview with H-psychiatrist.

72 CIA, 'China' (The World Factbook) < www.cia.gov/the-world-factbook/countries/china> accessed 1 July 2021.

73 *Training Textbook* (n 25) 201.

74 Ibid 174.

75 Karen Eggleston et al., 'Health Service Delivery in China: A Literature Review' (2008) 17 *Health Economics* 149, 155.

76 Chapter 5, Section 5.7.2; *Beijing Anding Hosptial v Yang* – Medical Service Contract Dispute First Instance Case, Basic People's Court of Xicheng District, Beijing Municipality, Civil First Instance No 24789, 19 December 2014.

77 Chapter 3, Section 3.2.5.

78 Zelin Yao, 'State Control and Doctors' Abuse of Clinical Autonomy: An Empirical Analysis of Doctors' Clinical Practice in Chinese Public Hospitals' (2019) 5 *Chinese Journal of Sociology* 29, 34.

79 Ibid.

willing to take responsibility by paying their hospital fee.[80] 'After all, it costs a lot of money'.[81] As suggested in Chapter 5, having your family members on your side is essential in retaining a service user's autonomy.[82] The fact that family members have earned their decision-making status in detention for involuntary treatment opens the door for abuse from family members. Interestingly, it also creates the possibility of preventing the coercion directly from the state through psychiatry.[83]

To conclude, family members' formal and factual decision-making role for the detention for treatment is primarily a result of their fee-paying status. It is built on the Chinese reality that mental healthcare is not free for most people, and family members bear the cost of providing treatment for a service user.[84]

6.2.2.2 Deciding discharge

Discharge is another decision in which family members have the final say.[85] It is a common phenomenon in Chinese psychiatry that, after some time in hospital, family members refuse to take service users back home and abandon them within locked wards.[86] This problem has been so prominent that some legislators proposed to explicitly criminalise family members' abandonment of service users in mental health facilities.[87]

By contrast, within the discharge procedure in Ireland, family members complained that they could not even get a notice before service users are sent home by the facilities.[88] Participating psychiatrists stressed that they very often have to make considerable efforts in persuading family members to approve service users' discharge and accept them at home.[89] It is because of the common practice that 'discharge must be completed by the family member who decided on the detention for involuntary treatment in the first place'.[90] Since family members have to invest considerable financial and emotional resources into care at home, without meaningful help in the community, practical difficulties are of course understandable when family members are unwilling to welcome service users back

80 Interviews with H-psychiatrist and I-psychiatrist.
81 Interview with H-psychiatrist.
82 Chapter 5, Section 5.3.1.
83 For a detailed discussion of the relationship among individual service users, families and the state, see Zhiying Ma, 'When Love Meets Drugs: Pharmaceuticalizing Ambivalence in Post-Socialist China' (2012) 36 *Culture, Medicine, and Psychiatry* 51.
84 *Training Textbook* (n 25) 174.
85 Chapter 4, Section 4.4.2; Chapter 5, Section 5.7.
86 *Training Textbook* (n 25) 235.
87 Ibid.
88 Shari McDaid and Agnes Higgins, 'The Paradoxical Role of Families in Mental Health' in Agnes Higgins and Shari McDaid (eds), *Mental Health in Ireland: Policy, Practice and Law* (Gill & Macmillan 2014).
89 Interviews with H-psychiatrist, K-psychiatrist, M-psychiatrist, O-psychiatrist, and P-psychiatrist.
90 Chapter 5, Section 5.7.1.

home.[91] This subsection, however, attempts to offer an institutional explanation of why a discharge has to be approved by family members.

This book argues that the motivation behind this problem is to clarify responsibility between psychiatrists and family members. A participating psychiatrist explains that

> Our hospital wants to make the boundary clear about who bears responsibility when incidents occur. We have encountered once that a patient was taken in by one of his family members but taken out by another family member. Later, the person who took the patient in came to our hospital and asked for the patient, saying 'I did not pick him up!' The patient travelled to another province by plane, and the family member made troubles with us. After this, we have to keep the rule that 'discharge must be completed by the family member who decided on the detention for involuntary treatment in the first place'. At least, if someone other than the person who signed the patient in wants to take the patient out, we need to hear the voice of the signing person by phone. After making sure the person who took the patient in acknowledges the discharge, then we can discharge the patient.[92]

This statement not only indicates how the service user is at the mercy of the family and the mental health system, but it also reveals the deep concern of the psychiatrists about how to prevent liability. An institutional basis of psychiatrists' worry of liability or 'trouble' is the fact that a service user's family members bear full responsibility after discharge. Chapter 3 and the subsection above have addressed family members' caring role at home and the lack of community support.[93] In this context, psychiatrists feel unsure about discharge unless family members have the necessary knowledge and ability to monitor the medication at home.[94] Nevertheless, if the family member insists on discharge but the psychiatrist still has concerns, the final decision is still up to family members.[95]

More importantly, in the situation that a discharged service user, usually deemed to be under guardianship, causes damage to the safety or property of others, family members bear a legal tort responsibility to compensate the damaged party.[96] As discussed in Chapter 4 about the guardianship law, guardians have the legal duty to compensate when the property of service user is insufficient.[97] As a result, when damage is caused by a service user, whose discharge is not approved by the responsible family member, it is common that the family member, who pays the compensation, asks the mental health facility for compensation. The

91 Chapter 6, Section 6.2.2.
92 Interview with K-psychiatrist.
93 Chapter 3, Section 3.2; Chapter 6, Section 6.2.2.
94 For example, interview with K-psychiatrist.
95 Ibid.
96 Chapter 4, Section 4.5.
97 The Tort Liability Law of the People's Republic of China (passed by the SCNPC on 26 December 2009, entered into force on 1 July 2010), art 32.

methods vary from litigation to petitions to administrative bodies, or even protests publicly inside or outside the facility, known as 'medical disturbance'.[98]

The claims by family members' against hospitals are not always valid in law, and sometimes the disturbance caused is extreme, for example physically hurting or killing medical professionals.[99] However, as long as a dispute attracts media or government attention, hospitals in many cases have to pay to settle the dispute, sometimes even under the government pressure of 'maintaining social stability'.[100] The deteriorated doctor-patient relationship arguably makes mental health facilities more sensitive to potential trouble caused by family members.[101] Therefore, regardless of the provision of the MHL, which says discharge procedure could be completed by service users independently in many cases, family members' approval is still necessary and in reality indispensable, for practical considerations.

6.2.2.3 Subsection summary

This sub-section explains why family members earn a significant decision-making role in deciding detention for treatment and discharge. It has argued that family members' fee-paying and responsibility-bearing role guarantees that their voices will not be overlooked. The reality differs from the mental health systems in many developed countries, where family members bear no such duty or at least receive supports from social benefits and community-based services.

6.2.3 Section summary

The section addresses why psychiatrists and family members share the decision-making power over the procedure for detention and involuntary treatment. Compared to their counterparts in other jurisdictions, Chinese psychiatrists have to share the decision-making power with family members. Nevertheless, the power imbalance over service users is still evident, as demonstrated at different levels. At the same time, the special fee-paying and responsibility-bearing obligations imposed on families, within the particular social and legal context of China, form the basis of family members' decision-making status.

6.3 Unpacking 'Silenced Users'

After exploring the shared power in decision-making, this section turns to explain why service users, the principal object of the shared power, are silenced. As addressed earlier, mental health facilities and psychiatrists cannot afford to

98 See, generally, Lina Chen and Shixiong Deng, 'Causes of Medical Disturbance and Its Countermeasures' (2007) 14 (4) *Journal of Law & Medicine* 253.

99 Ibid.

100 Ibid. Alex Jingwei He and Jiwei Qian, 'Explaining Medical Disputes in Chinese Public Hospitals: The Doctor-Patient Relationship and Its Implications for Health Policy Reforms' (2016) 11 *Health Economics, Policy and Law* 359.

101 Ibid. (n 100).

overlook the opinions of family members, who are in a better position to generate 'practical pressure' on the mental health facilities, either through lawsuits or informal medical disturbances.[102] Thus, the issue of 'inequality of arms' emerges between service users and family members in front of psychiatrists, who exercise the power imbalance over the decision-making and delivery of mental health treatment.

At first glance, the idea of 'inequality of arms' appears to be counterintuitive. Besides the newly adopted voluntary principle, in the MHL also provides the internal and external complaint mechanisms to prevent abuse.[103] As discussed in Chapter 5 the internal mechanism, namely reassessment and medical certification, is not in good use in practice.[104] More importantly, the MHL does not allow a service user to apply for reassessment or medical certification independently.[105] Hence, the external mechanism becomes critical in safeguarding a service user's rights. This section will have a closer examination of the question relating to whether service users have meaningful and effective access to justice, mainly in civil litigation against hospitals and family members. It argues that service users are facing significant legal barriers in accessing justice. These barriers place service users in a powerless position when their rights are violated by either hospitals or family members, or both.

This section focuses on the formal access to justice, not because it is the only reflection of service users' powerlessness. Instead, based on the qualitative interviews of the study, where it was shown that service users' voices are also routinely neglected when they make a complaint to the management sector of a mental health facility[106] or the government department which bears the duty of monitoring the MHL's proper implementation.[107] The access to judicial remedies merits special attention. However, judicial remedy serves as the last resort of redress when a service user's right is violated. This focus on the formal access to justice is also necessary because of the rich materials available for analysis, including legislation and court judgments. The author believes the analysis of the access to judicial remedy also helps to understand the mindset of other decision-makers in dealing with other types of complaints brought by people with a label of mental illness.

This section starts with a brief review of the situation of service users' access to justice before the MHL came into force in 2013. It is followed by an analysis of relevant Chinese law of so-called 'capacity to litigate', the primary legal barrier for service users to access justice. There will then be a review of both progressive and resisting practice since the MHL's entry into force. This section will also address the importance of legal empowerment of civil society organisations.

102 Chapter 6, Section 6.2.2.
103 Chapter 4, Section 4.4.2.
104 Chapter 5, Section 5.8.
105 MHL, Art 31, 32.
106 Interview with M-psychiatrist.
107 Interviews with Q-lawyer/NGO and X-lawyer/NGO.

6.3.1 Service users' access to justice before the Mental Health Law

A widely cited civil society report in 2010, also referenced in Chapter 3, which suggests that (ex-)service users and people with a label of mental illness[108] have great difficulties in accessing justice.[109] Cases brought by service users are nearly always denied by the courts because of their diagnosis of mental illness or experience of detention.[110] Rejection could be formal, by a ruling of inadmissibility, or informal. For example, some courts just gave no response after receiving lodgement materials for years or indefinitely.[111]

It is also worth mentioning here that the difficulties in accessing justice are not a problem for service users. Instead, it is a general problem for many litigants of different areas of law, including cases taken on environment law, administrative law, and constitutional law grounds.[112] This well-acknowledged problem has been subject to various projects of judicial reform and attributed to various reasons: excessive workloads for local courts, their weak political status compared to the executive branch, and so on.[113] Although the courts tend to avoid cases for different reasons, this section will only focus on the difficulties and barriers facing litigants with mental health issues.

Here is an example of the formally denied access to justice before the enactment of the MHL. Zhou had a dispute with the local government in his region for many years. In 2008, the government took Zhou into Shanghai Mental Health Centre which detained Zhou for treatment for two months.[114] After discharge,

108 As suggested in Chapter 1, the terminology used to refer persons who oppose psychiatry or reject their label of mental disorder/illness is controversial. The term 'suspected' is emphasised here because it is particularly common among people who actively and persistently seek access to justice, in order to deny their label. For clarity, however, 'service users' are used in an inclusive meaning in this section wherever possible.

109 Xuetao Huang, Jiajia Liu, and Xiaohu Liu, The Involuntary Commitment System in China: A Legal Analysis <blog.sina.com.cn/s/blog_66b9e1f30100m2h1.html> accessed 1 July 2021.

110 Ibid.

111 Bo Chen, 'Right to Litigate of Persons with Psychosocial Disabilities in China: From Mental Health Law to the UN Convention on the Rights of Persons with Disabilities' in Wanhong Zhang (eds), *Disability Rights Study in China 2015*, (Social Science Academic Press, Beijing 2015). Also, see interviews with Q-lawyer/NGO and U-lawyer/NGO.

112 See, generally, Yongjin Zhang, 'Study on a Sample of Law: The Difficulty in Filing Cases in Grass-roots Courts' (2010) 4 *Anti-Corruption and Integrity Culture Studies* 37.

113 The Supreme People's Court of the People's Republic of China issued a legally binding document in 2015 that requires local courts to register lodgements without undertaking a review before registration. See, generally, Xianxiong Huang and Ting Huang, 'Legislation Defect of Case-filing Register System in Administrative Litigation and Its Treatment' (2015) 6 *Administrative Law Review* 20.

114 *Zhou v the local government* – procedural ruling, Basic People Court of Changning District, Shanghai Municipality, Civil First Instance 3765, May 2010; as cited in Chen (n 111), 217–218.

with the assistance of his family members, Zhou brought a lawsuit against the mental health centre and the local government in August 2008, which was rejected by the receiving court in May 2010.[115] The court ruled that:

> The plaintiff, Zhou, received inpatient treatment in the mental health centre for two months, with a diagnosis of paranoia. A forensic assessment should be made to identify whether Zhou has the *capacity to litigate*. However, since Zhou refused to cooperate with the forensic assessment, this court is unable to judge whether Zhou has the *capacity to litigate*. Therefore, the lawsuit brought by Zhou does not meet the legal criteria for filing a case and shall be rejected.[116]

It is evident that the concept of 'capacity to litigate' plays a critical role in this decision. It is also reasonable to assume that similar logic is in place in those cases that denied access to justice informally. The next subsection will examine this concept in depth.

6.3.2 Capacity to litigate: a legal barrier to access to justice

The concept of the 'capacity to litigate' appears on the Civil Procedure Law (CPL).[117] This subsection addresses the confusing and problematic relationship between the capacity to litigate and the capacity for civil conduct in judicial practice[118], followed by an analysis of the implications for service users' in attempting to access justice. This subsection will suggest that the concept of 'capacity to litigate' and its interpretation by courts form the basis of the formal barrier to service users' access to justice.

6.3.2.1 Capacity to litigate under the current legal system

According to the CPL, a natural person can assume the role of plaintiff in civil litigation.[119] The CPL also provides that 'a person who has no capacity to litigate shall be represented by his guardian as a legal representative in civil litigation'.[120] Therefore, the court will deny a service user's status of participating in civil litigation independently from his or her family members, given the service user does not have the capacity to litigate. Interestingly, however, the CPL does not define the term 'capacity to litigate' nor provide judges or a potential plaintiff with any guidance on its application.

115 Ibid.
116 Ibid. Emphasis added.
117 The Civil Procedure Law of the People's Republic of China (adopted in 1991, amended in 2017) (Civil Procedure Law) (CPL).
118 Chapter 4, Section 4.5.
119 CPL, Art 48.
120 Ibid., Art 57.

As discussed in Chapter 3, the judicial interpretations issued by the Supreme People's Court is an official source of law.[121] The Supreme People's Court's Interpretations of the Application of the CPL contains the principal judicial interpretations for this book.[122] However, the judicial interpretations do not explain what the capacity to litigate is or guide judges on what to consider. The Interpretations of CPL only provide that 'in litigations, the guardians of *people having no or limited capacity for civil conduct* are their legal representatives'.[123] This clause arguably conflates people having no *capacity to litigate*, a term in the procedural law, with people having limited or no *capacity for civil conduct*, a term in the Civil Law.

This vague and confusing conflation also reflects on court rulings. In a civil case in which the plaintiff's capacity for civil conduct was assessed during litigation, the court of first instance ruled:

> Article 57 CPL provides that a person having no *capacity to litigate* shall be represented by his guardian as legal representative in litigation.... Yangdi Zhu is determined as having *no capacity for civil conduct* by a forensic assessment. Since neither party of this case objects to the determination, the court accepts the opinion of the forensic assessment as evidence.... Therefore, Rongwei He, Yangdi Zhu's first son, is Yangdi Zhu's legal representative and guardian in this case.[124]

The judgment above does not invoke the provision of the Interpretations of CPL. However, it accepts the same conflation between the two capacities. The determination that the plaintiff had no capacity for civil conduct led to an automatic result in the case: the plaintiff lost their independent standing in the litigation, and the court accepted the plaintiff's first son as the legal representative in the proceedings.

Possibly due to the vagueness of the provisions and the court's ruling above, few scholars in China have researched in more depth, either raising a clearer understanding of the two capacities or providing any guidance for legal practice.[125] A study states 'people having limited capacity for civil conduct can independently undertake civil activities that are appropriate to one's age and intellectual ability, but they cannot participate in litigation independently'.[126]

121 Chapter 3, Section 3.1 and 3.2.
122 The Supreme People's Court's Interpretations of the Application of the CPL (issued on 18 December 2014) (Interpretations of CPL).
123 Interpretations of CPL, Art 83. Emphasis added.
124 *Yangdi Zhu v Lishui Shan and others* – Traffic Incident Liability Dispute First Instance Judgment, Basic People's Court of Zengcheng Municipality, Guandong Province, Civil First Instance No 2761, 24 April 2014. Emphasis added.
125 Chen (n 111), 219.
126 Weixiong Cai et al., 'A Discussion on the Issues of Assessment of Capacity for Civil Conduct of Persons with Mental Illness' (2003) 2 *Chinese Journal of Forensic Sciences* 38, 38.

Without any justification for this statement, it is merely a repetition of Article 83 of the Interpretations of CPL and the court's reasoning was quoted above. Another piece of forensic research proposes that the determination of capacity for civil conduct should form the basis of the determination of one's capacity to litigate.[127] It provides a long list of factors that forensic experts should consider when they assess one's capacity to litigate. The factors include the person's ability to understand the legal issue at hand, to communicate with the attorney, to exercise procedural rights (for example the right to apply for a judge's recusal), and most problematically, whether the person can afford an unfavourable judgment.[128]

Possibly assessing any layperson as having no capacity to litigate, the reasonableness of this proposed list is highly questionable. The point here, however, is that these considerations, directed at procedural issues, differ significantly from the capacity for civil conduct which is about substantive issues. The legal definition of the capacity for civil conduct is the ability to 'account for his conduct'.[129] As Chapter 4 explains, several factors affect the determinations of the capacity for civil conduct. They include the relevance of the conduct with one's life, whether the person is able to understand the nature of the conduct and foresee its consequence, and the person's ability for self-protection.[130] These factors are no less subjective. Nevertheless, the difference between the two capacities and their determining factors is evident.

6.3.2.2 Implications for service users' access to justice

Although the differences between the two capacities are apparent, it is beyond the scope of this book to give a precise definition of the capacity to litigate or provide a practical guide for its determination. For the purposes of this book, the point is that the questionable equation of two supposedly different legal terms negatively impacts service users' access to justice. Chapter 4 has addressed the procedure of declaring someone as having no or limited capacity for civil conduct.[131] On the other hand, mental hospitals routinely treat service users as if they do not have the capacity for civil conduct, simply because of their psychiatric diagnosis, without any procedure before a court.[132] The court rarely, if ever, challenges this practice in dealing with the MHL-related cases.[133]

127 Jiasheng Wu, 'On the Legal Issues in Determining Capacity for Civil Conduct' (2002) *Collected Papers of the First Academic Conference of Forensic Psychiatry of the Professional Committee of Forensic Psychiatry of Chinese Forensic Medicine Association* 165, 168.

128 Ibid.

129 The General Provisions of Civil Law of the People's Republic of China (passed on 15 March 2017 by the National People's Congress, entered on 1 October 2017), art 21, 22.

130 The Opinions on Implementing the General Principle of Civil Law of the People's Republic of China (adopted by the adjudication committee of the Supreme People's Court of the People's Republic of China, entered into force on 26 January 1988), art 4, 5.

131 Chapter 4, Section 4.5.

132 Ibid.

133 Chapter 5, Section 5.9. Also, see *Training Textbook* (n 25) 17–18; Xin (n 43) 273.

Given this particular context, service users are in a doubly disadvantaged position. For many service users, their capacity for civil conduct is denied simply because of their psychiatric diagnosis and experience of hospitalisation, which are most likely against their will in the first place. Moreover, because courts are very likely to deny the capacity to litigate based on the presumed lack of capacity for civil conduct, the service user may also lose his or her standing in court. As a result, the service user is very likely to lose the opportunity of challenging any wrongdoings in a court, against either the mental health facility or the concerning family member, or both. According to the current understanding and application of the law, a service user must be represented in the litigation by his or her family member who assumes the role of the guardian. It then creates a paradox that a service user has to be represented by the family member in litigation against the same family member who decided on the detention for treatment. It is not only theoretically possible but well-documented in the literature.[134] The service users in this situation have no access to justice at all.

6.3.2.3 Subsection summary

This subsection addresses the concept of 'capacity to litigate' and its implication for service users' access to justice. After detention and involuntary treatment, a service user may automatically lose the capacity for civil conduct. Given the problematic conflation between the capacity to litigate and the capacity for civil conduct, his or her right to seek justice and a remedy is also at stake. This subsection aims to build a normative baseline of understanding in respect of service users' access to justice. The next subsection will now turn to identify any changing practice in this regard.

6.3.3 Changes and resistance in the new era of the Mental Health Law

In the developing the law, the design of the MHL's monitoring and oversight mechanism was subject to heated debate.[135] The tribunal model, like the mental health tribunals in Ireland, was, at one time, on the table.[136] It was later considered 'impractical' and replaced by the internal mechanism of reassessment and medical certification upon application.[137] The final text of the MHL added a clause explicitly granting service users and family members the right to sue in front of courts. Article 82 provides that persons with mental disorders and their guardians and close relatives who believe that administrative bodies, medical facilities, other relevant agencies, or individuals have violated the provisions of this law and infringed on the legal rights and interests of persons with mental disorders may legally initiate a lawsuit.[138]

134 Chinese Human Rights Defenders (n 33); Chen (n 111).
135 Xin (n 43) 93–98, 236–238,
136 *Training Textbook* (n 25), 88.
137 Ibid.
138 MHL, Art 82.

The provisions of 'capacity to litigate' under the CPL are still in place and applicable to cases brought by service users. So, MHL Article 82 appears to be a legislative response to the difficulties in accessing justice, as outlined above. Rather than a total replacement of the institutional barriers, it is more a restatement that the court should not deny service users' independent standing too easily.[139] A service user's access to justice is now up to the judge in individual cases, given that the law arguably leaves room for affirming or denying the standing of a service user at the same time. Different courts have adopted different approaches, suggesting a mixed picture of how effectively this legislative response has achieved its goal.

Since the MHL's entry into force several cases have emerged in which the court respected the service users' independent standing based on different reasonings. For example, this study collected a case in which a young man was taken into a mental health facility when his parents and newly married wife discovered his homosexuality.[140] He sued the hospital for unlawful treatment after discharge, and the court did not consider the issue of capacity to litigate and eventually ruled in his favour.[141] There is another case in which, the court ruled, after a full quotation of Article 82, '[a]lthough the plaintiff has a mental disability, he is still able and qualified to bring a lawsuit'.[142] Also, it has become possible that a service user who was formally declared as having limited capacity for civil conduct is assessed as having the capacity to litigate.[143] It indicates the possibility of delinking the problematic conflation between the capacity for civil conduct and capacity to litigate in practice.[144] All these cases reflect a progressive move in the direction of implementing Article 82 MHL and ensuring service users' access to justice.[145] However, based on the data collected, it could be argued that cases emerged due to the sympathetic or open-mindedness of individual judges.

This study also identified cases where the problematic conflation and discriminatory mindset still played a significant role. For example, there is one case where a service user sued the detaining hospital for unlawful psychiatric assessment

139 Chen (n 111), 223.

140 *Hu Yu v Mental Hospital of Zhumadian Municipality* – Right to Personal Liberty Dispute First Instance Case, Basic People's Court of Yicheng District, Zhumadian Municipality, Henan Province, Civil First Instance No 4122, 26 June 2017 (*Yu v the Hospital* 2017). In addition, there are more cases cited in Chapter 5 were addressed in this way.

141 Ibid.

142 *Hong Xia v The Third People's Hospital of Panzhihua Municipality* – Tort Liability Dispute First Instance Judgment, Basic People's Court of Renhe District, Panzhihua Municipality, Sichuan Province, Civil First Instance Case No 1260, 18 November 2013.

143 *Lixin Xu v Shanghai Qingchun Mental Rehabilitation Hospital and Canxing Xu* – Right to Personal Liberty Dispute Appeal Case, First Intermediate People's Court of Shanghai Municipality, Civil Appeal No 2108, 15 September 2015 (*Xu v the Hospital and Xu* 2015).

144 Chapter 6, Section 6.3.2.

145 Chen (n 111).

and false statement in the medical record.[146] The court denied the plaintiff's standing essentially based on his experience of hospitalisation.[147] The court ruled:

> A person having no capacity to litigate should be represented by his or her guardian as legal representative in the lawsuit. In this case, the plaintiff was considered to be a patient with a diagnosis of schizophrenia. The plaintiff's complaint also suggests that the plaintiff was registered into the National Database of Patients with Severe Mental Illness by [the local police]. In the court's proceedings, the plaintiff refused the representation by his family members and insisted that his family members believed his mental status is normal. The plaintiff's medical record confirms that the plaintiff's family members did not agree that the plaintiff had mental illness. Based on the plaintiff's health condition, the court finds the plaintiff's lawsuit, which is not represented by his legal representative, does not comply with the law. Therefore, the court finds the plaintiff disqualified to bring the lawsuit and rejects the plaintiff's complaint in accordance with the law.[148]

In another case an involuntary service user sued the hospital for a false statement in the medical record and unlawful medication.[149] The courts adopted an assumption of incapacity to litigate for people with mental health issues.[150] The court of first instance rejected the complaint because the plaintiff 'does not provide preliminary evidence to prove the plaintiff has full capacity to litigate' and is therefore disqualified from bringing a lawsuit independently.[151] The court of the second instance rejected the plaintiff's appeal with the same reasoning.[152]

By reviewing both progressive and resistive judicial practice, this subsection finds service users' access to justice remains vulnerable to judicial discretion on the capacity to litigate. The reaffirmation of a service user's right to protect his or her rights in front of a court has not achieved its full potential. It is a clear violation of Article 13 of the UN Convention on the Rights of Persons with Disabilities, which requires states to 'ensure effective access to justice for persons with disabilities on an equal basis with others' and provide necessary accommodation to facilitate participation.[153] Article 13 of the CRPD is argued to have a normative potential

146 *Weihua Yao v Beijing Anding Hospital attached to the Capital Medical University* – Medical Damage Liability Dispute First Instance Ruling, Basic People's Court of Xicheng District, Beijing Municipality, Civil First Instance 31441, 24 November 2017.

147 Ibid.

148 Ibid.

149 *Shuibing Cao v The Seventh People's Hospital of Hangzhou Municipality* – Medical Damage Liability Dispute Appeal Ruling, Intermediate People's Court of Hangzhou Municipality, Zhejiang Province, Civil Appeal No 1176, 17 March 2016.

150 Ibid.

151 Ibid.

152 Ibid.

153 UN Convention on the Rights of Persons with Disabilities (adopted 13 December 2006, entered into force 3 May 2008) 2515 UNTS 3 (CRPD), art 13.

beyond its literal meaning. For example, according to some commentators, Article 13 promotes the development of a state-operated advocacy system that supports people with disabilities in exercising their legal capacity.[154] In contrast, service users' access to justice, in its most literal and fundamental sense, is easily denied by the institutional discrimination among Chinese courts. It significantly worsens the service users' powerlessness when their rights are violated.

6.3.4 Importance of legal and community empowerment

Another theme from the analysis is that support from civil society organisations, including public interest law institutes and LGBT communities in China, is crucial in legal empowerment and beyond.

Xu v the Hospital and Xu 2015 is an excellent example where Equity and Justice Initiative (EJI), a Chinese public interest law institute, provided comprehensive litigation support to the plaintiff throughout the years of court proceedings.[155] After receiving a call for help from the plaintiff under detention at the end of 2012, EJI issued an online recruitment notice for lawyers who might be interested in the MHL-related case.[156] When the representing lawyer was found, EJI helped formulate the litigation strategy by bringing a lawsuit as soon as the MHL entered into force.[157] Before the trial, EJI also attempted to reach out to the community-based services, so that the plaintiff and the lawyer could have a better chance to convince the judge that the return to the community would not be a problem.[158] The effort, however, failed as the community-based resources were unavailable.[159] Even though the courts rejected the case and the appeal, the plaintiff was eventually discharged years later, arguably thanks to the representing lawyer and EJI's continuing pressure and advocacy.[160]

Yu v the Hospital 2017 not only echoes the above observation but also reflects the importance of community support other than the public interest law institute. In this case, the plaintiff, a homosexual man, was taken to the local mental hospital by his parents and wife who discovered his sexual orientation.[161] When the plaintiff was detained for treatment, his boyfriend contacted a national LGBT community centre for help.[162] The LGBT centre hired a lawyer to represent the plaintiff and later asked EJI for their MHL-related advice.[163] A staff member from

154 Eilionóir Flynn, 'Making Human Rights Meaningful for People with Disabilities: Advocacy, Access to Justice and Equality before the Law' (2013) 17 The International Journal of Human Rights 491. More discussion, see Eilionóir Flynn, *Disabled Justice?: Access to Justice and the UN Convention on the Rights of Persons with Disabilities* (Routledge 2016).
155 Interview with R-lawyer/NGO.
156 Ibid.
157 Ibid.
158 Ibid.
159 Ibid.
160 Ibid.
161 *Yu v the Hospital* 2017.
162 Interview with W-lawyer/NGO.
163 Ibid.

the LGBT centre travelled a long way to visit the mental health facility, negotiated with the hospital, and, when the negotiation failed, called the police.[164] Due to pressure from the LGBT centre, the hospital discharged the plaintiff after two weeks, which is unusually short by Chinese standards.[165] The plaintiff sued the hospital, and the court found in his favour. The court ruled the hospital had to compensate for its wrongdoings, namely the imposition of involuntary detention for treatment without legitimate grounds.[166]

These two atypical cases suggest that the 'inequality of arms' could be 'fixed' by adequate support for service users. The reality is, however, many MHL-related cases identified in this study reflect the unavailability of such support. Instead, a large number of court judgments which are unsuccessful suggest service users have underdeveloped litigation strategies. Many plaintiffs would have a better chance of winning if they had access to the support from a public interest law institute with expertise and a remit related to the MHL. EJI is the only civil society organisation that is capable of providing litigation support to service users in China,[167] but its functioning and existence are under threat with the changing political environment.[168] In the meantime, for those service users who do not belong to the LGBT community, it is difficult for them to access any support, since the development of peer support groups among service users is also at a very early stage of development.[169] There is no public interest body in China, similar to an Ombudsman or a National Human Rights Institution, that could help service users assert and protect their rights through other mechanisms.

6.3.5 Section summary

This section argues that the barriers in accessing justice silence service users in the decision-making for detention and involuntary treatment. As a result, the legal powerlessness means service users are unable to exert legal or social pressure on psychiatrists or family members who hold great power. As addressed earlier, there is no independent monitoring body over the decision-making process. Thus, the external mechanism of oversight is expected to carry more weight in preventing abuse and protecting the rights of service users. However, due to the problematic understanding and application of 'capacity to litigate', service users have significant difficulties in seeking a judicial remedy.

With the entry into force of the MHL, a number of cases have emerged in which the courts facilitated service users' access to justice. Among these cases, the judges' changing mindset is praiseworthy, and the NGOs' role in providing legal

164 Ibid.

165 Interviews with V-lawyer/NGO and W-lawyer/NGO.

166 *Yu v the Hospital* 2017.

167 Interview with R-lawyer/NGO.

168 Chongyi Feng, 'The NGO Law in China and Its Impact on Overseas Funded NGOs' (2017) 9 *Cosmopolitan Civil Societies: An Interdisciplinary Journal* 95.

169 Interviews with C-service user, E-service user, F-service user, S-lawyer/NGO, and U-lawyer/NGO.

support is also critical. However, as addressed in this section, the space for all civil society organisations, including those with a mission of promoting service users' rights, is closing down in China.

The MHL-related courts' judgments form the basis of the analysis in this book. This is only possible when the service users had a chance to be heard in courts. Regardless of the outcomes of the cases brought by the service users, the vague rules of the MHL could only be clarified when more cases are heard by the courts.

6.4 Final Remarks on Inter-connection of Factors

The previous sections consider the factors behind the 'shared power and silenced service users' respectively. This section provides some final remarks on the inter-connection between these different factors.

In many (if not most) cases, service users face significant barriers, both institutional and attitudinal, in accessing justice. Having both a formal status and a social or cultural authority in decision-making in health settings[170] (including health research[171]), their family members can make a formal complaint or cause a 'medical disturbance' for psychiatrists and hospitals reasonably easily. As discussed above, the different abilities to have their voices taken seriously creates an 'inequality of arms' between family members and service users.[172] Therefore, in cases where service users and family members disagree, psychiatrists may prefer the voices of family members over that of service users. Nevertheless, it is so because psychiatrists have discretion in various critical determinations. It leads back to the point that the lack of independent oversight reinforces psychiatrists' decision-making authority.

Due to the differing abilities in making financial contributions and maintaining social capital, most service users and their family members are also in an unequal position at home. The mental health issues compromise service users' ability to earn,[173] and the community resources and support are scarce and generally unavailable.[174] Most service users have to depend on their family members in everyday life. Family members' fee-paying and responsibility-bearing status not only carries enormous weight before psychiatrists, but it also creates a space of domination from which service users cannot escape.[175] The domination may silence service users' voices at home and prevent conflicts from being litigated. It is also why, in

170 See Chunyan Ding, 'Family Members' Informed Consent to Medical Treatment for Competent Patients in China' (2010) 8 *China: An International Journal* 139; En-Chang Li and Chun-Feng Wen, 'Should the Confucian Family-Determination Model Be Rejected? A Case Study' (2010) 35 *Journal of Medicine & Philosophy* 587.

171 See, generally, Deng Rui, 'A Family-Oriented Decision-Making Model for Human Research in Mainland China' (2015) 40 *Journal of Medicine and Philosophy* 400.

172 Chapter 6, Section 6.3.

173 Daphna Levinson et al., 'Associations of Serious Mental Illness with Earnings: Results from the WHO World Mental Health Surveys' (2010) 197 *The British Journal of Psychiatry* 114.

174 Chapter 3, Section 3.2.4.

many cases, service users have to earn the trust and understanding from their family members, before proceeding to sue the hospitals for wrongdoing.[176]

6.5 Chapter Conclusion

Chapter 5 questions why the progressive changes in the MHL have not been translated into practice. This chapter argues that this is because the power imbalance within and beyond the decision-making structure and process remains unchanged, conceptualised as 'shared power and silenced service users'.

This chapter has revealed the factors of psychiatrists' discretion, family members' full responsibility, and service users' barriers in accessing justice, respectively. First, psychiatrists still retain enormous power, displayed at various levels. Second, family members earn their decision-making status by paying the fees and bearing all responsibilities, including compensating third parties for their loss caused by service users. Third, the lack of effective mechanisms to challenge the decisions made for them against their will silences the service users. This book considers that the logic underlying the MHL's decision-making framework of mental health detention and treatment is no different to the system that existed before the MHL's entry into force. Therefore, no meaningful change is possible unless this hidden structure is altered.

Putting together the discussion in previous chapters, significant and comprehensive room for improvement becomes evident. For example, the current debates in international disability and mental health law focus on whether mental health legislation with safeguards complies with the CRPD, but the MHL has not yet adopted any substantive safeguards such as an independent oversight mechanism. A piece of mental health legislation equipped with adequate safeguards is not a magic pill to all of the problems nor does it make China CRPD-compliant. Nevertheless, it would provide an external and possibly multidisciplinary mechanism that would check psychiatrists' authority and discretion in a more meaningful way. Similarly, the development of community-based support and a safe space for service users' groups to provide support to each other would also go some way towards improving the power imbalance.

A comprehensive list of recommendations for law and policy reform is far beyond the scope of this book. Nevertheless, in light of the CRPD's values and principles, the next chapter compiles a list of the most fundamental issues that require further research and work on the ground. The next chapter will also give an overall summary of the findings and arguments presented in previous chapters.

176 Interviews with D-service user and G-service user.

7 Conclusion and Recommendations

7.1 Chapter Introduction

The primary purpose of this chapter is to summarise the findings and arguments presented in the previous chapters. It will also highlight the original contribution to the literature made by this book. The most critical added value of this research includes an empirical exploration of the implementation of the MHL[1] and a discussion of the barriers to the implementation of the progressive elements of the law reform in practice, thereby presenting a case study to the international debate on the tension between the United Nations Convention on the Rights of Persons with Disabilities (CRPD).[2]

This final chapter will also propose a list of recommendations for lawmakers and policymakers in China. Based on the findings of the research, the recommendations also draw insights from the CRPD. The book is primarily critical, aiming to offer a deep understanding of the legal phenomenon, rather than giving practical recommendations. Therefore, these recommendations only aim to initiate future constructive research projects, both practical and theoretical, exploring mental health law and human rights law within the Chinese context.

7.2 A Summary of Previous Chapters

Chapter 1 sets out the central research question that has guided the chapters in this book: does China's first national MHL take a step closer to the CRPD's requirement on mental health treatment decision-making? If not, why not?

The starting point is to understand what the CRPD require in terms of treatment decision-making in mental health services. Chapter 2 discussed the CRPD Committee has adopted an approach of recommending the abolition of mental health detention and involuntary treatment. Deprivation of liberty on the basis of mental health issues is prohibited. States Parties are obliged to provide non-

1 Mental Health Law of the People's Republic of China (passed by the Standing Committee of the National People's Congress on 26 October 2012, entered into force on 1 May 2013) (MHL).

2 UN Convention on the Rights of Persons with Disabilities (adopted 13 December 2006, entered into force 3 May 2008) 2515 UNTS 3 (CRPD).

DOI: 10.4324/9781003212034-7

coercive supports under which persons with mental health issues are supported to make free and informed consent or refusal to mental health treatment.

As discussed in Chapter 2, this approach has attracted enormous criticisms on the grounds of its practicality and desirability. Chapter 2 has reviewed the heated debate and suggested a consensus between both the opponents and supporters of the CRPD approach: States Parties should maximise service users' autonomy in mental health decision-making by providing a range of non-coercive supports. This approach has been raised as a tool in assessing whether or not the MHL has taken a step closer to the CRPD, with a view to facilitating pragmatic changes in reality. It does not, however, intend to challenge the Committee's interpretation of the relevant provisions of the CRPD.

Among the efforts at reconciling the need to reform mental health laws internationally and the need to protect lives in crisis, there emerges a school of proposals that the focus should be reinvested in voluntary services, before the eventual abolition of the involuntary system. However, others believe it is rebuttable because the problem would remain unless the power imbalance between psychiatrists and service users and the coercive environment is fundamentally altered. As Chapters 4–6 suggest, this study of the MHL may provide a case study that adds to this ongoing international debate.

Then, what does the MHL provide on treatment decision-making? And does this make a step closer to the CRPD requirement? In short, yes. After providing the context for mental health services and the political-legal landscape in China, the book presents a doctrinal study of the provisions of treatment decision-making under the MHL and applicable adult guardianship law in Chapter 4. It does so by comparing the relevant provisions in the seven municipal mental health regulations and two major drafts before the enactment of the MHL in 2012–2013.

Compared to its predecessors, the MHL significantly expands the scope of voluntary decision-making. The MHL adopts the voluntary principle in inpatient treatment by removing the limitation of exercising decision-making rights on the basis of insight or capacity for civil conduct. Under the MHL, the only exception to the voluntary principle is based on a dangerousness standard. The necessity of treatment, which is common to find in the mental health laws in other jurisdictions, has no place under the MHL. The recently reformed adult guardianship law in China also promotes the principle of 'maximum respect for autonomy' of the person under guardianship. The existing procedural safeguards and the promising concept of 'limited capacity for civil conduct', which has the potential of being applied in line with the functional approach of legal capacity, are also in place.

It must be noted that, since substituted decision-making is still clearly provided, the MHL and applicable adult guardianship law is not CRPD-compliant. Nevertheless, as discussed above, the law reform represents a step closer to the CRPD requirement, at least in theory.

Third and most importantly, have the relevant provisions of the MHL been implemented in the medical and judicial practice? Chapter 5 presents the findings of the research, suggesting that the progressive law reform in China, which in theory expands service users' decision-making rights in treatment, has not been well translated into practice. The most significant change introduced by the MHL is that the so-called 'medical protective admission' is no longer permissible. The medical protective admission means a service user posing no evident harm or dangerousness could be detained for treatment indefinitely upon the family member's request or approval. The findings from the qualitative interviews suggest this decision-making pattern of 'psychiatrists propose, and family members decide' is still prevalent in medical practice and rarely challenged by the courts.

The practice of 'psychiatrists propose, and family members decide' is interesting because it is also prevalent in cases where the decisions for detention for treatment should be made by psychiatrists. The MHL provides that if the harm or dangerousness posed by a service user is to others, his or her detention for treatment is ultimately up to the mental health facility; the family member only has a right to apply for reassessment or medical certification. What really happens is that, even in this scenario, the psychiatrist always let family members make decisions and limits their own role as a psychiatrist to making proposals only. The voices of service users, however, are largely absent, or at the mercy of their family members. The book conceptualises this as 'shared power and silenced service users'. The analysis of the court judgments shows that the courts are most likely inactive in challenging this medical practice, leaving a large margin of discretion to psychiatrists in most cases.

Finally, the book also discusses the institutional barriers to validating the progressive law reform. Chapter 6 provides a set of institutional explanations of why the progressive law reform above has not been validated, by unpacking the phenomenon of 'shared authority and silenced service user'. Overall, the book argues that the practice has not been altered because the power relationships among service users, family members and psychiatrists remain unchanged.

One reflection of the unchanged power relationship is that psychiatrists still retain huge discretionary power over service users. Psychiatrists in China have visible and explicit power, for example imposing restraint measures with extremely loose criteria and no oversight. They also exercise the hidden and invisible power of deciding what is true or valuable to consider in admission and treatment and what language other stakeholders have to use. Different from the decision-making structure in mental health treatment in many other jurisdictions, family members in China earn their status of decision-makers by bearing almost all responsibilities. They are primary caregivers and hospital fee payers to service users. According to Chinese law, they are also liable for civil compensation if the service users cause damage to a third party. Without accessible alternative forms of social support from the government or from society, family members are the sole source for the provision of the basic needs and support in all aspects of service users' lives. Hence, the family becomes a place of domination from which a service user cannot escape. It enlarges the power imbalance between service users and family members, which is already obvious in Chinese culture.

Chapter 6 argues that service users could potentially make their voices louder and better heard, given that their access to justice is ensured. As explained earlier, the MHL and applicable guardianship law provide a more useful normative framework than the previous ones for service users to challenge abusive decisions made by psychiatric facilities or family members, or both. However, this potential has not been fulfilled because service users' litigations before the courts have been routinely denied, which constitutes another form of denial of their legal capacity. The existing evidence suggests that legal empowerment and community support provided by civil society organisations could help in this scenario. However, the changes in the social-political environment have made it less likely to develop.

Overall, this book argues that the step closer to the CRPD requirement made by the mental health law reform in China has not been effectively translated into medical and judicial practice, due to the unchanged power relationships embedded in the wider social and legal reality. It contributes to the existing literature by (a) exploring the medical practice of mental health treatment decision-making through the 26 qualitative interviews with key stakeholders, (b) collecting and analysing all available the courts' judgement mentioning the MHL within five years after its entry into force, and (c) explaining the barriers in implementing the progressive law reform from a broader socio-legal point of view.

7.3 Further Research and Recommendations

During the research for the book, a number of issues were identified that are beyond the scope of this book but merit further research. First, the criminal procedure for offenders with mental health issues has also been challenged, motivated by the growing influence of the CRPD. As discussed above, China has reformed the criminal procedure for imposing compulsory treatment in 2013, transferring the decision-making authority from the police to the courts. This reform and its implementation also require scrutiny from the perspective of international human rights law and requires research to produce empirical evidence.

Second, Chapter 4 discusses the restrictions on accessing one's medical record relating to mental health treatment.[3] It appears to be common practice in mental health services that service users are restricted from accessing their own medical records. In the Chinese context, however, there also emerges a concern about the lack of a mechanism that ensures the authenticity of the contents contained in medical records. Since family members' descriptions of symptoms and dangerousness are critical to the lawfulness of detention for treatment, there is a need for further research on how to enhance the credibility of medical records, especially where the authenticity is called into question.

Third, access to justice for persons with mental health issues merits a comprehensive examination. This book raises the issue of capacity to litigate to explain why the voices of service users are ignored in treatment decision-making. This represents an institutional barrier that service users encounter in accessing justice. The CRPD also raises higher requirements in respect to service users' access to justice, including procedural accommodation, training for judicial professional, and even redistributive justice. The application of these requirements to service

3 Chapter 4, Section 4.4.2.

users merits further research.[4] For example, independent advocacy may be particular helpful for those service users who have no access to informal support from family members and are admitted by government bodies.[5]

In addition, introducing periodic review and establishing a multidisciplinary review mechanism for mental health detentions and involuntary treatment may also be helpful in balancing the discretion of psychiatrists and family members.[6] The research on the design and feasibility of this proposal requires further investigation. More importantly, however, this book holds the position that effectively tackling the power imbalance and its social embodiment is beyond the capacity of a piece of mental health legislation. Therefore, the following subsections will also discuss how the CRPD would benefit the future development of mental health and human rights in China, in a broader sense. As will be suggested below, the development in relevant social sectors with the close participation of persons concerned may be the ultimate solution.

7.3.1 Developing community-based services and non-coercive support measures

As mentioned earlier, Article 19 of the CRPD requires States Parties to recognise all persons with disabilities, including persons with mental health issues, have an equal right to live in the community and to ensure persons with disabilities 'have access to a range of in-home, residential and other community support services'.[7] However, commentators observe that mental health services in China are experiencing a worrying trend of institutionalisation. A huge amount of money has been spent in building or expanding institutions, many of which have more than 1,000 beds.[8] Of greater concern is that relevant policies increasingly encourage local governments to maintain institutions, increase the number of beds and commit persons with mental health issues for longer periods of time.[9]

On the other hand, community-based services and support remain largely underdeveloped.[10] Family members of persons with mental health issues assume the primary responsibility of taking care of them, with very limited social or public support.[11] It is

4 CRPD, Art 13. See, generally, Eilionóir Flynn, *Disabled Justice?: Access to Justice and the UN Convention on the Rights of Persons with Disabilities* (Routledge 2016)
5 Chapter 4, Section 4.4.2.
6 See Xiju Zhao and John Dawson, 'The New Chinese Mental Health Law' (2014) 21 *Psychiatry, Psychology and Law* 669, 677.
7 CRPD, Art 19.
8 Jiajia Liu, 'Dependent and Non-Community Living: Rethinking the Institutionalization Trend of Chinese Policies Regarding Persons with Mental Disabilities', in Wanhong Zhang (ed) *Disability Rights Study in China 2015* (Social Science Academic Press 2015).
9 Ibid.
10 Xuesong He, Zhiwu Li and Liandong Xu, 'Changes of Community-Based Mental Health Services after the Mental Health Law' (2014) 13 *Chinese Journal of General Practitioners* 255.
11 *Training Textbook for Healthcare Professionals on the Mental Health Law of the People's Republic of China* (China Legal Publishing House 2013), 201.

usually the case that the only 'help' available to them is the involuntary system provided by locked wards and specialised psychiatric hospitals or departments. Official data of a national report about mental health service providers in China suggests that there are 780 specialised psychiatric hospitals, 541 psychiatric departments in general hospitals and only 57 institutions working on rehabilitation which are likely to be community-based.[12]

The roaring trend of institutionalisation and the underdevelopment of community-based services may cause a number of problems, such as neglect and human rights abuses in these large and isolated settings that are usually lack independent monitoring and oversight. The sole focus on the regulation of involuntary mental health services may cause a lack of resourcing for and attention paid to the voluntary services, as argued in Chapter 2.[13] After all, one important component of promoting the autonomy of persons with mental health issues is to offer meaningful alternatives. Given the context that China has not built its community-based mental health services in the past,[14] it should be a prioritised development goal.

Similarly, as discussed in Chapter 2, the legitimacy of abolishing coercive mental health systems ultimately depends on the effectiveness and practicability of the alternative non-coercive measures, including supports in the decision-making process. Research has already emerged to give a systematic review of the use and development of these non-coercive measures in the world.[15] Many of the measures, such as peer support, advanced mental health directives, and lasting power of attorney, have been in use in many jurisdictions for decades.[16] A small number of advocacy and pilot projects seeking to introduce these measures into Chinese law and practice have also emerged, although they remain at an early stage of development. Attention and investment into these research and pilot projects are urgently needed.

12 Bin Xie, 'Impact of the New Mental Health Act on Mental Health Services in the Future' (2013) 13 *Journal of Neuroscience and Mental Health* 1.

13 Chapter 2, Section 2.4.2. Also, see Bernadette Mcsherry and Kay Wilson, 'The Concept of Capacity in Australian Mental Health Law Reform: Going in the Wrong Direction?' (2015) 40 *International Journal of Law and Psychiatry* 60.

14 The Ministry of Health and others, 'National Mental Health Work Plan (2015–2020)' (2015) <www.cdpf.org.cn/zcwj/zxwj/201506/t20150618_519355.shtml> accessed 26 May 2016.

15 Piers Gooding and Bernadette McSherry, 'Alternatives to Compulsory Detention and Treatment and Coercive Practices in Mental Health Settings' (2018) 26 *Journal of Law and Medicine* 300.

16 See Penelope Weller, *New Law and Ethics in Mental Health Advance Directives: The Convention on the Rights of Persons with Disabilities and the Right to Choose* (Routledge 2012). However Gooding also warns that introducing such 'singular elements' has a danger that governments use the language of the CRPD 'but without meeting core obligations'. See Piers Gooding, *A New Era for Mental Health Law and Policy: Supported Decision-Making and the UN Convention on the Rights of Persons with Disabilities* (Cambridge University Press 2017), 253.

7.3.2 Awareness raising of the Convention on the Rights of Persons with Disabilities and its human rights model of disability

The controversies around the freedom from involuntary mental health interventions as required by the CRPD reflect that States Parties and scholars in the field have taking this 'paradigm shift' in thinking seriously. Although significant challenges to implementation remain, the debate at least suggests that the CRPD is gaining increasing relevance in the discourse around the future and reform of mental health laws in different jurisdictions. For example, in addition to those reports cited in Chapter 2, the Mental Health Commission of New South Wales in Australia also published their report examining its obligations under international human rights law, and explicitly points out that involuntary detention in Australia appears to breach the right to liberty under the CRPD.[17] The tension between the CRPD and the MHL has received less attention by the legislative and public interest bodies in China. By contrast, the National People's Congress did make reference to the CRPD in its official explanation on the amended Regulation on the Education of Persons with Disabilities (Draft), suggesting its awareness of the obligation under the CRPD, in respect of a different topic.[18] This under-developed awareness is also reflected on the first state report by China to the CRPD committee. In the sections that China reported its implementation of the right to legal capacity, right to liberty and the right to health under the CRPD, the government did not mention the draft of MHL at all.[19] A similar situation could also be observed from the limited academic research of the CRPD and the MHL. However, China's most recent report on the CRPD implementation in 2018 mentioned the MHL, which at least indicates growing awareness of its relevance.[20]

This book has identified that the decision-making structure in mental health treatment is deeply embedded into the broader social and legal context in China. Breaking the existing decision-making structure and power relationships is highly dependent on whether the kinds of social support prescribed in the CRPD can be provided in line with the human rights approach. In order to achieve this, awareness raising, a State Party's obligation under Article 8 CRPD,[21] is one of the critical starting points. Based on a human rights approach to understanding disability and addressing disability rights, the government should support research and pilot

17 Bernadette McSherry, *Australia's International Human Rights Obligations* (Mental Health Commission of New South Wales 2014).

18 Legislative Affairs Office of State Council, 'Explanation on the Amended Regulation on the Education of Persons with Disabilities (Draft)' (2013) < www.cndcm.cn/html/zhenglan/falufagui/84_1.html > accessed 1 July 2021.

19 China, 'Implementation of the Convention on the Rights of Persons with Disabilities: Initial Reports Submitted by States Parties under Article 35 of the Convention' (2011) CRPD/C/CHN/1.

20 China, 'Implementation of the Convention on the Rights of Persons with Disabilities: 2nd and 3rd Reports Submitted by States Parties under Article 35 of the Convention' (2018) CRPD/C/CHN/2–3.

21 CRPD, Art 8.

projects made by Chinese academics and practitioners bridging the international human rights standards and the Chinese reality. Then, law and policy reforms based on the result and experience of the research and pilot projects should follow. This book suggests that this is the only way that meaningful change can happen.

7.3.3 Enhancing the participation of service users in all stages of decision-making

The book has earlier addressed that the CRPD itself stands out from other international human rights instruments because of its participatory nature: Disabled People's Organisations and self-advocacy organisations participated meaningfully in its negotiating and drafting process. The CRPD also requires States Parties to ensure the full and effective participation in all relevant public decision-making.[22]

For example, the WNUSP, led by people who have lived experience with mental health services, made contributions to a number of provisions that are pivotal to the rights and lives of people with mental health issues.[23] The WNUSP actively used the language and ideas of the global disability rights movement in reframing the human rights standards for treating persons with psychosocial disabilities.[24] However, their peers in China had less opportunity for participation in the legislative process of the MHL. Before the draft of MHL was handed to the State Council by the Ministry of Health in 2010, psychiatrists were the most important, if not the only, stakeholders involved in the formulation of the law. The Legislative Affairs Office of the State Council later made the draft public and asked for comments from broader society. Some psychiatrists suggested that this was when the draft moved beyond the control of medical professionals, while others suggest that the psychiatrists continued to dominate the process overall.[25] A few individuals who were 'wrongly' and involuntarily diagnosed, committed and treated by psychiatrists attempted to assert their voice through strategic litigation and media advocacy,[26] but it could only be done in an indirect, informal and irregular manner. This suggests significant room for improvement on the consultation with service users in future reforms in mental health services. After all, hearing their voices should be the first step in protecting and promoting their rights.

The CRPD also requires States Parties to facilitate meaningful participation at the level of daily life. It would include a number of softer measures, including training for healthcare professionals about how to work with people with mental

22 CRPD, Art 4(3) and 33.

23 Tina Minkowitz, 'CRPD Advocacy by the World Network of Users and Survivors of Psychiatry: The Emergence of a User/Survivor Perspective in Human Rights' [2012] Survivor Perspective in Human Rights (August 14, 2012) < papers.ssrn.com/sol3/papers.cfm?abstract_id=2326668 > accessed 1 July 2021.

24 Ibid.

25 Chengxi Yang, 'Staring at the China's Mental Health Law from the Third Eye' (2012) China Hospital CEO 74.

26 Harry Yi-Jui Wu, 'The Moral Career of "Outmates": Towards a History of Manufactured Mental Disorders in Post-Socialist China' (2016) 60 *Medical History* 87.

health issues, how to build and maintain a multi-trust relationship. In other words, 'Nothing about us without us', the slogan of the global disability rights movement, is not only applicable to public decision-making but should be followed in every aspect of the lives of persons with disabilities, including decisions in the context of mental health treatment.[27]

7.4 Final Words

This book explores the implementation of the MHL in medical and judicial practice, and it further explains why progressive mental health law reform in China, which supposedly expands the scope of voluntary decision-making in mental health treatment, has not been well translated into practice. It does so by incorporating qualitative research into doctrinal legal research, drawing insight from what is actually happening on the ground. Moreover, the book argues that the inadequate implementation of the law reform results from the unaltered power imbalance and other legal and social embedment. This final chapter also proposes recommendations in the spirit of the CRPD.

In the process of finalising the book, what has emerged is not a firm belief in finding the truth. The debate around international human rights law or domestic mental health laws reflects much deeper tensions about human nature and social institutions. The tensions not only reflect on the classical relationship between autonomy and coercion. There are also complicated interactions among the authorities in understanding one's mental health-related experience, a person's control of his or her body and mind, the broader context of one's social life, and, eventually, legal regulation of mental health services. Without any ambition of giving any solution to these tensions, the book seeks to add another layer of understanding of mental health treatment decision-making in China and its socio-legal embodiment into the growing literature of human rights and mental health laws.

27 See, for example, Lisa I Iezzoni and Linda M Long-Bellil, 'Training Physicians about Caring for Persons with Disabilities: "Nothing about Us without Us!"' (2012) 5 *Disability and Health Journal* 136.

Bibliography

Books and Chapters

World Health Organization Mental Health Evidence and Research Team, *Mental Health Atlas 2005* (World Health Organization2005)

Bartlett P, Lewis O and Thorold O, *Mental Disability And the European Convention on Human Rights* (Martinus Nijhoff Publishers2007)

Chen B, 'Right to Litigate of Persons with Psychosocial Disabilities in China: From Mental Health Law to the UN Convention on the Rights of Persons with Disabilities', in W Zhang (ed.), *Disability Rights Study in China 2015* (Social Science Academic Press2015)

Chen B and Huang S, 'Promoting the Autonomy of Persons with Mental Disabilities through Social Worker's Intervention: A Qualitative Study Guided by the Convention on the Rights of Persons with Disabilities', in W Zhang (ed.), *Disability Rights Studies in China* (Social Science Academic Press, Beijing2014)

Crossley N, *Contesting Psychiatry: Social Movements in Mental Health* (Routledge2006)

Degener T, 'A Human Rights Model of Disability', in P Blanck and E Flynn (eds), *Routledge Handbook of Disability Law and Human Rights* (Routledge2016)

Dhanda A, 'Universal Legal Capacity as a Universal Human Right', in M Dudley, D Silove and F Gale (eds), *Mental Health and Human Rights* (Oxford University Press2012)

Dudley M, Silove D and Gale F, *Mental Health and Human Rights: Vision, Praxis, and Courage* (Oxford University Press2012)

Fei X, *From the Soil: The Foundations of Chinese Society* (University of California Press1992)

Fina VD, Cera R and Palmisano G (eds.) *The United Nations Convention on the Rights of Persons with Disabilities: A Commentary* (Springer International Publishing2017)

Flynn E, *Disabled Justice?: Access to Justice and the UN Convention on the Rights of Persons with Disabilities* (Routledge2016)

Gooding P, *A New Era for Mental Health Law and Policy: Supported Decision-Making and the UN Convention on the Rights of Persons with Disabilities* (Cambridge University Press2017)

Halliday S and Schmidt P, *Conducting Law and Society Research: Reflections on Methods and Practices* (Cambridge University Press2009)

Hsü IC, *The Rise of Modern China* (Oxford University Press2000)

Keith RC, 'China's Struggle for the Rule of Law', in RC Keith (ed.), *China's Struggle for the Rule of Law* (Palgrave Macmillan UK1994)

Kelly BD, *Mental Illness, Human Rights and the Law* (Royal College of Psychiatrists2016)

Keys M, 'Legal Capacity Law Reform in Europe: An Urgent Challenge', in G Quinn and L Waddington (eds), *European Yearbook of Disability Law*, vol 1 (Intersentia2009)

Lewis O, 'Council of Europe', in L Waddington and A Lawson (eds), *The UN Convention on the Rights of Persons with Disabilities in Practice: A Comparative Analysis of the Role of Courts* (Oxford University Press2018)

Li X, *Research on the Legal System of Mental Health* (Shanghai Sanlian Bookstore2016)

Liu J, 'Dependent and Non-Community Living: Rethinking the Institutionalization Trend of Chinese Policies Regarding Persons with Mental Disabilities', in W Zhang (ed.), *Disability Rights Study in China 2015*, vol 2 (Social Science Academic Press2015)

Ma Z, 'In the Name of Love and Medicine? Understanding the Experience of Female Psychiatric Inmates from the Perspective of Rights', in W Zhang (ed.), *Disability Rights Studies in China* (Social Science Academic Press, Beijing2014)

McDaid S and Higgins A, 'The Paradoxical Role of Families in Mental Health', in A Higgins and S McDaid (eds), *Mental Health in Ireland: Policy, Practice and Law* (Gill & Macmillan2014)

McSherry B, 'The Right of Access to Mental Health Care: Voluntary Treatment and the Role of Law', in B McSherry and P Weller (eds), *Rethinking Rights-based Mental Health Laws* (Hart Publishing2010)

Minkowitz T, 'Advancing the Rights of Users and Survivors of Psychiatry Using the UN Convention on the Rights of Persons with Disabilities', in H Spandler, J Anderson and B Sapey (eds), *Madness, distress and the politics of disablement* (Policy Press2015)

Moeckli D et al. (eds), *International Human Rights Law* (New Edition, 3rd Edition, Oxford University Press2017)

Pearson V, *Mental Health Care in China: State Policies, Professional Services and Family Responsibilities* (Royal College of Psychiatrists1995)

Perlin ML, *International Human Rights and Mental Disability Law* (Oxford University Press2011)

Perlin ML and Szeli E, 'Mental Health Law and Human Rights', in M Dudley, D Silove and F Gale (eds), *Mental Health and Human Rights: Vision, Praxis, and Courage* (Oxford University Press2012)

Potter P, *China's Legal System* (Polity Press2014)

Quinn G, 'A Short Guide to the United Nations Convention on the Rights of Persons with Disabilities', in G Quinn and L Waddington (eds), *European Yearbook of Disability Law*, vol 1 (Intersentia2009)

Quinn G, 'A Short Guide to the United Nations Convention on the Rights of Persons with Disabilities', in G Quinn and L Waddington (eds), *Resisting The 'Temptation Of Elegance': Can The Convention On The Rights Of Persons With Disabilities Socialise States To Right Behaviour?, The UN Convention on the Rights of Persons with Disabilities: European and Scandinavian Perspectives* (Brill2009)

Quinn G, Degener T and Bruce A, *Human Rights and Disability: The Current Use and Future Potential of United Nations Human Rights Instruments in the Context of Disability* (United Nations Publications2002)

Ran M-S et al., *Family-Based Mental Health Care in Rural China* (Hong Kong University Press2005)

Seymour JD, 'Human Rights in Chinese Foreign Relations', in SS Kim (ed.), *China and the World* (Routledge2018)

Spandler H and Anderson J, *Madness, Distress and the Politics of Disablement* (Policy Press2015)

Training Textbook for Healthcare Professionals on the Mental Health Law of the People's Republic of China (China Legal Publishing House2013)

Wei YD, *Regional Development in China: States, Globalization and Inequality* (Routledge2013)

Weller P, 'Lost in Translation: Human Rights and Mental Health Law', in B McSherry and P Weller (eds), *Rethinking Rights-Based Mental Health Law* (Hart2010)

Weller P, 'Lost in Translation: Human Rights and Mental Health Law', in P Weller, *New Law and Ethics in Mental Health Advance Directives: The Convention on the Rights of Persons with Disabilities and the Right to Choose* (Routledge2012)

Whelan D, 'Protecting Rights in Mental Health Law: The Relationship between the Courts and Mental Health Tribunals', in M Donnelly and C Murray (eds), *Ethical and Legal Debates in Irish Healthcare: Confronting Complexities* (Manchester University Press2016)

Yang J, *Mental Health in China: Change, Tradition, and Therapeutic Governance* (John Wiley & Sons2017)

Xin C (eds), *The Interpretations of the Mental Health Law of the People's Republic of China* (Law Press China2013)

Journal Articles

Appelbaum PS, 'Protecting the Rights of Persons With Disabilities: An International Convention and Its Problems' (2016) 4 *Psychiatric Services* 366

Appelbaum PS, 'Protecting the Rights of Persons With Disabilities: An International Convention and Its Problems' 'Saving the UN Convention on the Rights of Persons with Disabilities – from Itself' (2019) 18 *World Psychiatry* 1

Arstein-Kerslake A and Flynn E, 'The Right to Legal Agency: Domination, Disability and the Protections of Article 12 of the Convention on the Rights of Persons with Disabilities' (2017) 13 *International Journal of Law in Context* 22

Bian J, 'They Are Bombs that Blow any Time: Experts Interpretation on Crimes Committed by the Mentally Ill' (2009) 13 *Law and Life* 8 [卞君瑜, '他们是一颗颗"不定时炸弹"——专家解读精神病人犯罪' (2009) 13 法律与生活 8]

Bartlett P, 'The United Nations Convention on the Rights of Persons with Disabilities and the Future of Mental Health Law' (2009) 8 *Psychiatry* 496

Bartlett P, 'The United Nations Convention on the Rights of Persons with Disabilities and the Future of Mental Health Law' 'The United Nations Convention on the Rights of Persons with Disabilities and Mental Health Law' (2012) 75 *The Modern Law Review* 752

Beauchamp TL, 'Informed Consent: Its History, Meaning, and Present Challenges' (2011) 20 *Cambridge Quarterly of Healthcare Ethics* 515

Bindman J, Maingay S and Szmukler G, 'The Human Rights Act and Mental Health Legislation' (2003) 182 *British Journal of Psychiatry* 91

Broderick A, 'The United Nations Convention on the Rights of Persons with Disabilities and the European Convention on Human Rights: A Tale of Two Halves or a Potentially Unified Vision of Human Rights?' (2018) 7 *Cambridge International Law Journal* 199

Brosnan L, 'Power and Participation: An Examination of the Dynamics of Mental Health Service-User Involvement in Ireland' (2012) 6 *Studies in Social Justice* 45

Brown J, 'The Changing Purpose of Mental Health Law: From Medicalism to Legalism to New Legalism' (2016) 47 *International Journal of Law and Psychiatry* 1

Cai W et al., 'A Discussion on the Issues of Assessment of Capacity for Civil Conduct of Persons with Mental Illness' (2003) 2 *Chinese Journal of Forensic Sciences* 38 [蔡伟雄等, '精神病人民事行为能力评定相关问题的探讨' (2003) 2 中国司法鉴定 38]

Chen B, 'Xu v the Hospital and His Guardian – Involuntary Inpatient Treatment' (2016) forthcoming *International Journal of Mental Health and Capacity Law*

Chen L and Deng S, 'Causes of Medical Disturbance and Its Countermeasures' (2007) 14 (4) *Journal of Law & Medicine* 253[陈丽娜, 邓世雄, '"医闹"事件的产生原因及解决对策' (2007) 14 法律与医学杂志 253]

Cohen JA, 'Chinese Common Law? Guiding Cases and Judicial Reform' 129 *Harvard Law Review* 2213

Das V and Addlakha R, 'Disability and Domestic Citizenship: Voice, Gender, and the Making of the Subject' (2001) 13 *Public Culture* 511

Davidson H, 'When Is a Voluntary Patient Not a Voluntary Patient? An Examination of the Degree to Which the Irish Courts Have Sought to Engage with the Jurisprudence of the European Court of Human Rights, in Relation to the Treatment and Detention of Voluntary or "informal" Patients' (2017) 2016 *International Journal of Mental Health and Capacity Law* 38

Dawson J, 'A Realistic Approach to Assessing Mental Health Laws Compliance with the UNCRPD' (2015) 40 *International Journal of Law and Psychiatry* 70

Dawson J and Szmukler G, 'Fusion of Mental Health and Incapacity Legislation' (2006) 188 *The British Journal of Psychiatry* 504

De Bhailis C and Flynn E, 'Recognising Legal Capacity: Commentary and Analysis of Article 12 CRPD' (2017) 13 *International Journal of Law in Context* 6

Deng J, 'The National Supervision Commission: A New Anti-Corruption Model in China' (2018) 52 *International Journal of Law, Crime and Justice* 58

Ding C, 'Family Members' Informed Consent to Medical Treatment for Competent Patients in China' (2010) 8 *China: An International Journal* 139

Ding C, 'Family Members' Informed Consent to Medical Treatment for Competent Patients in China' 'Involuntary Detention and Treatment of the Mentally Ill: China's 2012 Mental Health Law' (2014) 37 *International Journal of Law and Psychiatry* 581

Dong K, 'Medical Insurance System Evolution in China' (2009) 20 *China Economic Review* 591

Donnelley M and Murray C, 'The Role of Family in Mental Health Law: A Framework for Transformation' (2013) 25 *Child and Family Law Quarterly* 380

Duffy RM and Kelly BD, 'India's Mental Healthcare Act, 2017: Content, Context, Controversy' (2019) 62 *International Journal of Law and Psychiatry* 169

Dute J, 'Should Substituted Decision-Making Be Abolished?' (2015) 22 *European Journal of Health Law* 315

Eggleston K et al., 'Health Service Delivery in China: A Literature Review' (2008) 17 *Health Economics* 149

Li E-C and Wen C-F, 'Should the Confucian Family-Determination Model Be Rejected? A Case Study' (2010) 35 *Journal of Medicine & Philosophy* 587

Erdmane A, 'Liberty behind Closed Doors-Involuntary Placement and Medical Treatment in Psychiatric Institutions from the Human Rights Perspective' (2010) 4 *Vienna Online Journal on International Constitutional Law* 90

Feng C, 'The NGO Law in China and Its Impact on Overseas Funded NGOs' (2017) 9 *Cosmopolitan Civil Societies: An Interdisciplinary Journal* 95

Feng J et al., 'A Study on Health Insurance Equality in China Through the Lens of Coverage Rate' (2010) 18 *Modern Business* 96 [冯洁等, '从覆盖率角度研究我国医疗保险公平性' (2010) 18 现代商业 96]

Flynn E, 'Making Human Rights Meaningful for People with Disabilities: Advocacy, Access to Justice and Equality before the Law' (2013) 17 *The International Journal of Human Rights* 491

Flynn E, 'Mental (in)Capacity or Legal Capacity: A Human Rights Analysis of the Proposed Fusion of Mental Health and Mental Capacity Law in Northern Ireland' (2013) 64 *Northern Ireland Legal Quarterly* 485

Flynn E, 'Disability, Deprivation of Liberty and Human Rights Norms: Reconciling European and International Approaches' (2017) 2016 *International Journal of Mental Health and Capacity Law* 76

Flynn E and Arstein-Kerslake A, 'State Intervention in the Lives of People with Disabilities: The Case for a Disability-Neutral Framework' (2017) 13 *International Journal of Law in Context* 39

Freeman MC et al., 'Reversing Hard Won Victories in the Name of Human Rights: A Critique of the General Comment on Article 12 of the UN Convention on the Rights of Persons with Disabilities' (2015) 2 *The Lancet Psychiatry* 844

Gendreau C, 'The Rights of Psychiatric Patients in the Light of the Principles Announced by the United Nations: A Recognition of the Right to Consent to Treatment?' (1997) 20 *International Journal of Law and Psychiatry* 259

Gooding P, McSherry B and Roper C, 'Preventing and Reducing "Coercion" in Mental Health Services: An International Scoping Review of English-Language Studies' (2020) 142 *Acta Psychiatrica Scandinavica* 27

Gooding P, 'Supported Decision-Making: A Rights-Based Disability Concept and Its Implications for Mental Health Law' (2013) 20 *Psychiatry, Psychology and Law* 431

Gooding P, 'Supported Decision-Making: A Rights-Based Disability Concept and Its Implications for Mental Health Law' 'Navigating the "Flashing Amber Lights" of the Right to Legal Capacity in the United Nations Convention on the Rights of Persons with Disabilities: Responding to Major Concerns' (2015) 15 *Human Rights Law Review* 45

Gooding P and Flynn E, 'Querying the Call to Introduce Mental Capacity Testing to Mental Health Law: Does the Doctrine of Necessity Provide an Alternative?' (2015) 4 *Laws* 245

Gooding P and McSherry B, 'Alternatives to Compulsory Detention and Treatment and Coercive Practices in Mental Health Settings' (2018) 26 *Journal of Law and Medicine* 300

Gooding PM, 'Change and Continuity: A Historical Overview of the Significance of the United Nations Convention on the Rights of Persons with Disabilities to Mental Health Law' (2014) 20 *European Journal of Current Legal Issues* <webjcli.org/article/view/367> accessed 1 July 2021

Gostin LO and Gable L, 'The Human Rights of Persons with Mental Disabilities: A Global Perspective on the Application of Human Rights Principles to Mental Health' (2004) 63 *Maryland Law Review* 20

Guo Z and Feeney F, 'The New Chinese Mental Health Laws' (2018) 17 *Washington University Global Studies Law Review* 411

Hale B, 'Justice and Equality in Mental Health Law: The European Experience' (2007) 30 *International Journal of Law and Psychiatry* 18

Harding TW, 'Human Rights Law in the Field of Mental Health: A Critical Review' (2000) 101 *Acta Psychiatrica Scandinavica* 24

He AJ and Qian J, 'Explaining Medical Disputes in Chinese Public Hospitals: The Doctor–Patient Relationship and Its Implications for Health Policy Reforms' (2016) 11 *Health Economics, Policy and Law* 359

He X, 'Black Hole of Responsibility: The Adjudication Committee's Role in a Chinese Court' (2012) 46 *Law & Society Review* 681

He X, Li Z and Xu L, 'Changes of Community-Based Mental Health Services after the Mental Health Law' (2014) 13 *Chinese Journal of General Practitioners* 255

Huang Y et al., 'Prevalence of Mental Disorders in China: A Cross-Sectional Epidemiological Study' (2019) 6 *The Lancet Psychiatry* 211

Humphrey JP, 'The International Bill of Rights: Scope and Implementation Bicentennial Symposium: Constitutional Government – Strengths, Weaknesses, Future' (1975) 17 *William and Mary Law Review* 527

Iezzoni LI and Long-Bellil LM, 'Training Physicians about Caring for Persons with Disabilities: "Nothing about Us without Us!"' (2012) 5 *Disability and Health Journal* 136

Inamdar M, Stein M and Bunders J, 'Does "Supported Decision-Making" in India's Mental Health Care Bill, 2013, Measure up to the CRPD's Standards?' (2016) 1 *Indian Journal of Medical Ethics* 229

Jones M, 'Can International Law Improve Mental Health? Some Thoughts on the Proposed Convention on the Rights of People with Disabilities' (2005) 28 *International Journal of Law and Psychiatry* 183

Kayess R and French P, 'Out of Darkness into Light? Introducing the Convention on the Rights of Persons with Disabilities' (2008) 8 *Human Rights Law Review* 1

Keys B, 'Congress, Kissinger, and the Origins of Human Rights Diplomacy' (2010) 34 *Diplomatic History* 823

Lam CS et al., 'Chinese Lay Theory and Mental Illness Stigma: Implications for Research and Practices' (2010) 76 *Journal of Rehabilitation; Alexandria* 35

Large M et al., 'Systematic Review and Meta-Analysis of the Clinical Factors Associated with the Suicide of Psychiatric In-Patients' (2011) 124 *Acta Psychiatrica Scandinavica* 18

Lawson A, 'People with Psychosocial Impairments or Conditions, Reasonable Accommodation and the Convention on the Rights of Persons with Disabilities' (2008) 26 *Law in Context: A Socio-Legal Journal* 62

Lawton-Smith S, Dawson J and Burns T, 'Community Treatment Orders Are Not a Good Thing' (2008) 193 *The British Journal of Psychiatry* 96

Levinson D et al., 'Associations of Serious Mental Illness with Earnings: Results from the WHO World Mental Health Surveys' (2010) 197 *The British Journal of Psychiatry* 114

Li K et al., 'Mental Health Services in China: A Review of Delivery and Policy Issues in 1949–2009' (2012) 26 *China Mental Health Journal* 321 [栗克清等, '中国精神卫生服务及其政策对: 1949–2009 年的回顾与未来 10 年的展望' (2012) 26 中国心理卫生杂志 321]

Li L, 'The "Production" of Corruption in China's Courts: Judicial Politics and Decision Making in a One-Party State' (2012) 37 *Law & Social Inquiry* 848

Liu J et al., 'Mental Health System in China: History, Recent Service Reform and Future Challenges' (2011) 10 *World Psychiatry* 210

Liu X, 'Psychiatry in Traditional Chinese Medicine' (1981) 138 *The British Journal of Psychiatry* 429

Lord JE and Stein MA, 'The Domestic Incorporation of Human Rights Law and the United Nations Convention on the Rights of Persons with Disabilities' (2008) 83 *Washington Law Review* 449

Lu SY and Galli VB, 'Psychiatric Abuse of Falun Gong Practitioners in China' (2002) 30 *Journal of the American Academy of Psychiatry and the Law Online* 126

Ma H et al., 'An Important Pathway of Mental Health Service Reform in China: Introduction of 686 Program' (2011) 25 *Chinese Mental Health Journal* 725

Ma Z, 'When Love Meets Drugs: Pharmaceuticalizing Ambivalence in Post-Socialist China' (2012) 36 *Culture, Medicine, and Psychiatry* 51

Macias C et al., 'What Is a Clubhouse? Report on the ICCD 1996 Survey of USA Clubhouses' (1999) 35 *Community Mental Health Journal* 181

Maingay S et al., 'Mental Health and Human Rights: The MI Principles – Turning Rhetoric into Action' (2002) 14 *International Review of Psychiatry* 19

Maylea C, 'Tensions in the Work of Mental Health Tribunals' (2019) *Precedent* (Sydney, N.S.W.) 13

Mcsherry B and Wilson K, 'The Concept of Capacity in Australian Mental Health Law Reform: Going in the Wrong Direction?' (2015) 40 *International Journal of Law and Psychiatry* 60

Minkowitz T, 'The United Nations Convention on the Rights of Persons with Disabilities and the Right to Be Free from Nonconsensual Psychiatric Interventions' (2006) 34 *Syracuse Journal of International Law and Commerce* 405

Minkowitz T, 'The United Nations Convention on the Rights of Persons with Disabilities and the Right to Be Free from Nonconsensual Psychiatric Interventions' 'The United Nations Convention on the Rights of Persons with Disabilities and the Right to Be Free from Nonconsensual Psychiatric Interventions' (2007) 34 *Syracuse Journal of International Law and Commerce* 405

Minkowitz T, 'The United Nations Convention on the Rights of Persons with Disabilities and the Right to Be Free from Nonconsensual Psychiatric Interventions' 'Why Mental Health Laws Contravene the CRPD–An Application of Article 14 with Implications for the Obligations of States Parties' (2011) Available at SSRN 1928600 <papers.ssrn.com/sol3/papers.cfm?abstract_id=1928600> accessed 1 July 2021

Minkowitz T, 'The United Nations Convention on the Rights of Persons with Disabilities and the Right to Be Free from Nonconsensual Psychiatric Interventions' 'CRPD Advocacy by the World Network of Users and Survivors of Psychiatry: The Emergence of a User/Survivor Perspective in Human Rights' (2012) *Survivor Perspective in Human Rights* (August 14, 2012) <papers.ssrn.com/sol3/papers.cfm?abstract_id=2326668> accessed 1 July 2021

Minzner CF, 'Xinfang: An Alternative to Formal Chinese Legal Institutions' (2006) 42 *Stanford Journal of International Law* 103

Munro R, 'The Ankang: China's Special Psychiatric Hospitals' (2006) 1 *Journal of Comparative Law* 41

Nilsson A, 'Objective and Reasonable? Scrutinising Compulsory Mental Health Interventions from a Non-Discrimination Perspective' (2014) 14 *Human Rights Law Review* 459

Parry-Jones WL, 'Psychiatry in the People's Republic of China' (1986) 148 *The British Journal of Psychiatry* 632

Patel V et al., 'The Magnitude of and Health System Responses to the Mental Health Treatment Gap in Adults in India and China' (2016) 388 *The Lancet* 3074

Pearson V, 'Law, Rights, and Psychiatry in the People's Republic of China' (1992) 15 (4) *International Journal of Law and Psychiatry* 409

Pearson V, 'Law, Rights, and Psychiatry in the People's Republic of China' 'The Chinese Equation in Mental Health Policy and Practice: Order plus Control Equal Stability' (1996) 19 *International Journal of Law and Psychiatry* 437

Perlin ML, '"Salvation" or a "Lethal Dose?" Attitudes and Advocacy in Right to Refuse Treatment Cases' (2004) 4 *Journal of Forensic Psychology Practice* 51

Phillips MR et al., 'Prevalence, Treatment, and Associated Disability of Mental Disorders in Four Provinces in China during 2001–05: An Epidemiological Survey' (2009) 373 *The Lancet* 2041

Potter PB, 'The Chinese Legal System: Continuing Commitment to the Primacy of State Power' (1999) 159 *The China Quarterly* 673

Qian J, 'Mental Health Care in China: Providing Services for under-Treated Patients' (2012) 15 *The Journal of Mental Health Policy and Economics* 179

Qin Q and Chen J, 'The Rational Thought about Human Right Written in the Constitution [J]' (2004) 3 *Legal Forum* 7

Qu X, 'UN CRPD and rights protection of persons with disabilities' (2013) *Legal Studies* 105 [曲项霏, '《残疾人权利公约》与残疾人权利保障' (2013) 法学 105]

Quinlivan S, 'The United Nations Convention on the Rights of Persons with Disabilities: An Introduction' (2012) 13 *ERA Forum* 71

Quinn G, '"Rethinking Personhood: New Directions in Legal Capacity Law and Policy" (Ideas Paper)' (2011) <https://www.inclusionireland.ie/sites/default/files/attach/basic-page/846/rethinkingpersonhood-newdirectionsinlegalcapacitylawandpolicy-gerardquinn-april2011.docx> accessed 15 April 2019

Quinn G, '"Rethinking Personhood: New Directions in Legal Capacity Law and Policy" (Ideas Paper)' 'Civil Death: Rethinking the Foundations of Legal Personhood for Persons with a Disability' (2016) 56 *The Irish Jurist* 286

Reaume G, 'Mad People's History' (2006) 2006 *Radical History Review* 170

Rosenthal E and Rubenstein LS, 'International Human Rights Advocacy under the "Principles for the Protection of Persons with Mental Illness"' (1993) 16 *International Journal of Law and Psychiatry* 257

Rui D, 'A Family-Oriented Decision-Making Model for Human Research in Mainland China' (2015) 40 *Journal of Medicine and Philosophy* (United Kingdom) 400

Schalock RL, Luckasson RA and Shogren KA, 'The Renaming of Mental Retardation: Understanding the Change to the Term Intellectual Disability' (2007) 45 *Intellectual and Developmental Disabilities* 116

Series L, 'Relationships, Autonomy and Legal Capacity: Mental Capacity and Support Paradigms' (2015) 40 *International Journal of Law and Psychiatry* 80

Shao Y and Xie B, 'Approaches to Involuntary Admission of the Mentally Ill in the People's Republic of China: Changes in Legislation From 2002 to 2012' (2015) 43 *Journal of the American Academy of Psychiatry and the Law Online* 35

Solinger DJ, 'The Chinese Work Unit and Transient Labor in the Transition from Socialism' (1995) 21 *Modern China* 155

Stein MA and Lord JE, 'Monitoring the Convention on the Rights of Persons with Disabilities: Innovations, Lost Opportunities, and Future Potential' (2010) 32 *Human Rights Quarterly* 689

Sundram CJ, 'In Harm's Way: Research Subjects Who Are Decisionally Impaired' (1998) 1 *J. Health Care L. & Pol'y* 36

The Lancet, 'Mental Health in China: What Will Be Achieved by 2020?' (2015) 385 *The Lancet* 2548

Thyloth M, Singh H and Subramanian V, 'Increasing Burden of Mental Illnesses across the Globe: Current Status' (2016) 32 *Indian Journal of Social Psychiatry* 254

Tian W et al., 'A Brief History of the Development of Rehabilitative Services in China' (1994) 165 *The British Journal of Psychiatry* 19

Trevaskes S, 'Courts on the Campaign Path in China: Criminal Court Work in the "Yanda 2001" Anti-Crime Campaign' (2002) 42 *Asian Survey* 673

Wang B and Li X, 'Analysis of factors influencing hospitalization expenses of 5439 psychiatric inpatients' (2013) 20 (1) *Chinese Journal of Hospital Statistics* 30 [王冰洁,李喜平, '5439例精神疾病患者住院费用影响因素分析' (2013) 20 (1) 中国医院统计 30]

Waddington L and McSherry B, 'Exceptions and Exclusions: The Right to Informed Consent for Medical Treatment of People with Psychosocial Disabilities in Europe' (2016) 23 *European Journal of Health Law* 1

Wei L, 'Judicial Interpretation in China' (1997) 5 *Willamette Journal of International Law and Dispute Resolution* 87

Weller P, 'The Convention on the Rights of Persons with Disabilities and the Social Model of Health: New Perspectives' (2011) Spring *Special Edition of Journal of Mental Health Law* 74

Wen B et al., 'Inventory Survey on Clinical Features of Patients in Open Wards and Locked Wards of Psychiatric Department' (2018) 49 *Journal of Shanxi Medical University* 1378

Whelan D, 'Mental Health Tribunals: A Significant Medico-Legal Change' (2004) 10 *Medico-legal Journal of Ireland* 84

Wu HY-J, 'The Moral Career of "Outmates": Towards a History of Manufactured Mental Disorders in Post-Socialist China' (2016) 60 *Medical History* 87

Xiang Y-T et al., 'Mental Health in China: Challenges and Progress' 'China's National Mental Health Law: A 26-Year Work in Progress' (2012) 379 *The Lancet* 780

Xiang Y-T et al., 'Mental Health in China: Challenges and Progress' (2012) 380 *The Lancet* 1715

Xie B, 'Impact of the New Mental Health Act on Mental Health Services in the Future' (2013) 13 *Journal of Neuroscience and Mental Health* 1

Xie B, 'Impact of the New Mental Health Act on Mental Health Services in the Future' 'The law-making history of the Mental Health Law' (2013) 13 *China Hospital CEO* 86 [谢斌, '精神卫生法立法史' (2013) 13 中国医院院长 86]

Xu J et al., 'The Economic Burden of Mental Disorders in China, 2005–2013: Implications for Health Policy' (2016) 16 *BMC Psychiatry* <bmcpsychiatry.biomedcentral.com/articles/10.1186/s12888-12016-0839-0> accessed 29 January 2019

Xu Q, Perkins DD and Chow JC-C, 'Sense of Community, Neighboring, and Social Capital as Predictors of Local Political Participation in China' (2010) 45 *American Journal of Community Psychology* 259

Yang C, 'Staring at the China's Mental Health Law from the Third Eye' (2012) 6 *China Hospital CEO* 74 *[杨承忻*, '第三只眼睛看中国精神卫生法' (2012) 中国医院院长 74]

Yao Z, 'State Control and Doctors' Abuse of Clinical Autonomy: An Empirical Analysis of Doctors' Clinical Practice in Chinese Public Hospitals' (2019) 5 *Chinese Journal of Sociology* 29

Yip K-S, 'An Historical Review of the Mental Health Services in the People's Republic of China' (2005) 51 *International Journal of Social Psychiatry* 106

Zhang J, 'The Evolution of China's One-Child Policy and Its Effects on Family Outcomes' (2017) 31 *Journal of Economic Perspectives* 141

Zhang S and Zhang T, 'The process and major contents of the Mental Health Law' (2013) 20 *China Health Law* 4 [张世诚, 张涛, '精神卫生法的立法过程和主要内容' (2013) 20 中国卫生法制 4]

Zhang Y, 'Study on a Sample of Law: The Difficulty in Filing Cases in Grass-roots Courts' (2010) 4 *Anti-Corruption and Integrity Culture Studies* 37 [张永进, '基层法院 "立案难": 一个法律样本的解读' (2010) 4 廉政文化研究 37]

Zhao X and Dawson J, 'The New Chinese Mental Health Law' (2014) 21 *Psychiatry, Psychology and Law* 669

Zhou Y, 'On the Judicial Review under the System of People's Congress [J]' (2006) 3 *Jiangsu Social Sciences* 124

Zhu G, 'Constitutional Review in China: An Unaccomplished Project or a Mirage' (2009) 43 *Suffolk University Law Review* 625

Index